Tito Puente and the Making of Latin Music

Music in American Life

A list of books in the series appears at the end of this book.

(Max Salazar Collection.)

Tito Puente
and the
Making of
Latin Music

STEVEN LOZA

UNIVERSITY OF ILLINOIS PRESS

URBANA AND CHICAGO

Library of Congress Cataloging-in-Publication Data
Loza, Steven Joseph.
Tito Puente and the making of Latin music / Steven Loza.
p.   cm. — (Music in American life)
Discography: p.
Includes bibliographical references (p.   ) and index.
ISBN 0-252-02332-3 (cloth : acid-free paper)
ISBN 0-252-06778-9 (pbk. : acid-free paper)
1. Puente, Tito, 1923–
2. Musicians—Latin America—Biography.
I. Title. II. Series.
ML419.P82L6   1999
784.4'81888'092—ddc21   98-25507
[B]   CIP
MN

A song for my father,
Ruben G. Loza,
who taught me love . . .

and

 to Max Salazar,
  who loved the music;
   to Urs Jakob,
    who believed in the music;
   to Josie Powell,
    who danced the music;
   to Joe Conzo,
    who lived the music;
   and to Tito,
    who made the music.

Contents

Illustrations follow pages 48, 128, and 218

Acknowledgments

I am indebted to many individuals and agencies for their invaluable participation in the making of this book. Without their dedicated assistance, the book would not have been finished.

To UCLA agencies, including the Latin American Center, the Academic Senate Research Committee, the Cesar Chávez Center, and the Chancellor's Office of Academic Development, I express my gratitude for the various grants they have provided. Those grants funded fieldwork and research assistance that were integral to the project. I also extend my utmost thanks to Kanda University of International Studies in Japan, which assisted me in the final stages of the book with a research stipend and numerous other forms of aid during my year of teaching at that excellent institution during 1996–97. To the UCLA School of the Arts and Architecture and the Department of Ethnomusicology, my home base, I am most grateful for the sabattical time and their constant support of my research and teaching. To all my colleagues, students, and the staff at UCLA I especially wish to extend my heartfelt love for all the positive work and friendship we have experienced together for many years.

To Urs Jakob, a lifelong friend, I give my thanks for the great generosity he offered me during my extensive research trips to New York City, especially the living accommodations he provided me at his hotel in Manhattan, the Gershwin. I must also give thanks to a man who has been my mentor for over twenty years, Robert Stevenson. Dr. Stevenson was especially helpful to me in the writing of this book, for he provided me with living accommodations during the three months just prior to my departure for Japan. Without the solitude of that Westwood apartment, I would not have been able to complete the manuscript on schedule. As so many of us know, Dr. Stevenson is a godsend in many ways.

I deeply thank my colleagues Daniel Sheehy, Norma Cantú, and Danilo Lozano for carefully reading the text and for their invaluable suggestions.

I would especially like to express my gratitude to my graduate research assistants, on whom I have depended constantly for their generous, meticulous, and excellent work and dedication. To Jay Keister, my principal research assistant during the project, I extend my deep thanks for his always excellent editing, formatting, interview and musical transcriptions, and extensive administrative input on the project. David Borgo also dedicated a major amount of time in the preparation of the manuscript, interview transcriptions, and numerous musical transcriptions (including the intricate timbal solo transcriptions). Francisco Crespo worked extensively on a number of essential research tasks, including the transcription of various song texts and interviews, in addition to providing numerous translations. He also served as my principal assistant in securing permissions and releases of artists' industry materials. Also assisting in the detailed and tedious searches was Vicente Contreras. My heartfelt thanks go to Colleen Trujillo for her proofreading and to the indexer, George Olshevsky.

I also want to express my deep gratitude to various professionals in the field who have given me direct aid in the making of this book. Ramón Rodríguez, director of the Boys Harbor School for Performing Arts in New York, provided me invaluable assistance in the use of the school's rich archives of Latin music historical data. I am especially indebted for the permission he has granted to incorporate much of that data in the book. I also want to express my warmest gratitude to Max Salazar and Joe Conzo, two individuals without whose help and friendship throughout the research process I could never have written this book. Also indispensable in the work of the book have been Judith McCulloh, an assistant director at the University of Illinois Press; her assistant, Margo Chaney; and copyeditor Bruce Bethell.

I wish to pay a special tribute here to my mother, Carmen Miranda Loza, who has been with me throughout my struggles and joys, my periods of both "agony and ecstasy." She, my brothers (Mitch, Bob, and Jerry), my sister-in-law (Rebecca), and I recently lost my father. We still miss him, and we will until we see him again.

It was just over twenty years ago that a very great lady also passed from this earth. She always encouraged me, helped me, and believed in me. Maria Terry Miranda Roberts was my godmother, my aunt, and a refuge for me and many others. May the Lord and Tía Terry look down at us favorably for what we are trying to do.

I also wish to honor here the memory of Miriam Laskofsky, another great lady who has passed to the next phase.

To some of my close personal and professional colleagues, I simply want to say "thanks" for being my friends: Dwight Dickerson; Kenny Burrell; Alfonso Smith; Aaron

Ballesteros; Simeon Pillich; Reggie Waddell; Danilo Lozano; Francisco Aguabella; Nati Cano; Raúl Pérez; Charlie Tovar; Miguel Delgado; Rudy López; James Wilkie; Juan Carlos Torres; Héctor Calderón; Raymond Paredes; Kenzo Kitahara; Takashi and Hiroko Sasaki; Koichiro, Yoko, and Hiroaki Yaginuma; Carlos Haro; and Juan Gómez-Quiñones, among all the others who have been so important to me—you know who you are!

Finally, there is another person who has stuck with me "all the way." He is Maestro Tito Puente, and he has never given up on me. Thank you, maestro, for all you have given me.

◈◇◈

Introduction

H E has for decades been referred to as the "king" of Latin music, the art that encompasses everything from the mambo and the cha-cha to Latin jazz and salsa. In Spanish he is "el rey," but whatever language they speak, people everywhere have come to recognize him as the world's leading exponent of Latin Caribbean–based (notably Afro-Cuban) music. Tito Puente is, in the estimation of many musicians, musicologists, and critics, the most influential artist in the development of Latin American music in the United States during the twentieth century.

In his book *Louis Armstrong: An American Genius,* James Lincoln Collier characterizes that great jazz master as the archetypal twentieth-century figure: "First, he was an American, during a period when the world was looking to the United States as a source of new ideas, new ways of thinking and doing things. Second, he was Black, at a time when one of the most important international political movements was the struggle of Blacks for parity in the world. Finally, during a century in which personal expression has been both a philosophy of life and a leading principle of art, Armstrong was the creative genius who first demonstrated the possibilities inherent in improvised music" (1983, 3–4).

Genius is a term reserved for leading thinkers and creators in any field of life. The genius of Tito Puente can be compared to the twentieth-century legacy of Armstrong in a strongly parallel fashion: Armstrong was American born, and so was Puente; Armstrong was African American, with all the cultural and social implications that heritage entails, and Puente was Latin American, with all the relative associations of that heritage; and Armstrong was a creative genius with regard to the contemporary values of individual artistry and African-connected improvisations, and so is Puente.

A number of further comparisons have been made between Tito Puente and other musical masters. I have consistently referred to him as the "Ellington of Latin music." Puerto Rican colleagues of mine have referred to him variously as the Count Basie, the Bach, and the Beethoven of Latin music. With 116 albums to his credit (all with him as leader), Puente has recorded more, performed in more countries, and enjoyed a more illustrious career than has any other artist in the field referred to here as Latin music.

An inspection of any contemporary major record store will attest to the previous claims, for the bins of Puente's recordings will predominate the various Latin jazz artists included in the collection; additionally, Puente will predominate the collection of the salsa artists. Two worlds and two markets have thus largely become associated with Tito Puente's music: the English-speaking and Spanish-speaking Americas. Added to this cultural matrix are the extended geographies of Puente's popularity, including Africa, Asia, and Europe.

In this book my goal is to offer an analytical view of the historical, stylistic, and social progression of Latin music as embodied in the music and life of Tito Puente. The analytical framework of the book is thus structured on historical data, musical repertory, ethnographic interviews, and cultural theories and concepts. After providing a historical survey of Puente's musical career in chapter 1, I offer three chapters (2–5) drawn from extensive interviews that I conducted with Puente, Max Salazar, Joe Conzo, Ray Santos, Chico Sesma, Jerry González, Poncho Sanchez, and Hilton Ruiz. Chapter 6 comprises in-depth musical analyses of a selected repertory representative of Puente's work. Chapter 7 includes a number of conceptual, theoretical, and cultural perspectives on the social and cultural ambits of Puente's innovations and international impact, especially as related to the issues of cultural identity, the market, aesthetics, and the perspectives of other scholars, critics, and musicians. My concluding remarks in chapter 8 include an eclectic choice of philosophical and personal views of Maestro Puente from my own perspective and my own applications of the concepts of others.

I have known Tito closely through the past fifteen years. In the early eighties I began to invite him to conduct workshops and lecture at UCLA and to perform with the student ensemble I led, UCLATINO. In 1983 an issue of *Caminos* magazine for which I was the guest editor ran as its cover story an interview that I conducted with Tito. Throughout the eighties I continued to invite him to lecture and perform with UCLATINO, and this association most recently culminated in Tito's 1994 appointment as a UC Regents Lecturer. During this residency he lectured extensively on campus and performed with my own jazz/Latin sextet and Poncho Sanchez's ensemble in a sold-out concert at UCLA's Wadsworth Theater. Other concerts that I have produced and performed in with Tito have featured artists such as Linda Ronstadt, Los Lobos, Poncho Sanchez, Vikki Carr, Lalo Guerrero, Daniel Valdez, and Mariachi Los Camperos de Nati Cano.

It is thus as a musician and an academician that I have developed a deep and meaningful relationship with Tito. And it is for this reason that he has asked me to write this book.

Tito Puente and the Making of Latin Music

1

A Historical Sketch

Early Years

The world that gave birth to Tito Puente was that of New York City, just as New Orleans, the cradle of jazz, had given birth to Louis Armstrong. To many, New York ranks first among those places where Latin music—more specifically, the music that migrated from Cuba—was reshaped, just as Chicago and New York reshaped the music that migrated from New Orleans.

Ernest Anthony "Tito" Puente was born on April 20, 1923, at Harlem Hospital and raised in the East Harlem neighborhood known as both Spanish Harlem and El Barrio. His parents, Ernest and Ercilla, had migrated to New York from Puerto Rico, already a U.S. "possession" following the Spanish-American War of 1898. The family lived at 1850 Madison Avenue, and in 1928 a sister, Anna, was born. A brother, Robert Anthony, was born later, but he died in a tragic fall from a fire escape at age four. The young Tito attended elementary school at Public Schools 43 and 184, Cooper Jr. High School, and Galvanni Jr. High School before attending Central Commercial High School.

Tito's early childhood years represented the seminal development of what was to become a prolific Puerto Rican–Latino community. In her book on the music of Puerto Ricans in New York City during 1917 to 1940, Ruth Glasser makes the following observations:

Although Puerto Ricans had been arriving on the mainland since the mid-nineteenth century, it was not until they were granted U.S. citizenship, in 1917, that people began migrating from the island in substantial numbers. As U.S. citizens, Puerto Ricans were not included in census population counts of the foreign-born; therefore there is some controversy over their numbers, with estimates ranging between 45,000 and 100,000 by 1930 (Glazer and Moynihan 1963).

Members of this post–World War I migration settled in five distinct neighborhoods of Brooklyn and Manhattan, clustered near waterfront, factory, and cigar workshop jobs. Within these areas, Puerto Ricans found themselves living in scattered pockets among a constellation of ethnic groups. The population of these neighborhoods was not only variable but constantly shifting, as were the Puerto Ricans' residential, work, political, and social relationships with their multi-ethnic associates. . . . class stratifications within ethnic groups, true for [Jews], Irish, Germans, African-Americans, and Italians as well, meant that working class ethnics of different backgrounds lived together in pockets with affordable housing, as close as possible to their workplaces. Puerto Ricans carried on daily interethnic negotiations with these people among whom they worked and lived, often within the intimacy of boarding arrangements. (Glasser 1995, 94–95)

Tito's mother encouraged him and his sister, Anna, to become music and dance performers. In 1935 they became members of the "Stars of the Future," an organization assembled by the director of a local funeral parlor. Meetings were held at La Milagrosa Catholic Church, at 115th Street and Lenox Avenue, which was also the Puentes' parish church, where Tito made his first communion and confirmation. "The church sponsored a yearly coronation of its most talented children who were crowned king and queen for their artistic ability and popularity. There exists a photo snapped in 1935 at La Milagrosa which shows young Tito in a blue soldier's uniform and cap. Also in the photo is Anna and her girl friend, Olga San Juan, who years later became a movie actress. Tito was crowned king on four occasions because of his dancing skills" (Salazar 1994, 5).

Some years later, during World War II, Anna would die in her teens from a long illness. The time that Tito spent dancing with his sister, however, provided a productive base for a lifelong aspect of his artistry. In an interview with Bobby Sanabria, he recalled the experience: "Annie and I studied all forms of ball room dancing, including acrobatic tap. We were inspired of course by Fred Astaire and Ginger Rogers. I pride myself on being one of the few band leaders who really knows how to dance. It's something that more young band leaders should investigate" (Sanabria and Socolov 1990, 1–3).

Tito's musical world encompassed diversity, the diversity of multicultural New York City and of the bicultural, bilingual environment of El Barrio. His mother enrolled him at the New York School of Music on 125th Street and Lenox Avenue, near the family's home. The piano lessons cost twenty-five cents apiece, and Tito recalled that his mother "would take the quarter from [his] father while he was asleep" (ibid., 1). Tito took music lessons for some seven years, "also occasionally being tutored by pianist Victoria Hernández, sister of Puerto Rico's most renowned composer, Rafael Hernández, and Luis Varona, an early pianist in the Machito Orchestra who would one day play in the Tito Puente Orchestra" (ibid.) Tito also studied drums with a Mr. Williams, a show drummer and teacher. Tito recalled: "He knew absolutely nothing about Latin music, but I wasn't going to him for that. He gave me a good foundation; snare drum technique, how to interpret figures in charts and accompany shows. I would listen to the great dance bands of the day on the radio, Goodman, Artie Shaw, Duke Ellington, and I'd go to theaters like the Paramount and the Strand to see them perform. My hero was Gene Krupa. I even won a drum contest playing his solo on 'Sing, Sing, Sing,' note for note" (ibid., 3).

Max Salazar provides additional insight into these various periods of Tito's early musical experiences:

> In 1937, at age 14, Tito was a boy scout whose troop met weekly at the American Legion on 5th St. At the time, he attended Central Commercial High School. All he thought about was music. During his lunch break, Tito would be seen in the auditorium with a crowd around him watching him play Boogie Woogie. He and his sister had already been tutored by a pianist named Blue Mountain. During the day, Tito would be seen and heard as part of a trio or quartet on a school stairway or on a street corner singing "Sweet Sue," "Am I Blue," and other songs the Ink Spots Quartet made popular. The piano lessons began after Tito had been overwhelmed by Cuban pianist Anselmo Sacassas' solo for Casino De La Playa's RCA recording of "Dolor cobarde." Months later he added trap drum to his studies after Gene Krupa's drumming to Benny Goodman's "Sing Sing Sing" excited him. The alto sax was mastered after his parents rented a room to a Professor Millian, a music teacher.
>
> At age 16 in 1939, Tito dropped out of school to become a full time musician. Not old enough to apply for a Local 802 Musicians Union [American Federation of Musicians] membership, he managed to qualify for a New Jersey card. At this time he was living at 53 East 110th Street, between Madison & Park Avenues. It was during that year he met another 16 year old named Pablo Rodríguez who had left Puerto Rico to live in New York. Pablo lived with his brother Johnny at 65 East 110th Street. Pablo, who years later became famous in the Latin music world as "Tito Rodríguez," met Puente at La Casita María, a teenage hangout on the block they lived. Both of them were on the same ball team. They were close buddies, not only because they were proud Puerto Ricans, but mainly because of their interest in music.
>
> In December, 1939, Puente was at the Musicians Union, then located at 50th St. & 6th Ave., where he got a job drumming with a Latin band. On the same gig was the newly arrived Cuban pianist José Curbelo who was impressed with Tito's drumming skills. After being offered a 3 month gig in Miami, Curbelo recommended Puente for the drummer's job. "I thought," said Curbelo, "I had seen the best drummers in Cuba . . . until I saw Tito perform." For three months they were roommates, each paying $5.00 a week for room rental. (Salazar 1994, 16)

Meeting and working with José Curbelo led to one of the most significant apprenticeships that Tito Puente was to experience throughout his career. Curbelo became Puente's mentor both in music and especially in business. The relationship also represented the confluence of music from Cuban and Puerto Rican cultures in New York City; musical interests were a most important force driving such merging. Later another Cuban bandleader, Machito (Frank Grillo), who had come to New York from Cuba in 1937, would become Puente's principal musical model. By the thirties Cuban music not only had begun to pervade the dance halls of Spanish Harlem but was spreading throughout the city.

> By the late 1930s a number of elegant night spots had opened, in the midtown district as well. With names like Havana-Madrid, Club Yumuri, La Conga, and Casa Cubana, it was clear that they were trying to capitalize on the current craze for the rumba and other Cuban dance forms. The demand for Latin music among a general New York audience was by this era so widespread that even clubs and hotel ballrooms without an explicitly Latin orientation were compelled to hire Cuban-style relief bands to alternate sets with their swing bands. (Glasser 1995, 122–23)

Soon after meeting Curbelo, Tito was playing drums for Johnny Rodríguez's Stork Club Orchestra and afterward for Anselmo Sacassas's band at Chicago's Colony Club. In 1941 he recorded with Vincent López's suave Swing Orchestra ("Los hijos de Buda," "Yumba," "La conga," and "Cachita"); that same year he drummed for Noro Morales, recorded for Decca Records, and appeared in four film shorts featuring Morales: *The Gay Ranchero, Cuban Pete, Ella,* and *Mexican Jumping Bean.*

In June 1942 Tito replaced Tony Escolies in the Machito Orchestra, recording arrangements of "Oye negra," "El botellero," and "Eco" for Decca. Bobby Sanabria makes the following observations regarding Tito's early years with Curbelo and Machito:

> Tito made his early recordings with José Curbelo and Machito [and Tito Rodríguez], proving to be one of the first drummers in Latin music to use a combination of timbales, bass drum and cymbal to "kick" big band figures, often without bongó or conga accompaniment. Tito's concept of chart interpretation and "kicking" of figures was most likely influenced by Mario Bauzá, Machito's musical director. Bauzá had previously served as musical director for Chick Webb, whom jazz historians generally acknowledge as the first drummer to "kick" figures in a big band context. . . . With Machito, Tito was featured as a soloist, bringing his timbales to the front of the stage where he played standing up rather than seated as had been the approved method until this point. (Sanabria and Socolov 1990, 4)

At one point Tito left Machito, along with Chino Pozo, to join the Jack Cole Dancers. Later returning to the Machito Orchestra, he was soon drafted into the U.S. Navy. World War II had begun.

The war greatly changed the lives of many in this country's Latino population and profoundly affected their views of themselves and their culture. Glasser notes that "the musicians who migrated to New York City in the years between the world wars were born in a transitional era. They were the inheritors of older traditions and practices and the beneficiaries of some new ones" (Glasser 1995, 27). Latino soldiers became highly decorated war heroes both in Europe and the South Pacific, and Latino culture as a social force in U.S. society began to take new shapes and directions. On a cultural level, Hollywood and the film and music industries had already begun to capitalize on and incorporate Latin American themes. Xavier Cugat, Carmen Miranda, the Argentine tango, and the Cuban rumba had all become portrayed in film and on recordings, albeit often in largely trivialized forms. Rita Hayworth, the Spanish American actress, was a "glamour girl" of the war period, and Americans of various ethnicities were beginning to dance the mambo along with the big-band dances of the swing era. With the war came much cultural consolidation, and the industry grew.

When Puente was drafted in 1942, he was nineteen years old. On completion of boot camp, he was assigned to the U.S.S. *Santee,* a converted aircraft carrier that escorted supply and passenger ships. Tito played alto saxophone and drums in the ship's band, entertaining the crew with arrangements of tunes such as "Sunny Side of the Street," "Sweet Georgia Brown," "Green Eyes," "Just Friends," "How High the Moon," and "One O'Clock Jump." In addition to performing with the band, he was also assigned to loading ammunition into artillery.

During this tour of duty Puente learned a great amount of arranging techniques from a pilot who played tenor saxophone and served as arranger for the big band of Charlie Spivak. Puente recalled, "[He] showed me the foundation of writing a good chart, how to lay out voicings and get colors out of the brass and reeds. I began writing at this time" (Sanabria and Socolov 1990, 4). While still in the navy, Puente completed an arrangement based on the tune "El bajo de Chapotín." He mailed the arrangement to Machito, who had it performed by his orchestra. It was also while at sea that Puente was informed of his sister's death from spinal meningitis. "He was given an emergency furlough. During his one week at home, he escorted his parents to La Perla del Sur, a Puerto Rican social club at 116th Street and Madison Avenue. At the urging of the audience, he sat down at a piano and performed dedications to his mother of 'Mis amores' (a Puerto Rican danza) and Debussy's 'Clair de Lune' in memory of his late sister" (Salazar 1994, 18).

Puente served in nine battles while in the navy, in both the Atlantic and the Pacific. Discharged in 1945 with a presidential commendation, he returned to New York to seek his previous position with the Machito Orchestra (a federal law required that all returning servicemen be offered their prewar jobs). Uba Nieto, who had taken Puente's job as percussionist with Machito, had a family to support, and both Machito and Tito agreed that it would be best if Nieto kept the position. Puente proceeded to be contracted by Frank Martí's Copacabana band. He then worked in José Curbelo's orchestra and in a Brazilian band led by Fernando Alvarez (which featured Charlie Palmieri on piano) before becoming drummer, contractor, and musical director for the Pupi Campo orchestra in September 1947. It was in Campo's orchestra that Puente met trumpeter Jimmy Frisaura, a big-band veteran who would continue to perform with and serve as contractor for Tito's bands for over forty years. The two also became the closest of friends. (Frisaura died on Feb. 26, 1998.)

New York City would change dramatically during the postwar period, especially with regard to the Puerto Rican and other Latino sectors. Although migration from Puerto Rico to New York and elsewhere in the United States had been substantial since Puente's childhood, the massive movement to the mainland occurred after World War II. The reasons for this migration were largely economic, but Puerto Ricans were also lured by the presence that their compatriots had already established in New York City. Cultural relevance, including music, was part of El Barrio. It was, after all, in New York that Canario and Rafael Hernández, Puerto Rican musical leaders, had been performing and recording extensively. Hernández's composition of "Lamento borincano," which signified so much to Puerto Rico during the war, had been composed and recorded in New York City. Another factor of the postwar period is what Jorge Duany alludes to as "the continuous exchange between New York and San Juan," which, "intensified by cheap commercial flights after World War II, has created a migratory circuit between the two cities that maintains kinship and friendship ties on both shores" (Duany 1984).

Immediately after the war, while he was working with the bands of Martí, Curbelo, Alvarez, and Campo, Puente spent time studying at the Juilliard School of Music. The G.I. Bill enabled him to cover the cost of tuition at the prestigious school, where he studied conducting, orchestration, and theory from 1945 to 1947. During this period he also expanded his composition and arranging skills by studying the Schillinger system with Richard Bender. "Developed by mathematician and theorist Joseph Schillinger, the system was a popular method among jazz musicians including Stan Kenton, whose writing influenced Tito greatly" (Sanabria and Socolov 1990, 5). Puente himself reflected, "My goal in studying Schillinger was to write for music scores, but I got sidetracked by becoming a band leader" (ibid.).* Another facet of his musical life that Puente had developed extensively by this period was the vibraphone, which was being used considerably by young musicians and which he began to feature on his interpretations of ballads.

Among the various pianists to play with Pupi Campo's orchestra during Puente's tenure with the group was José Esteves Jr., known to the public as "Joe Loco," who was also a talented composer and arranger. Loco and Puente collaborated on a number of arrangements performed by Campo's orchestra, which began to be recognized as one of the top Latin bands at the time. Each man made sure that his name appeared on the labels of recordings of his arrangements. A few of Tito Puente's arrangements were "How High the Moon," "Son de la loma," "Está frizao," and "Piérdate," in addition to arrangements of his own tunes "Pilarena," "Cuando te vea," and "The Earl Wilson Mambo" (Salazar 1994, 18).

The Palladium Era

One of the most important stages in the development and popularization of Latin music was the Palladium Ballroom period of the late forties through the fifties (the club remained in business until 1966). It was at the Palladium that the orchestras of Machito, Tito Puente,

---

* Joseph Schillinger was a Russian academician who taught, composed, and wrote extensive theoretical works. Among the various institutions at which he taught were the New School for Social Research, New York University, and Columbia University. He wrote the highly significant book *Mathematical Basis of the Arts*. For information on the Schillinger system, see Schillinger 1940.

and Tito Rodríguez, among others, changed the course of musical style in New York City and elsewhere. Located in downtown Manhattan, the club became a multicultural forum for what might now be called performance art. Jazz musicians became interested in the mambo, and Latin musicians such as Mario Bauzá were incorporating jazz and bop in dance arrangements. A hotbed of new musical interchange was emerging. Tito Puente played a major role in the development of the Palladium and its exploding popularity.

> During late summer 1948, Federico Pagani, dance promoter, visited the Embassy Club to hear the Campo orchestra. After a tune ended, Puente huddled with Loco and played a phrase on the piano. Tito then sang out a melody he wanted duplicated by bassist Manuel Patot (Pachó) and trumpeter Chino González. What followed was one of Latin music's rare moments as the haunting melody raised goose bumps. Pagani said, "The music was so arousing it made my blood turn cold." After the tune ended, Pagani asked Puente for the name of the tune. "I haven't titled it yet," said Puente, "es un picadillo" (it's a mish mash).
>
> Years later, at his office located at 1674 Broadway, Tito Puente said, "I was going to give the tune an oriental title because of the strong oriental feel of the melody." In 1949 Tito Puente recorded it as "Picadillo." A year later Miguelito Valdés recorded it as "Chang."
>
> Pagani offered Puente a Sunday matinee dance at the Alma Dance Studios (which the following year became the Palladium Ballroom) with a pick up band. After Tito agreed to play, Pagani said, "I'll present your group as The Picadilly Boys." The Boys, the majority Campo sidemen, were: Jimmy Frisaura, Al Di Risi, Tony Di Risi (trumpets), Manuel Patot (bass), Angel Rosa (vocals), Chino Pozo (bongós), and pianists on different occasions Al Escobar, Luis Varona and Charlie Palmieri, with Tito Puente on timbales and vibes.
>
> "Tito was incredibly good," recalled Pagani, "He had a fresh sound with a jazz influence. For weeks thereafter his name kept popping up . . . dancers wanted to hear more of his music." During the week before the June 1, 1949, Spanish Music Center Alfredito Valdés recording session, Tito wrote the arrangements of "El Mambo de Broadway," "Enchanted Cubano," "Afro-Cuban Serenade" and "Picadillo" which SMC owner Gabriel Oller retitled "The Arthur Murray Rumba." (Salazar 1994, 18)

By March 1949 Puente was ready to become an independent bandleader. After giving Campo notice, he proceeded to take a number of Campo's musicians who constituted the core of his Picadilly Boys. Puente's new band now included Jimmy Frisaura (lead trumpet), Chino González (second trumpet), Luis Varona (piano), Angel Rosa (vocals), Manuel Patot (bass), Manny Oquendo (bongos), and Frank (Frankie) Colón (conga). Puente played timbales, vibraphone, and drum set. According to Salazar (1994, 20), the ensemble primarily performed arrangements of American pop instrumentals in which Colón (congas) did not play, but the significant aspect of the effort is well expressed by Sanabria: "Dating from that first matinee performance, Tito Puente would never stop being a bandleader" (Sanabria and Socolov 1990, 5).

One of the most essential aspects of Pagani's decision to feature major Latin orchestras at the Palladium was the intercultural context of the dance halls. "For the first time, Latinos and Blacks were coming downtown to listen and dance to the exciting new sound of mambo performed by the likes of Machito, José Curbelo and Noro Morales [as well as Miguelito Valdés and Marcelino Guerra]" (Sanabria and Socolov 1990, 5). In assessing the seminal role of the Palladium, Vernon Boggs offers another point of view:

> Latin music had been served [in] two varieties at the time: one for Harlem residents, largely Hispanics, and the other for "downtown" residents, largely whites. In the ensuing years things began to change and drastically so; Latin music moved downtown and became "unified." . . . By the turn of the decade (1950), the Palladium Ballroom had become one of the most important Latin dance clubs in New York City. Even though the Park Palace dance hall on 110th Street and 5th Avenue could still boast about major Latin bands playing on its premises, the Palladium, situated on Broadway, began taking on the form of a Latin dance institution. (Boggs 1992, 127, 128)

The Palladium had existed since 1942, and in 1949 Max Hyman purchased the club from Tommy Morton and renovated it. Excited by the growing numbers of Latin clients, Hyman displayed the club's new name and began to schedule more Latin music at the venue. Puente became one of the major attractions, and he recalled that "the Palladium was a phenomenon. . . . On Wednesday nights, 'Killer Joe' Piro would teach the current mambo steps to the crowd. The place was a big melting pot—Jews, Italians, Irish, Blacks, Puerto Ricans, Cubans, you name it. Everyone was equal under the roof of the Palladium because everyone was there to dig the music and to dance" (in Sanabria and Socolov 1990, 6). Sanabria also makes the following note: "The Palladium attracted the elite of New York's art and literary community along with a host of Hollywood stars. On any given night Sammy Davis Jr., Jackson Pollack, Marlene Dietrich, Allen Ginsberg, Le Roi Jones (Amiri Baraka) or Kim Novak might be spotted on the dance floor or Marlon Brando might be found sitting in on bongó with the Machito Orchestra" (ibid.). To borrow from a comment by Max Salazar quoted in a later chapter of this book, it could be said that the Palladium and its Latin music did more for integration than all the theories and methods of social scientists. Music, dance, and the art of it all seemed to captivate the soul, exorcising the physical and cultural restrictions of a historically segregated society.

The Tito Puente Orchestra

Puente's newly formed orchestra made its formal debut at the El Patio club at Atlantic Beach, New Jersey, on July 4, 1949. The engagement lasted until Labor Day of the same year; a week afterward Puente expanded the seven-member ensemble to nine with the addition of a third trumpeter, Tony Di Risi, and bongo player Chino Pozo. It was also during this time that bandleader Tito Rodríguez, who had known Puente since childhood, hired him to arrange charts for recordings of "Un yeremico," "Frisao con gusto," "Guararé," and "Mango del monte." Rodríguez's recording session took place on August 31, 1949, at the Spanish Music Center studio.

In September 1949 Cuban *sonero* [lead vocalist] Vicentico Valdés began singing with Puente's orchestra, premiering with the band when invited as a guest to sing the bolero "Tus ojos" (one of the first of Puente's recordings on which the bandleader played vibraphone) at the Palladium. By the end of 1949 Puente was recording orchestrations for four trumpets, three trombones, four saxophones, and a full rhythm section of piano, bass, timbales, congas, and bongos. He used this instrumentation to record "Un corazón," "Solo tú y yo," and "Mambo macoco." On the initial recording of "Abaniquito," his first major hit, he eliminated the saxophone and trombone sections, retaining the four trumpets (Frisaura, Di Risi, González, and Mario Bauzá). On vocals he used Vicentico Valdés, Graciela, and Frankie Colón. Disc jockey Dick "Ricardo" Sugar, hired by Tico Records to host a fifteen-minute program and air its recordings, played "Abaniquito" nightly and enabled Puente and Valdés to enjoy instant recognition (Salazar 1994, 20). In an article on Valdés, Salazar wrote that "it was Valdés's fiery ad-libs and Mario Bauzá's thrilling trumpet solos which had adrenaline flowing and enabled 'Abaniquito' to be identified with the Palladium Ballroom" (Salazar 1993, 29).

Personnel changes continued in Puente's orchestra, and in 1950 Charlie Palmieri replaced pianist Gil López. In 1951 Mongo Santamaría replaced Frankie Colón on congas. It was also during this period that the noted, sometimes exaggerated, rivalry began between Tito Puente and Tito Rodríguez. In an interview conducted by musician Willie Rosario in 1967 on radio station WADO, New York City, Tito Rodríguez responded to a number of the sensationalized myths about his relationship with Puente.

Rosario: Let's clear something up here for the public of New York, for your admirers. There's been a question mark in the matter about you appearing as Rodríguez/ Puente. What do you think . . . your orchestra . . . they always used to say that if the two Titos appeared together it was going to be the dance of the year.

Rodríguez: Yes. [*Laughter*]

Rosario: The dance that was going to produce the most money. What's the truth about that matter, Rodríguez?

Rodríguez: No. The truth is that when I used to have the orchestra, he and I, we were friends for a long time, no? At least on my part, I don't have anything against Rodríguez/Puente. And I never have. But it turns out that we were rivals, and you know how rivalry is good for business.

Rosario: Yes.

Rodríguez: And of course, when you have a business, well you protect it, just like I protected my orchestra. Like he protects his. And that's something he can't be blamed for [for] the simple reason that he has an investment there. That's the way that he earns a living. And that was mine. The way I used to earn my living. And then every time they called us to play for a dance he wanted them to put his name first. And when they called me, well I wanted [*laughter*] them to put me first. And that is why that dance never took place. But it wasn't because he had something against me nor that I had anything personal against him. It just was a problem that arose about the billing, about how the two names would appear on the ticket booth, on the tickets, in the "throwaways," and posters, and the rest.

Rosario: Or, in other words, these were clauses that were in your contract?

Rodríguez: My contract specified that I had 100 percent of the "bill" in all the contracts of the dances that I played. And he had the same.

Rosario: The same?

Rodríguez: The same clause. Therefore it was never possible to make a single event.

Rosario: So that was the truth . . . it was a question of—how do you say it—professional friction?

Rodríguez: No, no, no.

Rosario: Well, you know that this also occurs in the film industry. For example, an artist of Richard Burton's stature when he works with Richard Harris. Both want to have "top billing," as they call it.

Rodríguez: Yes, yes.

Rosario: Because they are big stars, so to avoid those problems they are listed in alphabetical order.

Rodríguez: In that case, I don't want to get into that. Just imagine. Already I was last if mine started—

Rosario and Rodríguez:—with "R." [*Laughter*]

Voice: Presenting the two Titos!

Rosario: No, but it wasn't possible because of the rules in the contracts.

Rodríguez: Of the clauses that existed in the contracts that we both had.

Rosario: Exactly.

Voice: So you definitely never appeared together?

Rodríguez: Well, yes. In the beginning when we started, we worked together. I don't know who was the one who came up with that, and unfortunately, you know that sometimes you tell people a little thing, you tell them some words, and you go on repeating. It sometimes goes on repeating, and when it's been through fifty or a hundred persons, it changes.

Rosario: Yes.

Rodríguez: What actually happened already changes. And that's why many people . . . think that other things exist. But no. It's not true! That's what happened in this case. He had that clause, and I had mine, and that's why they never could present me together with him. But as to whether something exists . . . on my part nothing exists, nothing has existed, and nothing will exist. Because I consider him a great talent . . . enormous. He is a good musician, and besides that, he's Puerto Rican, just like me.

Rosario: Exactly. That's something you have to keep in mind all the time. Well, the public that recognizes you as a singer, as much in the area of the *guarachas* as the boleros, but also many people haven't seen you perform. They didn't see your presentations with your orchestra, they don't know the number of musical instruments that you like to play. For example, I know that you used to play trap drums for a while.

Rodríguez: Yes, well, truthfully, I never studied trap drums. I made some recordings on the timbales and I took a few bongo solos on some records, but I . . . it wasn't something that I studied. I . . . I don't know. I felt like this . . . the natural ability. I have a natural talent for that. The only instrument that I really studied, and I studied it for four years, was the vibraharp. I studied it with the music teacher from

Juilliard . . . of the Juilliard School of Music. I recorded a few records with it. But I decided not to use it any more because when the matter of whether the Titos were in competition with each other came up, I didn't want to form an orchestra that sounded the same as his, you see.

Rosario: Oh, yeah.

Rodríguez: I always thought that to succeed with the orchestra, I had to have my own style and my own sound.

Rosario: And you had it.

Rodríguez: And I achieved that. (interview on radio station WADO, New York, Mar. 12, 1967; trans. Willie Rosario)

Sanabria, also aware of the "billing" exaggerations of the period, notes the commonalities in the impacts of the orchestras of Machito, Rodríguez, and Puente: "By 1950, Tito was churning out 78s for Tico, RCA, SMC, and Verne under names like Tito Puente y Los Diablos del Mambo, Tito Puente and his Conjunto, and Tito Puente and his Mambo Boys. Mambo was the rage, and it had developed two distinct factions; the more commercially palatable sounds represented by the Xavier Cugat Orchestra and Pérez Prado, and the hybrid Afro-Cuban jazz sound of the Machito Orchestra, Tito Puente, and later Tito Rodríguez" (Sanabria and Socolov 1990, 6).

Puente in large part emulated the work of Machito, Mario Bauzá, and pianist-arranger René Hernández, who also arranged many works for Puente, Rodríguez, and others. Puente has commented, "The Machito Orchestra was way ahead of its time, combining jazz and Latin. I wanted to keep that going" (in Sanabria and Socolov 1990, 6). Puente's recording output began its productive pace. "At this time Cubop was at its height of popularity and Tito Puente had swinging Afro-Cuban charts which were heard live from Birdland on September 22, 1952. [On Symphony Sid Torin's radio show one evening] Tito Puente conquered New York with 'Babarabatiri,' 'Carl Miller Mambo,' 'Ran Kan Kan,' 'Mambo Inn,' 'Mambo City,' and 'Esy'" (Salazar 1994, 20).

The controversy over the "authentic mambo" was fueled largely by the comparison between Pérez Prado's internationally popular mambo style and that of the Palladium orchestras. John Storm Roberts boldly proclaimed the following in his book *The Latin Tinge: The Impact of Latin American Music on the United States:*

Prado proved to be less successful in New York, where his heavy brass sound and his over-simplification did not sit well with Waldorf-Astoria clientele used to Xavier Cugat, nor with a hard-core Latin public accustomed to the greater sophistication of Machito and Curbelo, Tito Puente and Tito Rodríguez. But to a greater extent than any of these, Prado symbolized the mambo to the American public—and its commercialization to most Latins. . . .

Ultimately Prado rarely transcended the problems caused by his great popularity. The tension between the showman and the creative artist has frequently been fruitful, as the work of both Machito and Puente illustrates. Even at his best, Prado's work almost always suffered from it; perhaps because he lacked a clearly defined constituency, capable of relating to both elements at once, so that he succumbed to the temptation to overmuch dilution posed by his considerable success during the early 1950s. . . .

If Prado symbolized the mambo's impact on the American public at large, Tito Puente and Tito Rodríguez symbolized its creative achievement. The great era of the New York mambo can be said to date from 1952, when the Palladium Dance Hall switched to an all-mambo policy featuring the big bands of Puente, Rodríguez, and Machito. (Roberts 1979, 127–29)

There are, however, contrasting views concerning Pérez Prado's achievement and innovation. In the estimation of many critics, the importance of his version of the mambo equaled not only that of the New Yorkers but also that of the original mambo interpreters, Orestes and Cachao López during their time performing with Antonio Arcaño in Cuba. Pérez Prado's style was not only commercially viable; it was virtuosic, highly danceable, superbly orchestrated, and at different points interpreted by some of the finest musicians from Cuba, Mexico, and the United States. Nevertheless, it must be recognized that the New York Palladium mambo exerted a profound influence, becoming a social and artistic force that eventually molded many younger, emerging musicians and affected not only Latin music but jazz, pop, and classical as well. This influence is especially pertinent with respect to the beboppers of the forties and fifties. Dizzy Gillespie, Charlie Parker, Max Roach, and Thelonious Monk were among the leading jazz musicians who incorporated the mambo and its related forms. Many musicians at the Birdland jazz club, a block away from the Palladium, were exposed to the new Latin music being created there. The mixing of jazz and Latin, frequently referred to at the time as "Cubop," began a movement that would eventually evolve with other labels such as jazz mambo, Afro-Cuban jazz, and Latin jazz.

The period 1951–60 was a fertile one for the Puente orchestra. Conga player Mongo Santamaría and bongoist Willie Bobo joined the orchestra, and both later had highly successful careers as solo artists with their own bands. Puente was recording during this time (1952–55) with Tico Records, where he was afforded much freedom to experiment. One of his most innovative albums, *Puente in Percussion,* was recorded in 1955. The album was recorded with percussion and bass only, no horns or piano. Featured were Santamaría, Bobo, and Patato Valdez in addition to bassist Bobby Rodríguez. Albums featuring only percussion eventually became more common on commercial Latin music labels, but at the time the effort was a creative milestone. In an interview with Bobby Sanabria, Puente recalled the project:

George Goldner, an executive at Tico, was resistant to the project at first. He couldn't see my making an album without piano and horns. I explained to him the significance of the drum in Africa; its use in religious dance rituals and communication and how the tradition was handed down to us in Latin America. He finally gave me the go ahead on the condition that we use the studio late at night to keep the cost down. We recorded everything in one or two takes and the album was very successful both from the standpoint of sales and quality drumming. (in Sanabria and Socolov 1990, 22)

The year 1955 was especially important in terms of Puente's earlier recordings, for RCA released a compilation album of his previously recorded 78-rpm records. It was also the year that Puente agreed to an exclusive recording contract with RCA. In the ensuing years the bandleader's output of LPs for the label was prolific, although he was never satisfied with the company's role. He made the following comments to Sanabria:

> At the time, RCA was pushing Pérez Prado and Luis Alcaraz whom they felt appealed to a wider audience because of their toned down approach to Latin music. Here I was ready to record with new arrangements and compositions and they put me on the back burner for three months. I finally had to go up to their offices and raise hell. From that time on at RCA they called me "Little Caesar." . . . RCA didn't know what to do with Latin music and they still don't. They treated me like some small time local artist yet I would consistently sell records. (in Sanabria and Socolov 1990, 22)

Between 1955 and 1960 Puente's orchestra experienced various personnel changes. In 1956 *sonero* Santos Colón left the orchestra of José Curbelo to join Puente, becoming one of the more dynamic and popular figures of the Puente orchestra. In 1957 Mongo Santamaría and Willie Bobo left Puente's orchestra to join the Latin jazz group of Cal Tjader.

Puente's first highly successful album with RCA was *Cuban Carnival,* recorded in 1956. Later that same year Puente recorded *Puente Goes Jazz,* which also attained major commercial success, with 28,000 copies sold within a period of two weeks. The album featured Puente's instrumental arrangements of various jazz standards and one of his original compositions. On a 1992 reissue of the album, Gene Kalbacher wrote the following:

> Reheard from a remove of some thirty-five years, the exciting big-band Cu-bop on the 1956 album *Puente Goes Jazz* loses none of its immediacy and incendiary shape. Little about it is staid or dated by 1992 standards. Though dissed in some quarters as an attempted crossover—Puente's never had to cross over, because he helped build the bridge between Afro-Caribbean music and jazz. *Puente Goes Jazz* struts and sways with the rhythmic intensity of mambo while it swings with the harmonic complexity of mainstream swing. The leader, displaying his mastery of the timbales and vibraphone, directs his thirteen-man crew of four trumpets, four reeds, bass, piano, and four percussionists through the Great American Songbook: Jerome Kern's "Yesterdays"; the bop lexicon "What Is This Thing Called Love?" and Oscar Pettiford's "Birdland After Dark"; the pen of Ted Sommer (three tunes); Gil Evans-ish Impressionism (the tone poem "Lotus Land," replete with shimmering vibes answered by gleaming brass in an almost Oriental ethos). Top-flight jazz players such as trumpeter Bernie Glow and saxists David Schildraut bring real verve, not merely a jazzy verisimilitude to arrangements that alternately swagger and seduce in the best tradition of Ellington and Herman, Gillespie and Kenton. (Kalbacher 1993)

In 1957 Puente recorded two sequel albums to previous efforts. One was a sequel to the *Puente Goes Jazz* album titled *Night Beat,* which featured jazz arrangements and musicians including trumpeter Doc Severinson. The other album again explored Afro-Cuban drumming, similar to the *Puente in Percussion* album of 1955. Titled *Top Percussion,* the recording featured percussionists Mongo Santamaría, Willie Bobo, Francisco Aguabella, Julito Collazo, Enrique Martí, bassist Evaristo Baro, and a chorus (El Viejo Machucho, Mercedita, and Collazo) interpreting the Lucumí (Yoruba) praise chants of the Afro-Cuban *santería* religious tradition. Tito had become interested in *santería,* and in later years he would become an initiate of the *orisha* Obatalá. *Top Percussion* exposed a largely unknowing listening public to the inseparable nature of African religion and music and their deep links to Latin music.

Another major event to occur in 1957 was the Cuban government's formal recognition of Puente in a ceremony honoring the great Cuban musicians of the previous fifty years. The inclusion of Puente was largely enacted through the efforts of Mario Bauzá, and Puente became the only non-Cuban so recognized at the affair.

In late 1957 Puente and his orchestra recorded his most commercially and, for many, artistically successful album, *Dance Mania,* which by 1994 had sold over 500,000 copies. Lead vocalist Santos Colón was featured on a variety of arrangements based on different Cuban dance rhythms, including *son montuno, guaguancó,* mambo, cha-cha, and bolero. The percussionists featured on the album were Ray Barretto, Julito Collazo, and Ray Rodríguez. Puente did the musical arrangements and played timbales, vibraphone, and marimba. In the notes to the reissue album, Cuban Domingo Echevarría and Puerto Rican Harry Sepúlveda wrote the following:

> [The recording] also features the singing debut of Puerto Rican sensual and sonero (ad-lib) vocalist Santitos Colón (previously the featured band vocalist for famous Cuban pianist and arranger José Curbelo); the young and dynamic conga drummer and upcoming bandleader Ray Barretto; Puerto Rican pianist, arranger, and composer Ray Coen; Cuban master drummer Julito Collazo; the famous and great Bobby Rodríguez on bass; bongósero Ray Rodríguez; as well as the powerfully polished trumpet and saxophone sections—complemented by the outstanding chorus work of Vitín Avilés, Otto Olivar, and Santitos Colón. Here is great sound and great music—a tribute to all the great dancers of the New York Palladium Ballroom Era. . . . If ever an album was deserving of its title, this one is it! For here is a dancer's paradise, a harvest of colorful, rhythmic music played by one of the world's finest Latin and Afro-Cuban dance orchestras. (Echevarría and Sepúlveda 1991)

One of the major hits on *Dance Mania* was "Cayuco," which became, and continues to be, a favorite among dance aficionados. Also on the LP was Puente's original "Hong Kong Mambo," featuring Puente on marimba playing a riff imitative of a Far Eastern melodic structure. "3-D Mambo," an instrumental arrangement composed by Ray Santos, was representative of the jazz influence on the recording. "Varsity Drag Mambo" was another arrangement on the album adapting an even earlier jazz influence, that of the big-band swing style converted to a mambo rhythmic base.

In his excellent biographical sketch of Tito Puente published in *Hip,* Bobby Sanabria offers the following synopsis of Puente's work after *Dance Mania:*

Tito maintained a busy and varied recording schedule during the last years of the decade, producing *Tambo*,* a further delving into Afro-Cuban themes, *More Dance-mania*, a straight dance album, and big band recordings with Count Basie, Woody Herman, Charlie Barnett and Abbe Lane. In 1960 Tito collaborated with trombonist Buddy Morrow on the recording *Revolving Bandstand*. Tito's radical concept for the album placed two big bands, one with a Latin rhythm section, the other with a jazz rhythm section, in a studio together. "First," Tito explained, "the jazz big band would play a tune like 'Autumn Leaves' and give it their treatment and then the Latin band would play the bridge of the tune in authentic style." The album, which wasn't released until the 1970's, featured Tito's conducting and arranging skills, blending his thorough knowledge of both the Latin and jazz idioms. *Revolving Bandstand* would be Tito's last recording for RCA. Joe Conzo, producer and longtime Puente publicist, states, "Tito recorded literally hundreds of unreleased tracks for RCA. They just never understood how great a talent they had with Tito." (Sanabria and Socolov 1990, 22)

After leaving RCA, Puente recorded an album in 1961 that was to become one of his favorites, *Puente in Hollywood* (retitled *Puente Now*). The album was produced by Norman Granz for his GNP label. Puente thereafter returned to recording with his former label, Tico Records. The next year began a period of international recognition and acclaim for the bandleader, as he made the first of many subsequent concert tours to Japan, popularizing Latin music there along with Pérez Prado and other Latin artists. Salazar notes that from the 1960s to the present, Tito Puente survived the new rhythm trends of *pachanga*, boogaloo, Latin soul, and disco, whose hits served as coronations of new kings of Latin music such as Johnny Pacheco, Charlie Palmieri, Joe Cuba, Johnny Colón, Eddie Palmieri, Ray Barretto, and Larry Harlow (Salazar 1994, 20).

Puente also began to receive numerous opportunities outside the realm of the Latin music industry. In 1967 he presented a concert of his own compositions at New York's Metropolitan Opera, and in the late sixties he hosted his own television program, *El Mundo de Tito Puente*, on a Spanish-language network. In 1968 he served as grand marshal for the Puerto Rican Day parade in New York City, and he received the key to that city in 1969 from Mayor John Lindsay.

During the sixties Puente recorded a number of significant LPs with two important female vocalists, Celia Cruz and La Lupe. Among these Tico recordings were *Cuba y Puerto Rico son . . .*, *Quimbo, Quimbumbia* (both with Celia Cruz), *Etc., Etc., Etc., with Celia Cruz*, *Puente Swings La Lupe*, *Tú y yo: Tito Puente and La Lupe*, *The King and I—El rey y yo*, and *Homenaje a Rafael Hernández* (with La Lupe). La Lupe actually became the featured vocalist with Puente's orchestra at different periods between 1965 and 1969. An extraordinary vocalist and performer, she was highly instrumental in enhancing the role of women not only in Puente's orchestra but also in Latin music generally. Although Celia

---

* *Tambo* featured the highly significant Cuban flutist Alberto Soccarrás in addition to trumpeters Bernie Glow, Ernie Royal, and Doc Severinson.

Cruz has been the more dominant personification of this aspect of Latin music, La Lupe's contribution to the art should not be underestimated. (La Lupe died in 1992.)

The Seventies: Salsa, Santana, and Latin Jazz

With the demise of the Palladium in 1966, an evolving nuance was beginning to characterize Latin music not only in New York City but around the globe. By the late sixties rock music had revolutionized the music industry and its audiences, and the borders of musical style seemed to become more irrelevant than ever. Artists throughout the United States were experimenting with various combinations of blues, rock, soul, jazz, and Latin concepts, and various new styles emerged.

In New York the confluence of these currents produced boogaloo and Latin soul but became exemplified most importantly by the style that came to be known as "salsa." Although not based on any particular rhythm or musical form, salsa basically adheres to the traditional structure and instrumentation of Afro-Cuban dance forms, but with significant embellishments, adaptations, and new formats and influences. Among the various artists spearheading this movement were Eddie Palmieri, Johnny Pacheco, Ray Barretto, and Willie Colón. Artists such as Tito Puente and Mongo Santamaría, who had been performing the same basic musical forms for the previous thirty years, adapted well and opportunistically to the new popular format, but they also remained outspoken about the "salsa" concept. Puente and Santamaría made the following statements, respectively:

> Salsa means sauce, literally; it's just a commercial term for Afro-Cuban dance music which was used to promote the music. My problem is that we don't play sauce, we play music, and Latin music has different styles; cha-cha, mambo, guaguancó, and son. Salsa doesn't address the complexities and the rich history of the music that we play. But it's become accepted now and it helped to get the music promoted. (Puente in Sanabria and Socolov 1990, 23)

> Whatever is salsa here is "música tropical" in Mexico. It's just another label for basic Cuban music. It means "saucy" or "tropical," two elements of Cuban life. The musicians emigrated from Cuba. Machito was here forty-five years ago when there were no Latin musicians here. When I came here in '48, the only Latin bands I heard were Machito, Marcelino Guerra and Noro Morales, a Puerto Riqueño. In the '50s I finally heard Puente and Tito Rodríguez. (Santamaría in Smith 1977, 19–20)

The early seventies also witnessed Carlos Santana's highly successful experimentations with blending blues, Latin, and rock. Mexican by birth, Santana had in his early youth come to San Francisco and was exposed to blues artists such as Muddy Waters and B. B. King, yet he retained his authentic base and interests in Latin music. After his first album, which included a Latin-rock version of Willie Bobo's "Evil Ways," he included in his second Columbia LP, *Abraxas* (1970), a version of Puente's "Oye como va." The recording of Puente's cha-cha, originally recorded in 1962, was an international hit, eventually becoming a classic in popular music. Santana's merging of Latin and rock gave impetus to Puente's music and the period's salsa movement. Another Puente standard,

"Pa' los rumberos,"* originally recorded in 1956, was also recorded by Santana on his third Columbia release, *Santana III* (1972), and also became a substantial international hit. The year 1977 marked the first time that Puente and Santana were featured in concert together, with both groups playing at New York's Roseland Ballroom. In his review of the concert for the *Village Voice,* Pablo Guzmán referred to Puente as "the Muhammed Ali of Latin music, complete with shuffle and rope a dope. After forty years, when faced with a challenge, the old man can still put it all together" (in Sanabria and Socolov 1990, 23). It is of interest to note that in 1977 Puente was already being referred to as "the old man," especially in the light of his continued performance and recording schedule into the late nineties.

As noted by Sanabria, "the late seventies saw an increased interest in percussion instruments in the United States and abroad" (Sanabria and Socolov 1990, 23). Martin Cohen had developed a company, Latin Percussion, Inc. (often called simply "LP"), that manufactured Latin percussion instruments. The enterprise eventually acquired an international market, becoming the world's leading manufacturer of Cuban and other Latin American–style percussion instruments. Cohen decided to tour a group of Latin musicians through Europe. In an interview with Sanabria, Cohen recalled the project:

> I signed up Johnny Rodríguez, who plays bongó with Tito, and he got Tito involved. Carlos "Patato" Valdez played conga and pianist Eddie Martínez and bassist Sal Cuevas rounded out the quintet. I was thrilled to have Tito involved in the project. He made a major impact on me dating from the time I first saw him perform at the Palladium back in the early sixties. It wasn't until a few years later that I got to know Tito on a personal level. . . . By this time Latin Percussion was in its infancy and I used a set of Tito's Cuban-made timbales and timbalitos as a basis for the prototype of my ribbed shell design. I based the "Trust the Leader" promotional campaign on Tito's supreme skills as a bandleader and musician. . . . It was a unique privilege for me to hang out with one of my heroes. Through all the traveling and things that can go wrong on the road, Tito remained a constant source of inspiration. His sharp wit always kept me smiling. Probably the most memorable occasion for me was when Tito performed with Toots Thielman, the jazz harmonica player, in a concert commemorating the 1,000 anniversary of the city of Brussels. It was electrifying. (in ibid.)

The ensemble, which Cohen named the LP Jazz Ensemble, gave numerous concerts and seminars in Europe, eventually touring Japan in 1979 with highly positive public response. Cohen commented, "It was here, I believe, that Tito realized the worldwide popularity he had achieved" (ibid.).

The same year, 1979, marked Puente's first Grammy Award, which he won for his 1978 album *Homenaje a Beny* (he had been nominated the previous year for his LP *The Legend*). The recording, dedicated to the memory of Cuban *sonero* legend Beny Moré,[†] featured his large orchestra and vocalists Celia Cruz, Cheo Feliciano, Santos Colón, Ismael Quintana, Adalberto Santiago, Junior González, Héctor Casanova, Néstor Sánchez, and

---

*This composition is also frequently documented as "Para los rumberos."

[†]Moré's first name is also often spelled "Benny."

Luigi Texidor. *Coros* (choruses) were sung by Tito Allen, Rubén Blades, Adalberto Santiago, and Puente. The LP was produced by Louie Ramírez and released on the Tico label under the executive production of Jerry Masucci. Masucci was the owner of Fania Records, which by 1978 had become the leading producer of the music being marketed and referred to as "salsa."* Included on the recording were classics composed by Moré, such as "Qué bueno baila usted," "Bonito y sabroso," "Dolor y perdón," "Se me cayó el tabaco," and "Santa Isabel de las lajas." Arrangements were done by Puente, Eddie Martínez, Jorge Milet, Frankie Colón, Marty Sheller, Louie Cruz, and Sonny Bravo.

After receiving the Grammy, Puente was honored with a testimonial "roast" by members of the Latin music community and *Latin NY* magazine.

> At the end of the affair, Joe Conzo remembers, "We had received all of these checks given by the patrons of the roast and we didn't know what to do with them. We decided to set up a scholarship fund in Tito's name to help support the education of musically gifted youth." "The scholarship fund," states Tito, "was a dream of mine for a long time. In the Latin community we have a lot of gifted youngsters who don't get an opportunity to develop their talent because of lack of money. Long after I'm gone," says Puente, "the fund will be helping kids." (Sanabria and Socolov 1990, 23)

Since the establishment of the scholarship fund in 1980, annual fundraisers featuring Puente's ensembles and other artists have continued to underwrite the foundation. Originally affiliated with Juilliard School, where Puente had studied, the project eventually became independent. As of 1995 over 100 scholarships had been awarded to diverse young musicians interested in studying music at the university, college, or conservatory level.

The Concord Years

During the early eighties, Puente was invited to sign a contract with Concord Records, a San Francisco–based company owned by Carl Jefferson, which had previously marketed mostly jazz recordings. Cal Tjader, already recording for the label, played a key role by recommending Puente as a Concord artist. Puente quickly adapted to the new momentum that had built up to this point through the performances of the LP Jazz Ensemble. He added a small horn section to the group and changed its name to the Tito Puente Latin Jazz Ensemble (later called Tito Puente and His Latin Ensemble). With the release of the ensemble's first LP, *On Broadway,* a whole new era of Puente's career began to take full shape.

This transition was profoundly significant and exciting for the music industry and the public. Although Latin jazz had established itself as a viable, somewhat marketable style since its inception among artists such as Mario Bauzá, Chano Pozo,† and Dizzy Gil-

---

* Masucci died in December 1997.

† Chano Pozo, widely recognized as the *conguero* who performed and composed with Dizzy Gillespie, should not be confused with the previously cited Chino Pozo.

lespie, and although it had maintained its directions through the efforts of Mongo Santamaría, Cal Tjader, and Willie Bobo, it had not received the market attention that many felt it deserved. In Puente's pact with Concord, a major Latin music bandleader who had been associated largely with dance music that produced international hits and received media exposure was making a recording and performance commitment to Latin jazz. In fact, and especially after the death of Cal Tjader in 1983, Puente often expressed the sentiment that he felt an obligation to continue the musical legacy of Latin jazz and its stylists such as Tjader and others. Soon after signing Puente, Concord began to arrange recording contracts with other Latin jazz artists, including Clare Fischer, Poncho Sanchez, and Jorge Dalto.

Artistically *On Broadway* and the subsequent releases by Puente's new ensemble redirected aficionados of Latin music and jazz toward much traditional material in both genres, but with refreshing, innovative new arrangements penned by Puente, among others. *On Broadway* was named after one of the album's tracks. An older, standard R&B tune originally recorded by the Drifters, "On Broadway" had recently become a major hit for the highly popular guitarist and vocalist George Benson. The Grammy-winning album also included versions of Duke Ellington's "Sophisticated Lady" and Freddie Hubbard's "First Light," the title track of an album recorded by trumpeter Hubbard that had been highly successful in the jazz market. *El rey* (1984), Puente's second Concord release, featured arrangements of some of the most notable jazz classics, including John Coltrane's "Giant Steps" and "Equinox," plus the standards "Autumn Leaves" and "Stella by Starlight." Included on the album was a remake of Puente's "Oye como va," by then a popular classic recognized worldwide. The album also included a new arrangement of Puente's "Ran Kan Kan," originally recorded by Puente's orchestra in the fifties. Puente's sixth Concord release, *Salsa Meets Jazz,* featured guest soloist Phil Woods on alto saxophone.

Through the years of his Latin Jazz Ensemble and recording for Concord, Puente has used some of the leading virtuosos of Latin music. The personnel of his ensembles has included Jorge Dalto (piano), Alfredo De La Fé (violin), Jimmy Frisaura (trumpet, bass trumpet), Bobby Rodríguez (bass), Johnny Rodríguez (bongos), José Madera (congas), Jerry González (congas, trumpet, flugelhorn), Ray González (trumpet), Edgardo Miranda (guitar, *cuatro*), Mario Rivera (soprano and tenor saxophone, flute), José "Piro" Rodríguez (trumpet), Francisco Aguabella (congas), and Sonny Bravo (piano). Bravo replaced pianist Jorge Dalto, who died in 1984 after having attained much international recognition as a member of Puente's ensemble and through his own distinguished career and recordings.

The success of Puente's Latin Jazz Ensemble also resulted in the nomination of its recordings for more Grammys, one of which was awarded for 1985's *Mambo Diablo* and another for 1989's *Goza mi timbal.* As of 1994 Puente had received four Grammy Awards and eight nominations. Numerous other awards and recognitions began to be bestowed on Puente with great frequency as the nineties approached. In 1987 he was voted the top percussionist in the *Downbeat* readers' poll, and in the same year he was honored by the National Academy of Recording Arts and Sciences with the Eubie award, in recognition of Puente's fifty-plus years of making significant artistic contributions to the recording industry.

It was also during the mideighties that Puente collaborated with playwright María Irene Fornes, a recipient of six Obie awards, on her play *Lovers and Keepers*. Puente composed the score for the work, which was presented by the INTAR Hispanic America Theater in New York. During the same period Puente had been commissioned by legendary bandleader Xavier Cugat to conduct the Cugat Orchestra for a television special produced in Barcelona Hall and devoted in part to Cugat's music.

Another significant aspect of Puente's more recent work has been an association with other artists and projects. He has played on numerous film sound tracks in addition to appearing in various films, including Woody Allen's *Radio Days, Armed and Extremely Dangerous,* and Luis Valdez's *Zoot Suit*. In 1992 the film *The Mambo Kings* was released, and Puente was a major figure in the Universal Pictures production. He worked as musical coordinator for the film, recorded sound tracks, and acted in the film, portraying a major bandleader of the Palladium era. In his compendium of his numerous *Chicago Sun-Times* reviews, Roger Ebert notes that *The Mambo Kings* contains a "wonderful scene where [actor] Assante climbs up on the stage with the legendary Tito Puente and insinuates himself into a performance with sheer gall" (Ebert 1996, 446). At the internationally televised Grammy Awards ceremony for that year, Puente performed the film's title song along with Plácido Domingo, Arturo Sandoval, and other major Latin music artists. Puente has also worked with contemporary artists ranging from the Sugar Hill Gang to Tower of Power to Gloria Estefan, playing on her Grammy Award–winning album *Mi tierra* in 1993. He again performed for the Grammy ceremony, accompanying Estefan along with Sheila E, Cachao, and Arturo Sandoval, among others who had recorded the album. Puente has also worked closely with various television programs and celebrities, including Bill Cosby, Regis Philbin and Kathie Lee Gifford, Arsenio Hall, Jay Leno, David Letterman, and television series such as *The Simpsons* and *Sesame Street,* among many others. In 1986 he was featured along with Dizzy Gillespie on *The Cosby Show,* which the February 13 issue of *TV Guide* described as an episode where "Cliff [Cosby's character] talks some jazz greats into a jam session."

During the nineties Puente also frequently appeared as a special guest on recordings by the younger generation of Latin music, considering many of them to be the inheritors and bearers of the tradition. Examples include his timbal performances and extended solos on Poncho Sanchez's *Chile Con Soul* (1990) and similarly featured solos with the highly acclaimed and popular Japanese salsa group Orquesta de La Luz's 1991 *Salsa no tiene frontera* (released in the U.S. as *Sin fronteras*), in addition to the group's video, *Live at Madison Square Garden*. Puente also recorded an important album with Pete Escovedo and Sheila E titled *Familia*.

On August 4, 1990, Puente was honored by the Hollywood community with a star on the Hollywood Walk of Fame. Celia Cruz had received one shortly before, and a committee was convened in Los Angeles to propose to the Hollywood Chamber of Commerce that Puente receive a star as well. As a member of that committee, I can personally attest to the excitement and long hours of work involved in the project. Especially active in the effort were Josie Powell, a former professional dancer and longtime associate of

Puente; Joe Conzo; KXLU (Alma del Barrio) disc jockey Carmen Rosado; actor Dennis Cole; and a number of other important figures in the music and Hollywood industry, including masters of ceremonies Johnny Grant and Bob Welsh. Puente was highly gratified and energized by the award, and a large group of his professional friends and family made a special trip to Hollywood to be present at the festivities. Puente's Latin Jazz Ensemble performed for both the star ceremony (where both Poncho Sanchez and Francisco Aguabella guest performed with the band) and the special banquet held at the historic Hollywood Roosevelt Hotel (directly across the street from the star).

The 100th Album

For some time before the Hollywood Star event, there had been much speculation about the fact that Puente was quickly approaching the recording of his 100th album, a feat accomplished by few major artists in the music industry. The album was finally recorded and released in 1991. Although Puente was still under contract to Concord Records, a special arrangement was made to record the album on RMM Records, a new label initiated by Puente's longtime agent Ralph Mercado. The recording was produced by Sergio George and coproduced by Johnny Pacheco. Recorded with a consortium of artists interpreting Puente's older dance orchestra style, the album featured singers Celia Cruz, Oscar D'León, José "El Canario" Alberto, Tony Vega, Tito Nieves, Ismael Miranda, Millie P., Santos Colón,* Danny Rivera, and Domingo Quiñones. Musical arrangements were written by Sergio George, Ray Santos, Paquito Pastor, José Madera, Mandy Visozo, Louis (Louie) Ramírez, and Tito Puente. Titled *Mambo King,* the album borrowed its theme from the film *The Mambo Kings,* on which Puente was then working. On the back of the cover was a dedication "to Tito Puente's lifelong friend and companion, Jimmy Frisaura," who at the time was suffering from poor health and was not able to play on the recording.

Having met the challenge of his 100th album, Puente seemed energetically prepared to begin his second hundred. Returning to the Concord label, he recorded his next album in 1992 with his Latin Jazz Ensemble, now expanded to eleven musicians besides Puente. The album, *Mambo of the Times,* included what was by now Puente's unique blend of Latinized jazz standards and "straight-ahead" Latin pieces. Jazz standards on the recording included Gil Fuller and Dizzy Gillespie's "Things to Come," Fats Waller's "Jitterbug Waltz," and Billy Strayhorn's "Passion Flower." The liner notes were written by Bill Cosby, who had become a close friend and associate of Puente through various projects and television work. Cosby concluded his notes as follows:

> And so with this 101st album, I would say, ladies and gentlemen, this is an historic album, because the man has gone past the century mark. But it also means that you're listening to a musician with 100 albums of experience. Therefore it is safe to assume that this man knows what he is doing. The album requires, first of all, the purchase. If you're reading the liner notes and you haven't made up your mind yet . . . trust

---

* Santos Colón died on Feb. 21, 1998, in Puerto Rico.

me. You can't—no way, as young people would say (which they've been saying for a long time)—make a mistake. Whether starting your Tito Puente collection, or adding to your Tito Puente collection, it's all here. And don't forget, ladies and gentlemen, you're listening to a man who has recognition all around the world, and the connection is there. It has nothing to do with whether Tito can speak Italian, Yugoslavian, Russian, Chinese, or Japanese. The beautiful thing about it is, once he bangs those two sticks together counting off the rhythm like sign language, they all come together and they dance, and they tap their feet, and they feel good. This man has earned Grammy Awards, has a star on the Walk of Fame, is a legend. A Latin Legend. A Latin Jazz Legend.

Mr. Puente will always be a musician, a composer, a family man, and a friend to me. You will notice that he is also an excellent businessman. And the proof of it is that I am not, and I have not played cowbell on any of his first 100 albums. And now the 101st . . . I'm not there. The man knows what he's doing. Enjoy.

As with many artists of Puente's stature, the number and variety of honors and recognition have been considerable. Puente received honorary doctorates from the State University of New York (Old Westbury) in 1987, Long Island University in 1994, and Hunter College (CUNY). Additionally, he has been invited to numerous universities to conduct workshops, give lectures, and perform with student jazz bands and other ensembles. He has performed for various presidents (Carter, Reagan, Bush, and Clinton) at the White House and other venues in Washington, D.C., and for other heads of state throughout the world. On March 4, 1993, George Wein produced a tribute to Puente. Staged at Carnegie Hall in New York City, the concert featured an all-star jazz orchestra directed by trumpeter Jon Faddis and featuring, among others, saxophonist Paquito D'Rivera. In 1994 ASCAP (Association of Songwriters, Composers, Authors, and Publishers) awarded Puente the organization's most prestigious honor, the Founder's Award, presented by Latin percussionist Sheila E at ASCAP's second annual El Premio celebration. Past recipients of the award include Don Henley and Glen Frey, Hal David and Burt Bacharach, Jerry Leiber and Mike Stoller, Smokey Robinson, Paul McCartney, Bob Dylan, and Julie Styne. Puente has also received major awards and recognition from magazines, including *Downbeat, Metronome,* and *Billboard,* the last of which bestowed him a 1995 Lifetime Achievement Award. In January 1997, as he had many times before, Puente again won the *Downbeat* critics' poll for "number one" percussionist for the previous year. On September 29, 1997, he was bestowed the National Medal of the Arts by President Bill Clinton at the White House. In honoring Puente with the medal, Clinton commented that the mere mention of his name makes "everyone want to get up and dance" (*Los Angeles Times,* Sept. 30, 1997).

A recent stage in Puente's career has been the development of his Golden Latin Jazz All Stars, the third of his performing groups (the others being his Latin Jazz Ensemble and his orchestra). Recording on the Tropijazz label distributed by Sony, the group recorded its first album live during 1992–93 at the Village Gate in New York City. The album featured leading contemporary artists Paquito D'Rivera (alto saxophone), Mongo Santamaría (congas), Dave Valentín (flute), Claudio Roditi (trumpet), Giovanni Hidalgo (congas), Hilton Ruiz (piano), and Ignacio Berroa (drums), with a guest appearance by

Mario Rivera (tenor saxophone). A second album was released in 1994 and featured the same personnel except for D'Rivera (replaced by Mario Rivera) and Roditi (replaced by Charlie Sepúlveda). Titled *In Session,* this recording was done in the studio and also featured a guest performance by jazz saxophonist James Moody, who sang his highly popular composition "Moody's Mood for Love."

In recent years the momentum associated with Puente's Latin jazz has been characterized by the bandleader's tours throughout the world—according to many critics, at a faster pace than ever before in his career. Throughout the early nineties Puente was performing twenty to thirty jazz festivals per year in countries around the world, including England, Greece, Holland, Finland, Germany, Spain, Sweden, France, Italy, Singapore, Russia, Japan, Australia, Mexico, Argentina, Puerto Rico, and Canada. He also continues to perform concerts, club dates, and dance hall engagements in numerous cities throughout the United States, from the Blue Note jazz club in New York to the Hollywood Bowl. In a September 16, 1993, *Los Angeles Times* review of one of Puente's Hollywood Bowl concerts, Enrique Lopetegui made the following observations of the evening's performances, which also featured Eddie Palmieri and Rubén Blades.

> At the end of the "Latin Jazz Explosion" on Tuesday at the Hollywood Bowl, Tito Puente achieved what had seemed impossible during the previous 2½ hours: breaking the ice and making the crowd dance in the aisles.
>
> It was a near-capacity crowd that had chatted, picnicked, laughed and held family discussions while Eddie Palmieri, Rubén Blades and Tito Puente offered a sample of some of the most important Latin music of the second half of the century.
>
> Five-time Grammy winner Palmieri opened the show with a 40-minute journey through all aspects of his music. Playing piano and directing his seven-piece orchestra, the New Yorker offered both sustained *salsa* grooves and long compositions that represent the ultimate in Latin fusion.
>
> Unfortunately, Palmieri's short set predicted the absurd concept of the whole evening: three geniuses of Latin music reduced to abridged versions of themselves, playing for an audience that for the most part was definitely not their crowd . . .
>
> After Blades' bittersweet performance [he was performing this last show in Los Angeles for some time, returning to Panama to enter politics], Puente closed the show by adding some spice to the evening. Several people were literally falling asleep in their boxes (to the puzzlement of die-hard fans nearby) and throngs were leaving the Bowl with their picnic baskets when the king of *timbales* grabbed his last card and began playing his greatest hit: "Oye como va," popularized worldwide by Santana in the early '70s.
>
> It was like pressing a button that changed the whole night. Hundreds of salsa and Latin jazz fans descended from the cheap seats and occupied the emptied boxes and aisles, doing for two songs what they couldn't for the rest of the night. (Lopetegui 1993, F1, 11)

In 1996 Puente recorded on the premiere album of his son, Tito Puente Jr., whose Latin Rhythm Crew (*Guarachando,* EMI Latin) was a Latin rap project that achieved considerable attention in the market. In the same year Puente Sr. also recorded what many consider to be a remarkable album, *Jazzin'*, featuring Puente, the young popular vocalist India, and a special guest—the Count Basie Orchestra. Along with Sheila E, Puente was a featured solo artist with Gloria Estefan in the internationally televised closing ceremonies at the 1996 summer Olympics in Atlanta. Also appearing in the midnineties was the RMM *Latin All Star Tribute to the Beatles* album featuring Puente, among numerous other contemporary Latin music artists. In 1997 the *Jazz Latino* album was released on the Tropijazz (RMM) label, featuring recordings by the ensembles of both Puente and conga drummer Giovanni Hidalgo. In the same year the video *Tito Puente* was released as part of the *RMM Best of Series,* including five musical performances and a "Tito Puente Documentary." Featured on the video are India, Millie P., Hilton Ruiz, Dave Valentín, Mongo Santamaría, Celia Cruz, Oscar D'León, Tony Vega, and Tito Nieves, among others. In 1998 Puente's new arrangement of Mario Ruiz Armengol's classic "Brassmen's Holiday" was included by trumpeter Arturo Sandoval on his *Hot House.* In addition to using Puente's remarkable arrangement, Sandoval also included his own tribute to Puente entitled "Tito." In his liner notes Sandoval wrote, "This piece is an homage to the Latin musician who, in the name of our race, has risen above all and has been a true inspiration for so many musicians" (Sandoval 1998).

In 1997 RMM Records also released an album celebrating Puente's fifty years in the music industry. Titled *50 Years of Swing,* the double album included a variety of Puente's recordings representing his diverse and dynamic career as a continually leading artist of Latin music. He was also one of the featured artists on the highly distributed *Nuyorican Soul* album (1997) and project led by hip-hop artists and producers Kenny "Dope" González and "Little" Louis Vega. Other musicians featured on the project included Roy Ayers, Eddie Palmieri, George Benson, Jocelyn Brown, Jazzy Jeff, India, Vincent Montaña Jr., Dave Valentín, Hilton Ruiz, David Sánchez, Steve Turre, Charlie Sepúlveda, Lisa Fisher, Paulette McWilliams, and Richie Flores. In the liner notes to the album, Carol Cooper made the following remarks:

> At first González and Vega only planned to approach a few guest artists. Philly soul writer/arranger Vince Montaña, Jr., fusion jazz artist Roy Ayers, and Latin jazz master Tito Puente were the initial choices. All men with reputations as writers and bandleaders. And all, incidentally, expert vibes players. The central ideas for original and cover material came from Vega's fond memories of the 1970s, a decade of remarkable diversity and hybridization. By centering on these first three artists, Vega and González were already mapping areas of emphasis, with each guest star signifying a major musical movement. Puente symbolized the 70s salsa explosion that was spearheaded by the Tico, Alegre and Fania labels. Roy Ayers symbolized a rich stream of politicized jazz funk bounded on one end by Weather Report and on the other by Earth, Wind and Fire. Montaña's contributions to the Salsoul label, and his association with the kind of big orchestral funk arrangements that Gamble and Huff (among others) marketed globally as "the Philly Sound," made him a symbol of all that was innovative, smart and serious about American disco.
>
> See, M.A.W. [Masters at Work, stage name for González and Vega] were never suckered into the glib, revisionist propaganda depicting the 1970s as "the decade that

taste forgot" because they have record collections that prove otherwise. Both Latin and black musicians created work of unprecedented sophistication during this period, often working together on tracks which combined jazz, rock, funk and Afro-Latin elements. Nuyorican Soul is a fond look back at that period filtered through a post-hip-hop, post-techno sensibility. Vega talks of taking listeners on a journey with Nuyorican soul. A trip through different eras and musics not with nostalgia, but with a firm vision of how to carry these traditions boldly into a new, improved future. (Cooper 1996)

In a feature article on the Nuyorican Soul project in *Straight No Chaser,* Puente, referring to González and Vega, was quoted as saying, "These guys are geniuses. When I die, they're taking over." In the same article Vega expressed his strong respect for Puente's knowledge and participation in the project: "We've got a lot better at dealing with musicians but this album has definitely made us want to learn more musically. It's being able to talk their language; it's knowing what we want to do but not being able to do it 'cause we're basically from the street. A lot of the musicians in the project have got street sense . . . people like Tito Puente, he's like, 'Hey, what you wanna do . . . ticaticatica . . . ticaticatica . . . ticaticatica . . . you want it this way?' It's like dealing with someone your own age" (Bradshaw 1996, 24).

In 1997 *50 Years of Swing* was released on the RMM label. The three-CD boxed set included selected tracks representing Puente's fifty years of recording and performance. The liner notes included personal testimonials dedicated to Puente from the following artists: Johnny Pacheco, Eddie Palmieri, Carlos Santana, Dr. Billy Taylor, Hilton Ruiz, Ray Barretto, Michael Camilo, Lou Rawls, Mario Rivera, Dave Valentín, James Brown, Andy García, Cristina Saralegui, Graciela, Celia Cruz, and Israel "Cachao" López.

As of 1998 Tito Puente had 116 albums, over 450 compositions, and over 2,000 arrangements to his credit. The figures do not include the numerous other recordings he has done with other artists, his recompiled recordings, or his appearances on film, television, and radio. It is difficult to estimate how many times he has performed live during his career, but the number is certainly over 10,000.

For over fifty years Puente has led his own bands, emerging as the most enduring leader and musician in the field of Latin music. This duration has many sources, especially his high level of performance ability and musical knowledge throughout his career, his innovative creative accomplishments, his resilient and consistent affinity for the promotion of his enterprise, and his competitive verve. Not the least of this artist's outstanding character has been the unique and universal flavor of his powerful charisma.

2

A Conversation with the King

THIS chapter is a transcript of an interview I conducted with Tito Puente in November 1994 while I was doing the principal research for this book. After knowing Tito closely for more than ten years, I finally had the opportunity to conduct an in-depth and personal interview with him. The goal of my questions and topics is more related to Tito's musical concept and philosophy than his biography, which is surveyed in the previous chapter. The videotaped interview, which took place at the Gershwin Hotel in New York City, lasted about two hours.

My goal in this interview with Tito included looking at his life in Latin music, examining some of the important events in the development of Latin music in New York City and therefore throughout the world, and investigating not only how Tito Puente has become a popular cultural icon but how he represents this whole movement that has been referred to as Latin music, mambo, cha-cha, and salsa. Why is Tito considered the king (el rey de la salsa, del timbal)? It was also important to me that I interview him in his native city, New York.

❖❖

Loza: Tito, I want to start off with a very basic concept. Everybody starts with this concept, where did you come from, where were you born, but going a little beyond that, how do you feel that you became a musician here in New York City? What is the importance of people like your parents, your family, the barrio where you grew up, Spanish Harlem? And why is it that you became a musician? Why did you choose to become a musician? Why did you have the talent?

Puente: That's an easy question to answer. I was born in Spanish Harlem. My parents were Puerto Ricans. They were one of the first pioneers coming here from Puerto Rico, to Atlanta, then Brooklyn. I was born in New York and went down there (Puerto Rico) when I was one year old, then they brought me up when I was three years old, and I grew up in Spanish Harlem. I mixed with jazz and Latin music all the time while I was a young kid, you know, studying. My mother put me to study immediately because they saw that I had a lot of talent musically, and they put me to study piano. I was always banging around cans and the walls and doing a lot of percussion things. Some of our neighbors told my mother, "Hey, why don't you put him to study drums?" Twenty-five cents a lesson, right there in the New York School of Music. Once a week I used to go. That's on Saturday. Thanks to her, I developed my musicianship. I studied there. I studied saxophone, studied drums. I had dancing, also tap dancing. Then I got heavy into the percussion. As a young man, I started playing with the local bands around the neighborhood, and that's where I developed, more or less, my reputation and my experience. This type of instrument, you need a lot of experience in the street to play, which is the percussion that I play, timbales.

Loza: Now Tito, you mentioned a word that is very important, the "neighborhood," Spanish Harlem. What are some of the things that you feel were important in the way that you were being raised—for example, the household, your house? Your parents spoke mostly Spanish; they were preparing the typical foods that they brought with them from Puerto Rico. Your neighbors were speaking Spanish, and these local bands were delivering a service to the local clientele. What was that local life like?

Puente: Well, we did have a lot of barriers, you know, because the neighborhood wasn't really a Spanish neighborhood. A lot of Jewish people used to live there at that time. In fact, I was born in Harlem Hospital. That was one of the best hospitals here in New York. So my upbringing was pretty rough. Around the neighborhood, one side we had the Italians, the other side we had the blacks, and the Puerto Ricans were smack in the middle! One of those things we had a lot of difficulties in getting was our music across, particularly. So we had to incorporate our music within the neighborhood, all the neighborhood clubs—all the Latin music was played there. It wasn't exposed like jazz, until a much later time. We were all very close neighborhood Latins there. Puerto Ricans particularly, anyway, and as the years went by, naturally a lot of Cubans and Dominicans, and all kinds of people. Today we have South American people, Colombians, Central Americans, but at the time I was growing up, it was a little difficult. We were very poor. My family used to move . . . a lot to different buildings, you know. Sometimes I'd come from school and I'd find out that they had moved across the street because they gave them two months' rent.

Loza: Now today they use the word *minorities* for people of Latin descent or African Americans. Here in a place like New York or Chicago or L.A., you've got over one hundred cultures thriving in those cities, but today they use the word *minorities,* and in a lot of the work I've done, I've looked at the issue of conflict. This is something you brought up, "barriers," because you start living two worlds, don't you? One is in English and one is in Spanish. Did that ever represent to you a conflict in what you were trying to do? Did you see conflict early, or was this more of an advantage to you?

Puente: Well, it was an advantage to me. My kids now, they speak very little Spanish. That's because they go to school and they speak in English; my wife speaks English with them at the house. When I was growing up, my parents insisted that we speak Spanish and read Spanish. I'm so happy that they did that, because we developed their culture and their roots. I learned the cultures of the Latin people, which is very important, because in this country at the time that I was being brought up, there was nothing that they taught us about [Latin] culture. America-only history you learn; but Latin American cultures are very big, and I'm very glad that my mother brought me up that way. I never had any difficulties really, because I spoke English, naturally—since I was born here—and Spanish. So today that's a big advantage to me, being bilingual.

Loza: Being in the area of Spanish Harlem, and being also near a lot of the African American culture in addition to the other cultures—because there were Jewish, Italian, among others I would imagine in the neighborhoods you lived in—did you confront or did you consider the issue of discrimination? Did you look at what was happening to the blacks and compare that to what was happening as a Latino?

Puente: Well, I was very much into the black people. We used to call them "colored" people in those days, you know. I was involved with jazz, I went to black schools—they were right there in the neighborhood. I never had any conflict with them, and musicwise, they were my heroes. Some of them were my mentors, like Ellington and Basie at the time, and Lucky Mullinder, and Chick Webb . . . all those bands. I was a young fellow, so I used to listen to a lot of the jazz music in those days, and all Latin music. We got that in the neighborhood because it wasn't as exposed as the jazz music was. So I'm very happy I got brought up with both cultures, and we really got along and developed all our music together through all these years.

Loza: And in a way this is the gist of what happened with Latin music. People like you, of Puerto Rican background, a lot of Cubans, Puerto Ricans, other Latinos, but especially some of the great people like Machito, and before that Arsenio Rodríguez, had come here to New York, and it started what you might call a transplantation of the Caribbean music, especially the Cuban music here. Some of the young ones, like yourself, started emulating these people and at the same time were exposed to the heavy jazz thing of the Ellingtons, Gillespie, and Charlie Parker. How do you feel this was essential in molding Latin music here in New York City?

Puente: Well, Machito, like you mentioned, was my mentor when I was a very young man, and Mr. Mario Bauzá, who just passed away two years ago. Those are my two main mentors in the Latin field, and then in the jazz field I was young and I had Count Basie, Duke Ellington, the Stan Kenton Orchestra, Woody Herman, and all these big jazz orchestras that sometimes used some of their . . . oh, of course Dizzy Gillespie was another one; they used a lot of Latin influence in their music too. They used to love our Latin rhythms. Of course, when I was a kid the king of the rumba was Mr. Xavier Cugat, who did many movies because his music was very commercial, but the music that we played in Spanish Harlem, or here, was music that was very modern, very typical, coming from Cuba—like Arsenio Rodríguez you mentioned, people like that and other heavy stars. But then Machito and Mario [Bauzá] were the ones that really got into the Latin jazz, which we call [it] today, and really developed that style many years ago. That's what made our music more modern to the Latin people and the jazz people, because it involved our percussion rhythm at the same time, and the harmonic and melodic concept of the jazz feel, which is very modern. So that was emerging at that time, in the early forties. Machito is responsible for that.

Loza: How did your relationship with Machito begin?

Puente: I must have been thirteen or fourteen years old, and I played with him in the neighborhood, during the weekend, because he used to perform on 110th Street and Fifth Avenue near the [Park] Plaza, we used to call it. And I used to come in on Sundays and sit in, and I was still going to school and all that, so naturally we got along, they saw my talents and all that. They really loved me. They loved my parents—you know most of the people in the neighborhood, they all knew each other. So I used to come in and play all the time. I was gaining a lot of experience, and that's how they really got to me. They taught me a lot about the street musician, because it was very important to play, jamming a lot with the Cubans, playing timbales and drums. I used to play saxophone. I used to play piano with them, and so that's how I developed my experience, hanging around with these musicians. Then eventually I was working for him anyway. I became a drummer.

Loza: And at that time were you already experimenting with arranging and notating music?

Puente: Oh yes, and much later I went to arranging. I went to the Juilliard Conservatory of Music, and I went to Richard Bender and I studied arranging. But that was nothing. I was already nineteen or twenty years old. In fact, it was in the world war, late forties, when I started my education as an arranger, conductor, orchestrator, and copyist, but as an instrumentalist I was already studying before the war.

Loza: Let's get into that period going up to the war, because you mentioned Machito had already sort of taken you under his wing. Are there some other musicians—because you mentioned the street musicians in Spanish Harlem—are there other people that you think are important to mention, that maybe don't get mentioned a lot, that really inspired you or taught you things?

Puente: Oh yes. There are a lot of them which I don't even remember. But there were quite a lot of them. Of course, the more later years we have the great Charlie Palmieri . . . Eddie Palmieri. These are all musicians that we all grew up together . . . Pacheco . . . this clan was with us at the Palladium.

Loza: You remember those guys when they were younger, in their teens?

Puente: Well, you're talking about the real old-timers, like Rafael Hernández; we had the Happy Boys Orchestra. These people aren't mentioned at all, except Machito and Mario. [There were also other important musicians who influenced me, such as] Noro Morales, Marcelino Guerra, Miguelito Valdés, and Arsenio Rodríguez, because they always kept active throughout the years. These are the musicians, the neighborhood musicians, very popular in the neighborhood and then they faded out.

Loza: Now one of the interesting things also at this time was that the majority of the Latino population in New York was becoming Puerto Rican, but you also had this heavy Cuban influx, and where[as] Machito and Mario Bauzá were Cubans, René Hernández and others such as Eddie Palmieri and Charlie Palmieri were Puerto Ricans. Johnny Pacheco was Dominican. How did this thing mix? You know, the Puerto Ricans and the Cubans? Did it come together very easily? What was that all about?

Puente: It came very [easily] because the Puerto Ricans are very good musicians too. The Cubans have their own style of music; that's what we play, really. We're not playing Puerto Rican music, because Puerto Rican music is *la bomba, la plena;* they had their own typical music in the island. But at that time we were playing Cuban music, and that's what developed really—the jazz, the Cuban bebop and all that throughout the years. Now it's different. Now the Puerto Ricans are so hip into the music we don't even have many Cuban bandleaders around. Puerto Ricans are the ones that have kept this music going from the late fifties until now.

Loza: It's almost like some people have said, that what developed from the thirties up to, let's say, the late forties was a school of music largely based on some of the older Cuban masters from Arsenio Rodríguez to Machito, and then it was people like you, Tito Puente, among others—perhaps Tito Rodríguez, or perhaps eventually Johnny Pacheco—who started emulating these musicians.

Puente: Well, we grew up in that environment. We loved that music anyway. We were into it and we grew up with these heavies around us all the time—Arsenio, and all the greatest—and we used to listen to records. That's very important. We listened to all the records that used to come in from Cuba, and we used them to develop our own style.

Loza: And eventually because the migration of Puerto Ricans kept increasing, the majority of these younger students in this so-called school were mostly Puerto Rican.

Puente: Oh yeah, sure. A lot of the young Puerto Rican musicians developed a lot of good Cuban-style playing. As I grew older I became a big-band leader, [and] then I catered to all kinds of people, but I really played Cuban music—which I still play, because that's the good dance music: the mambo, the *guaguancó,* the cha-cha-chá, the *guajira,* all that kind of music.

Loza: How about some of the important percussionists that were coming from Cuba—especially Patato Valdez, Mongo Santamaría, some of these people that were coming by the early to late forties, your contemporaries—how did those people influence you?

Puente: One of the biggest influences was Chano Pozo. He was here with Dizzy Gillespie. He did "Manteca" and all that. That was the beginning of Latin jazz and all these jazz orchestras that utilized conga drums. He was the big influence within the jazz and the Latin. Then some of the Latin bands started putting conga drums and bongo players and timbales in the bands, because in the early days the jazz orchestras or Latin orchestras didn't even have a drum player, maybe a timbale player, maybe, but they didn't have no congas and all that. In the late fifties, that's when they all started. Machito and Noro Morales were very important influences here. They started adding percussion instruments.

Loza: One of the things that has earmarked your musical style is the diversity of your instrumentation—the fact that you became an orchestrator and arranger and composer. You composed all these important songs, tunes, arrangements, and . . . you also started experimenting with different instruments. Now, the Chano Pozos and the Mongo Santamarías may have influenced you as a percussionist among the street players that you're talking about. What made you start expanding? You even played saxophone, and of course you played the trap set. You experimented with conga drums and bongos. You ended up doing a lot of timbal, which became your major percussion instrument. What made you start experimenting with a diversity of percussion instruments, and even harmonic and melodic instruments beyond that—the vibraphone, which became your second mainstay?

Puente: Well, you have to realize that these percussionists that came up from Cuba, they're not really musicians. In fact, in Latin America and Central America they call percussionists street musicians, but I studied. I went to study music. I went to music school, which they didn't. They had all that percussion ability, which today is very respected, but at the time they weren't musically inclined, so by my studying music and becoming an arranger, and being a percussion man at the same time, I tried to give the percussion instrument more class and bring it out front in the music. Like today, that's what's happening around the world. The people love our Latin American music. Sometimes they don't understand our lyrics, but they love our rhythms, and that's what's important in Latin American music—in our music from the Caribbean or Brazil or wherever. The percussion is what really makes the music exciting.

Loza: And so that when you started picking up, let's say, on piano, it enabled you to do other things, for example, the orchestrations and the arrangements?

Puente: Oh yes, orchestrations. I did three or four percussion albums too. I learned how to play 6/8 rhythms and *santería* rhythms, and it's very important too.

Loza: So the ability to relate to both the percussion and to the harmonic and the melodic forms became an important asset of what you became as a bandleader?

Puente: Very important, because there are arrangers that are great ballad arrangers and harmonically they're great, but when it comes to the percussive end of the music, which is very important—a little clave, or the bass figuration or the piano figuration—they're not hip to that yet. See what I mean?

Loza: For example, Stan Kenton attempted to do that, and he had probably hired people to arrange some of these things, because it was not the kind of knowledge that he had easy access to. He hadn't played clave.

Puente: It still happens today. Latin musicians can play better jazz than jazz musicians play in Latin. It always happens.

Loza: In fact, Dizzy Gillespie has said that. You said the exact same thing that he did.

Puente: Oh yeah, sure. Well, he loved our music. He was always into it . . . all the time. He composed [and performed] a lot of Latin-influenced things, like "Cubano Be" and "Cubano Bop," "Tin Tin Deo," "Manteca," and then "Night in Tunisia."

Loza: But the big difference is the rhythmic foundation. In other words, a lot of jazz musicians haven't played around arrangements that rely on clave, or on the heavy piano with *guajeo,* or on the *tumbao,* and these are things that one has to know. One has to do them for a long time. It's just like doing changes in jazz.

Puente: Oh yeah, sure. They used to come up and visit us a lot at the Palladium. The Palladium was like our home of the mambo here on Fifty-third Street and Broadway, and all the best bands and everybody used to come up and listen to the music or watch the dancers. Down the block was Birdland, around the corner of Fifty-second Street. So all the fellas that were into jazz used to come up here to listen to the Machito orchestra or my band playing these Afro-Cuban rhythms and these exciting mambos, and they loved it. That's where they got the influence, too.

Loza: Besides Dizzy Gillespie, who were some of the other jazz musicians coming up to the Palladium to listen?

Puente: Most all of them . . . Charlie Parker, he recorded with Machito . . . the trumpet player Howard McGee, very famous at the time. Oh, a lot of the trumpet players and jazz players . . . tenor saxophonist Dexter Gordon. They all used to come to the Palladium and jam with us and record. Of course Stan Getz and all them too.

Loza: You're mentioning the Palladium and the Latin scene and you're comparing it to what was happening on, I guess Fifty-second Street and the jazz thing. What were the Latin clubs? What were the main ballrooms, the main places of Latin music? Where were they, and why were they so important in the development of this music?

Puente: They were very important because . . . we had the Roseland, which is a very important ballroom. We had the Palladium. We had the Arcadia, and uptown we had the Plaza, and in the Bronx we had ballrooms. Downtown, there was a hall there, and all these places. Then the hotels used to give a lot of Latin dances because they have beautiful ballrooms. The music was really very popular, and we used to play all the resorts up in the mountains, and all the big hotels and out on the beach clubs up in Long Island too. The music itself was becoming very popular, and you didn't have to be Latin to love the music. All non-Latinos used to love our music too.

Loza: Now Tito, you mentioned, of course, Juilliard. You had gone there to study, and of course a lot of . . . well, people certainly like Miles Davis actually came to New York back in the late forties to study at Juilliard. You also studied there probably sometime during the same time. Why is it that . . . people from jazz—and in the case of yourself, Latin—all of a sudden were deciding to go to Juilliard? What was it that was pulling them there? Was it the prestige, or was it the technical skill that you were looking forward to learning, because basically it was still the classical music tradition that you were going to study there. What made you go to Juilliard?

Puente: Well, originally when I went to Juilliard it was to study orchestration, because I didn't go there for percussion. I went for composition, orchestration, and arranging, and naturally transcribing and copying. I had different subjects there, but I realized that studying at Juilliard wasn't enhancing what I wanted to learn to play, because they were mostly into the classical field. Like now, I have my scholarship fund. I've given scholarships and all that, but then I realized that these scholarship funds didn't mean anything to them because that wasn't my field. I was more into the jazz and the Latin fields, and I feel that those musicians needed that education or some scholarships, so then I pulled out and I started giving these scholarships to these people, see, and most of them are jazz musicians too, because to go to Juilliard it's naturally a conservatory of music. They're more involved with the classics. They're not really into the Latin music that we play. The percussion that they teach is timpani, drumming, cymbals, and symphonic work.

Loza: So, whereas your scholarship originally was specifically associated with Juilliard, now you've opened it up to a more free base?

Puente: Oh yes, I opened up Boys Harbor, and I opened up for all universities and conservatories of music; and its mostly for young people that have been studying already music for two or three years and then they need that last year to get their bachelor's or their master's, and they need funding. That's why I have to help them out, so they can get their degree. Because if you go on with too many young people, they may change their mind after a year. They may become a dentist or a lawyer, or anything else, you know what I mean? These people have really been studying music, you know, the performing arts. That's what I do now. I give them [scholarships] to dancers—ballet dancers like the lady in Ballet Hispánico, Tina Ramírez. Well, I give it to performers, to arrangers, composers, instrumentalists who are studying.

Loza: It's interesting that this has happened with so many musicians who attempt to go to, let's say, Juilliard. The same thing, I think, of what you're describing that happened to you in the late forties at Juilliard happened with Miles Davis. I remember from reading his autobiography that after about a year or so, he just got tired of the constriction of just studying Western European harmony, and he just didn't see how he could use it in what he wanted to do. This was the same feeling you had?

Puente: No. What happened was that after the war the government would pay half of your studying fees if you went to study. So, first . . . I gave the audition—because you have to make an exam before joining Juilliard . . . , and then I was studying the Schillinger system with Mr. Richard Bender, but those lessons at that time were $15.00. They were very expensive, so I used to pay $7.50, and the government paid the other $7.50. While I was studying there I was trying to learn how to write motion picture music. I was interested in that, and graphs and all that—you know, permutation of melodies—and that's what I was really studying there. I found that I wasn't involved in that end. That wasn't really my main interest, so then I stopped studying that. I have my books and everything, but I stopped there about a year or two later and developed my style and all that by actually performing and playing, because everybody has the same books. Everybody goes to school. Everybody studies. Everybody graduates. They get a big diploma. They go home and put it up against the wall, and they just stare at it all the time. "What did you do?" Don't do nothing. You know dentists and doctors, everybody, it's the same thing.

You've got to go on and practice. Take every practice and gain experience playing. It's the same thing for musicians. In those days there used to be a lot of jam sessions at places—you could hang out a lot and play—and at places where the musicians used to get together and discuss different arrangements and different tunes, or "Did you hear this record?" and all that, you know. All that is part of your growing up and gaining experience in whatever profession you're in.

Loza: One more little comment on the Juilliard issue. It's an interesting issue because now you got people like Wynton Marsalis formerly associated with Juilliard. I believe he went there. He's done a series of PBS broadcasts with Juilliard. He's now doing a thing with Tanglewood, with PBS, and Sony. . . . The thing, though, is that, as you were saying, Tito, for a lot of musicians—and it's something that is important for the public to realize—that sometimes it's important for maybe a Miles Davis or a Tito Puente or whoever else to be at a Juilliard, where they can compete with this so-called other standard but at the same time start demonstrating the fact that, well, there's another standard of excellence, and two or three years may be enough at that point. You felt there was a time that you had to go and enter the world of performance, to really use the tools that you had assimilated, right?

Puente: Of course. Sure. The performing end is very important; that's what my end is now. I'm still in the performing end. It's a very rough end of the profession, because you have to keep your chops up, like we say. You've got to play your horn. You've got to be up to date with what's happening and with the young generation—the kind of music that they want—and you got to keep up with new harmonic and melodic concepts and phrasing and all that. A lot of the jazz orchestras that they have at universities, like in Indiana, . . . [and] all these jazz orchestras around the United States anyway, they're hungry for something new. And so Latin jazz has become very popular now, see? You combine the jazz with the Latin. Never lose your authenticity in the Latin percussions, but maintain a good conception, a good concept of harmony and melody for the jazz musician to be interested in playing solos behind that Latin rhythm, and that's what causes the excitement. And they're beginning to like it a lot, because I get a lot of calls for that now. I was in residence at UCLA; I was in residence five days. I had a residence in Northern Illinois, [University of] Miami—three or four days at the university in workshops, seminars . . . actually performed with them and did concerts with them, and that's very important. By the time I leave there they learn something different in the music, and they love it.

Loza: And you've been doing this throughout the country for quite a few years now. You've also received numerous honorary doctorates from . . .

Puente: Oh yes, four of them now, but I'm up there for every one of them. I have Westbury, and I have a Long Island University and I have a Hunter College, and that's nice recognition because not many on the percussive end of Latin music get these awards. I'm getting the Hispanic Heritage Award in Washington and President Clinton is going to give it to me, and I play the White House and I play a lot of these dignitary places with all Latin music. Naturally I play all these festivals around the world and go all over

Japan, Singapore, and Australia. We just came from Europe, so our music is really getting a lot of recognition around the world and I'm very happy to be still around to be able to perform it.

Loza: Tito, I wanted to cover one area that you and I were discussing the other day that I feel is something important, because we don't have that many master musicians that really represent that experience so much anymore. You're still out there competing with the young *timbaleros*.

Puente: Yes, and they're coming up good, and they're all good too—but more or less part of my school, which I'm very happy to see—and I may hang up anyway in about a year or two. I'll probably just cool down on the performing end of it and concentrate mostly on my scholarships and developing new young talent.

Loza: Now you've been saying that for about ten years, that you're going to hang it up in about a year or two. I could show you a videotape of ten years ago where you said that, so we'll see if that really happens or not. I'm not sure that that's going to happen with you.

Puente: Well, my health is there—you know, I'm playing, that's why. As long as I have my health I'll be okay. My main ambition is to be the first band to play on the moon. I've been telling you that all the time. It could happen in the year 2000. Two thousand and something, sure.

Loza: Now this issue that we were discussing, though, was the fact that you are a World War II veteran. Before this Juilliard period, and after your days as a teenager and as a young adult in the streets of Spanish Harlem being exposed to this great music—in between we had this big world war, and you were inducted. You went into the navy. How did this affect not only your musical career but your whole philosophy about it? You've experienced something that a lot of the younger musicians haven't, even though there have been wars since then. Certainly this was, unfortunately, the war of the century, probably of the last many centuries. How did that affect you?

Puente: Yeah. I was lucky, and . . . first of all I was on an aircraft carrier. I was there three years. I was in nine battles. I have a presidential citation. I mean, I was in action, but I was on a ship. We had formed an orchestra there, and then one of the lieutenants was a pilot who used to be chief arranger of a band [led by] Charlie Spivak. In those days, naturally, a lot of arrangers, directors, and instrumentalists were in the navy. I was in the navy, and they used to come in as pilots. So they took a liking to me; they were teaching me about writing music, arranging, and making the scores and all that—how they used to write for Benny Goodman and all these big bands that were out there. So I learned a lot also while I was in the service besides doing my duties there on the ship. My professional life was at a standstill, but I was still learning, studying. I used to play drums on the ship, and then I went over to saxophone. We used to have five saxophones. I used to play alto, and then I was writing, already scoring for the bands the nice jazz-pop music at the time; not heavy jazz bebop or anything like that. There I developed a lot of experience in writing. During the service I had time for that.

Loza: Now one of the things that I found in writing my other book, on the music of

Mexican Americans in L.A., was that a lot of these veterans that had gone into the war—people like Eddie Cano went in at the heightened end of the war . . . it was already over, but other people like Andy Russell and Lalo Guerrero had been there, involved in those years—and one of the comments that has come out from many social historians has been that a lot of the Latins in this country really emerged out of the war with a very different sort of social, or even political, feelings because all of a sudden there were a lot of Latins overseas fighting for the country, and in a sense they sort of developed a feeling of, "Well, we're defending this country also." It sort of enabled many of the Latins and the Afro-Americans, for example, to become a bit more outspoken when they came back about being Americans. Did you ever have that kind of a feeling about it?

Puente: Well, I don't know. That feeling is around today more than during the war years. See, I was a young man at the war years, and I more or less went to fight for my country, which was this country, like all the veterans did. And of course there was a law passed that when you came out of the service, you can always go back to get your job. Now, naturally when I came back—I had left Machito's orchestra—and so when I came back to Machito, I told him, "Gee, ahh . . . you know, you think I could get a job? You know, with the band? I'm trying to look for work." His drummer was my friend Uba Nieto; he passed away many years ago. He told Machito, "You tell Tito that I can't give him back his job, 'cause I have five kids I have to support." But then I went to José Curbelo, who was a big-band leader at the time, and I had no problem getting a job. At that time the Latin bands were playing nightclubs in downtown, like the Conga and the Havana Madrid. We had nice clubs, but you had to be a good musician because we had to play the shows also, not just dance music, and you had to play waltzes, tangos, sambas, boleros. You had to play all kinds of music, not just barrio music like Spanish Harlem. I was gaining a lot of experience playing all that kind of music for drumming, so that's how I developed, more or less, my experience in reading and playing all types of music . . . show music. And we were at Bill Miller's Riviera up in New Jersey, a very big club . . . big, big shows I used to play also, and recording-wise too. In the studio, man, you had to know how to read music. You went in and you stopped at the eighth bar and you start on the ninth, see, because most of the Latin percussion musicians didn't read much music and they always depended on the ear. Your ear can only go so far. Really, you just have to learn your profession, your instrument. This is it. You have to study, which all the fellas are doing nowadays, and we're getting a lot of good, talented musicians in our profession now.

Loza: Now Tito, you came back from the war. You studied some at Juilliard. You got into the band of José Curbelo, as you mentioned. This is the period of Machito, Tito Rodríguez, other bands, and of course your own band eventually started, you might say, hitting it. This became the very intense period of ballroom dancing . . . of Latin music in New York City, and it spread out into other areas of not only this country but into the Caribbean, back to where it came from, and then into other parts of Latin America. What were some of the essential events, recordings, artists, that became very important during this postwar period and that made the Latin thing shoot to its eventual high degree of success and popularity?

Puente: Well of course one of the main names at the time after the war was a man named "king of the mambo." They used to call him Pérez Prado. Mr. Pérez Prado had a big name, particularly on the West Coast with the Mexicans, and in Mexico too. In New York my music was different than his. My music I played for dances mostly, like more Cuban-type, or American-style cha-chas. What you wanted. So I had a big non-Latino following, while Prado, he made some good hits 'cause he was recording with a major label, RCA Victor, at the time, and that's when he did "Mambo Jambo" and "Patricia" and "Cherry Pink and Apple Blossom White." Beautiful hits that he did, but that music wasn't dance music. You could listen to it and it was semicommercial, if you want to call it that. He was a very talented man, and he did some great records in Mexico with Beny Moré, singles and things like that, but in this country Machito, Tito Rodríguez, myself, we were more like an obstacle to him, because our music would be followed by people who really loved our type of music . . . good dance music, while his wasn't really. So that's why RCA signed me, naturally put me away in a shelf for a few months, you know, so I don't hurt the sales for Prado and all that.

We sold because I had . . . my music was . . . like *Cuban Carnival,* the *Dance Mania* album, which is still out today and people still buy it because it's a very good dance album, because I was ahead of my time playing the music like Machito, see? Now, with these CDs that come out now, the young generation—their parents told them about many of these bands—now they listen to these CDs and they're blowing their mind away! That's why we're so busy now, because they say, "Geez . . . This is great! Mom, you know that crazy guy you used to talk about? Puente is in town. He's playing a concert here. I want to catch him." And when they come home, they tell dad or mom, "Gee, it was great! He really plays beautiful."

So that's where we're at now because of the enhancement of the music into the CD era, because if now we would have left those tapes down there, nothing would have happened. By them coming out again, all the jazz . . . it's happening in the jazz field too! People are listening to the Blue Note recordings of old Charlie Parker days, and Miles, and the old days, and all the great Ellington old things are coming out from the walls that were never released. So now people are more open. Their ears are more open. They know they have a concept of music, of jazz . . . even the Latinos. They're very hip to that, and naturally you travel all over the United States and they know about the jazz artists and they know about the Latin artists. They give them recognition.

Loza: Now this difference between the two mambos, which is a very interesting thing, even John Storm Roberts in his book, if you want to use that as a source, made the differentiation between Pérez Prado, and on the other hand he mentions Tito Puente and Tito Rodríguez and Machito of course, but especially Tito Puente and Tito Rodríguez. If the Pérez Prado mambo personified the commercialization of the mambo throughout the world, Tito Rodríguez and Tito Puente personified the artistic destiny or the artistic culmination of the mambo. In other words, he was actually saying that the mambo here in New York was a much more complicated complex of things going on.

Puente: It was authentic. Not artistic. It was more authentic music we were trying to play, from the Caribbean, while Prado didn't go into that. His was more commercial, more pop, with the "huuhh" and the gimmicks and the high-note trumpets and all that. You know, it was his own sound, really. He had a nice sound for him. That's his sound, definitely, but that wasn't Rodríguez's sound or Machito's or my sound, see? And yet the three bands had different sounds too. If you're really a musician you get into it. You feel the excitement that Machito gave you. Machito concentrated more on vocals, and I was mostly into instrumentals, and good vocalists also, but my instrumentals were very exciting.

Loza: Exactly, and of course Tito Rodríguez being a singer . . .

Puente: Well, naturally. Sure, he appreciates that more.

Loza: You being the arranger, the orchestrator, the percussionist, right?

Puente: Well, arranger, orchestrator, percussion, vibes . . . you know I was more on the musicianship end. Meanwhile, Machito was also a singer, so he had to depend on Mario [Bauzá] and arrangers. You always need a third party to give you ideas. Not me, I was on my own thing. I'd sit down. I'd write what I wanted, or I'd ask the singer to get his keys or, "What do you think about this?" and I'd do the writing, see? That was the difference there.

Loza: It was the Cuban mambo, which in Cuba ironically had never really taken off as it did either in Mexico with Prado or here with the three bands you're referring to, Puente, Rodríguez, and Machito. Was part of the authenticity also the fact that here in New York City and beyond that your music was, along with Machito and Rodríguez, most commonly in the context of a dance hall? You mentioned that Prado was doing a lot of concertizing. He went on tour with Stan Kenton to Europe. He was on the West Coast a lot. How important was this in the music? Because a lot of people skip the fact that, "Hey, remember, people were dancing," and that was as much part of the art as the guys on stage playing the music. What was the bottom line, the essence of that relationship to the dance? How important were the dancers?

Puente: Very important, because a lot of rhythms came out during the years, even the bossa nova, which was very popular. Any rhythm that comes out, if you don't have a dance to it, that rhythm dies. Like they had the boogaloo era? That passed. The shingaling, you know? Nothing happened. That's why Latin music has always maintained itself, because there's a beautiful dance to it. You could do a nice cha-cha, you do a bolero, you know, couples get together and they dance. Very important in those days. We had dance studios all over the place, Arthur Murray, Fred Astaire Studios, all these studios all over the country teaching the tango and the mambo and the cha-cha, and all these kinds of dances. And all the resorts up in the Catskills, all the mountains had dance lessons every day. All the beach clubs, they had studios. So besides the people learning how to dance, they're listening to records at the same time, then they would come to a ballroom and they'd have concerts and champagne hours in all these places—Miami Beach, very popular Latin music all around the beach there. So the concept of having a dance studio was very important for the music, because the music alone was marvelous and everything, but you had to dance to it to keep it popular together. Sometimes I couldn't play way-out music. I would have to play music so that they really feel that mambo, exciting, and they can get up and dance to it and feel it! I still tell the people, "Did you feel it?" They say, "Yeah Tito, I feel it." I gotta get to them, see?

Loza: And if there hadn't been this context of ballroom dance rooms like the Palladium, Roseland, et cetera, the music probably wouldn't have survived, right? That's what made the music happen.

Puente: Oh yeah. Well, it went down a little when rock and roll came out. Rock and roll came, then Latin music started dying. It never left . . . the scene was there, but it wasn't that popular anymore, because we had great bands in them days too. We had Carlos Molina, who was a very big orchestra here. Nano Rodríguez and Noro Morales, they used to play theaters like Miguelito Valdés and Xavier Cugat. They used to play the Strand Theater, the Paramount Theater. These are Latin bands doing that. But the concept of dancing is different in the theater bands. In the theater you play more commercial and artistic, like you said . . . dancing . . . a Cuban team dancing the rumba and all that, with the *guarachera* and all the coloring. But the music that we played was mostly for ballroom dancing, and the people for society dancing. Here on the East Side they had these nice clubs, the private clubs always had a little rumba band that they used to call, four or five pieces, and everybody would get up and dance to "Frenesí." Very important in those days that dancing went with the music, and that's what's happening now too.

Loza: Tito, you recorded . . . I believe it's a hundred and five albums . . .

Puente: Yes.

Loza: It's certainly a world record in the field of Latin music. Most jazz artists have not recorded that much. Most symphonic artists have not recorded that many albums. So you may be way ahead of most artists in general. Among those albums, which are some of the particular ones that you felt demonstrate the changes you made, the innovations that you were making in the field of Latin music, and even beyond Latin music? Because you started to engage upon a thing called "Latin jazz." Eventually people started calling this music "salsa" in the sixties, something that had never been used before. You made a lot of interesting statements upon why all of a sudden this word came out after the music had really existed before that. What are some of the major arrangements and orchestrations and compositions that you have recorded through those hundred and five albums that you feel really stand out as things that can be called your innovations in Latin music?

Puente: Well, when I first started recording—naturally I say [I was] stubborn now, but it's not that I was stubborn. I had my ideas musically, and that's what I wanted to record. In those days the recording company was the one telling you what to record, or the a&r man, they used to call him. You had to record what they wanted. "No," I told them, "I had my own style and this is what I want to do," and I kept doing that until my first album came out, which is still around today. *Cuban Carnival* is the name of it, and then I did *Dance Mania*. I used to bother those people so much, because always the heads of these departments, they never know nothing about music. Most of the heads of all recording companies, they're businessmen, they're not musicians. They got somebody else working, and then they tell the guy how to record this because they had in those

days the publisher, who used to pay them to have this artist record that kind of number. So you had to go in the studio and do what they told you. See, nowadays it's different. The artist goes in with his own composition, his own arranging, or his own publishing house too. And then they try to do what they wanted you to do, and that's why
I recorded different types of albums. I had a beautiful string album. I had guitar albums.
I got percussion albums. And luckily I was fortunate that a man came in, his name is
Marty Gold. He's still around today. He writes for movie pictures. We did a revolving
bandstand album with Buddy Morrow's orchestra and a Latin orchestra. Two bands in
the same studio, playing jazz and Latin on the same tune. That's my favorite album. Now
that was a concept really ahead of its time, see? It just came out now on a CD. That was
in 1960, that album, and it was so progressive . . . and so all these things were being
recorded during that era. It's not like now. Today you go in a studio and you tell the
company what you want to do, and you record. Except the vocalists. Sometimes you want
to consult with somebody that knows what he's talking about, or to give the material
and you pick out what you want. But in those days, you recorded what they wanted
you to do, like the cha-cha, grocery goods. You know they made me do a cha-cha album
up in the mountains which I had nothing to do with. "I don't want to record there. That's
not my style." I had to do it and I did it.

   Loza: One of the differences, of course, if you compare today, is the fact that there
was this huge audience, a market for these particular dances . . . the cha-cha . . . for
mambo.

   Puente: And I was into that audience. That's the audience that buys my records.

   Loza: So the record company wanted another cha-cha album back then, right?

   Puente: Right. Well, I had plenty of them. That's why I had so many albums. All my
albums are all listed. Everything is there, and when you hear the music, it's beautiful
dance music, you know what I mean? That's what I was doing at that time, because I
believed in it, and I'm a dancer too anyway, and I saw that all these places that I played
at and all the studios were always involved with dancing, teaching people how to dance—
and people love it! Even today, you know, they love to dance and still take lessons as a
form of exercise, if you want to call it that. Eddie Torres, a beautiful friend of mine who's
a choreographer, has dance lessons in ballrooms, and there's 100 or 200 people in the
class. All ages, all colors, all kinds of people learning how to do the cha-cha or the merengue or a tango, all kinds of dances. People love to dance when they go out. They love
the music at the same time.

   Loza: Tito, it's funny how sometimes we look at the fifties as an era that sort of went
by and there was a lot of self-absorption, Americans buying and producing, but so many
incredible styles of music went down [emerged] during that period. Eventually, of course,
in the fifties the word *Latin jazz* started being thrown around. By the sixties we hear the
word *salsa*. In other words, Latin music started to change, didn't it? And a lot of the ex-
ponents of Latin jazz, a lot of the practitioners of salsa, of Latin music, were even going
through social change. They didn't speak as much Spanish as they used to. They were
assimilating more and more the English language, the music of James Brown. You men-

tioned boogaloo; this was an example of combining, of fusion of the Latin music with R&B or jazz. Well, how did these changes affect your approach, your arrangements, your engagement as a Latin musician, and as a jazz musician for that matter, and as a musician in general? Especially the so-called new terms that came into use, *Latin jazz* and *salsa*?

Puente: Well, you know, when rock came out it was very heavy, very popular. The problem that I find with rock is that they were utilizing our percussive instruments, but they never gave recognition, see? There was always a conga drummer or even a jazz drummer, but a swing band, as long as they had somebody playing that had conga drums, they never gave you recognition, until many years later. During the last ten or fifteen years, they're doing that now. All the bands have some sort of Latin feeling in it, a cowbell or maracas or a conga, the timbales or bongos, a tambourine. They're all involved. It gives more excitement to the music, even if it's jazz music.

Like the lindy hop, that was a dance in them days. Nobody dances to the lindy hop anymore. Now, they're dancing the, you know, the dance music that they call the . . . well, they just stand looking at each other, you know; they don't even have the right timing when they're dancing. You know, it looks something like the boogaloo, not really heavy dancing, you know what I mean? Disco dancing was nice, but it wasn't easy to do that three-step thing in disco music, and even I left the scene, see? And there were people going to discos all over the place; you'd find yourself sitting on the floor on a pillow and paying a hundred and twenty dollars for spending that night there listening to records. That's what you were listening to. I said, "What, am I crazy? Let's go listen to a live band!" You know, that kind of thing, so that's why the disco fell down.

Of course, the discotheque that they have now is a different type of music, with the hip-hop, and you got a lot of young people, the beer drinkers, that go over there and listen to the music and hang out. It's the hang out all night, but Latin music at that time was music with people who used to come . . . they'd come into the city to go to a Broadway show or something like that. From the Broadway show they'd have dinner or something and they'd come to the Palladium to watch dancers and to listen to the music . . . or the people that used to go away on vacation, they used to always get involved with Latin music.

Loza: When this word *salsa* came out, one of the interesting things is that there were a lot of younger . . . young musicians. I don't want to say younger necessarily, because I'm not sure that Eddie Palmieri, Ray Barretto, or Johnny Pacheco are that much younger than you. They might be a few years younger, but not too much, but yet you were able to sort of make a conversion. You also became one of the *salseros*. Why did you permit yourself to become part of the salsa movement, when you've gone on record . . . saying, "Well, salsa is just a word. What does it mean?"

Puente: Well, I mean yes, what does it mean? There's no salsa music. They just put that word to the music that we were doing all the time, the mambo, the cha-cha, the merengue: they called it "salsa." Salsa is a condiment of food. You eat salsa. You don't listen to it. You don't dance to it, you know? It became a popular word and all American people . . . "Tito could you play me a salsa?" So I said, "Do you have a headache? I'll give you an Alka-Seltzer." You know, something like that. Now I've joined them. I'm not going to fight it anymore, you know? The mambo, call it whatever you want! You know, "Could you play me a salsa tango?" They don't know what they're talking about. Salsa is everything. Salsa is actually the condiment that you put on food. *Salsa tomate,* tomato sauce, spaghetti sauce. The Mexicans have been using the word *salsa* for centuries. Mexican salsa all the time, the hot salsa, you know, for tamales. So they gave it to the music, you know to give it heat. It makes it exciting. It's easy for everybody to say. You know even in my concerts I always tell everybody, "Now you know, we're gonna play for you salsa!" "OHHH!" It's the same mambo I've been playing for forty years.

Loza: Salsa is hot, though. It's hot, and so is the music, and that's probably one of the associations.

Puente: Yeah, maybe that's the issue. When you play salsa you play hot music.

Loza: But the word *salsa* still exists even though it's become very different now. If you listen to Tito Nieves or Eddie Santiago . . .

Puente: Oh yeah, that's a different type of salsa. That's a ballad type with a nice swing that they have . . . good and very nice, very good music, very well recorded. They recorded with me too up here, Tito and the boys, on my 100th album. I had thirteen of the top singers, and when I did my Beny Moré albums, you know I won a Grammy. I have good singers there, so I recorded salsa, but they were still singing that all the time, *son montuno* and all that with the guitars.

Loza: We were talking about Latin jazz, Tito, and we're gonna talk about Latin jazz and then Latin rock, 'cause those are two things that came out of Latin music, really. Two different musical worlds receiving or adapting to, however you want to consider it, Latin music. The jazz world all of a sudden said, "Hey, Latin can be used as a base for jazz," [and] eventually a rock guy by the name of Santana did the same thing. What is it that made you so accepted in the jazz world, and how is it that you entered also the field of Latin jazz simultaneously with the heavy Latin dance music and the salsa scene? At the same time you were developing your Latin jazz group, you still had your big-band Latin group, your large orchestra. What is it that enabled you to do that?

Puente: Well, I still have it. I still have my big band, and I have my Latin jazz ensemble. See, it depends what kind of jobs that I get. If I had a concert, or I have to play a jazz festival, some jazz club, then I play my Latin jazz there, but if I have to play a dance where people are dancing, and they want to hear some good Latin dance music, then I use my big band because that kind of music calls for vocalists and a complete sax section; the book is completely different. It's a different type of music—with the jazz, naturally, you improvise more, more modern, you know, exciting for clubs so people could understand it. So I was always involved with both.

Loza: So what made this Latin jazz thing start? Who were the people that got it going, and how? Why did you get into that also?

Puente: The truth of the matter, I got into Latin jazz very late because some of our boys were involved into that already. George Shearing was playing Latin and Latin jazz many years ago, and naturally Cal Tjader and Mongo Santamaría were involved with

Latin, Latin rock, or Latin jazz. And Eddie Cano on the West Coast was involved also. A lot of the Latin groups were into Latin jazz, but I wasn't really into it. My music was typical dance . . . good Latin dance music. But in the last ten years, the last eight years, when Cal Tjader was alive, he was the one that put me in contact with Concord Records. Now Concord is the jazz company. It's not like Fantasy, you know what I mean? They [Concord] weren't into Latin, and being that I was a good Latin jazz musician, and Cal Tjader used to record a lot of Latin jazz music, he was the one that got me in there, and I started recording Latin jazz for the Concord label.

And I won a Grammy award there. In fact, I won three Grammy awards in my Latin jazz category. It wasn't a category in the Latin field. The first one I won was real typical music of 1978, the music of Beny Moré with the big band, and I won it for my good dance music. But in my Latin jazz albums, I always play a nice cha-cha, something real typical. Latin instrumental with a nice Latin beat, and then I go into the Latin jazz. I mix it up a little, see, because I couldn't lose my Latin audience.

And that's what happened for my 100th album: I had to go record a Latin album for them because the newspaper people and the radio and all the critics were criticizing me that I had forgotten all the Latin music and I went into jazz. So just to show them I can always go back, I did my 100th album, and then I did four more after that with Latin jazz. This year Grammy Awards, or now NARAS [National Association of Recording Arts and Sciences], has given us a Latin jazz category. That's where I should've been all the time, because a lot of us play good Latin jazz, you know, like Paquito D'Rivera, Arturo Sandoval, Michel Camilo, and there's a whole lot of them, and I can't remember all of them now. I'm involved in there too with very good Latin jazz groups which are not typical of Latin music.

So the year Machito won his Grammy Award he was in the same category with Julio Iglesias, you know what I mean? They don't know what they were doing there. They still don't know what they're doing anyway. They had a lot of problems with the classical music. They have problems every year, and with the Latin music they always have problems. We just have three categories; they have the Mexican, then they have the pop, and now tropical, or whatever they call it. But they mix in there the merengue. They mix in there all kinds of music . . . Colombian music, *cumbia*. Like in jazz, they got the blues. They have the gospel. They got the jazz. They got all different kinds of categories in jazz music—pop singers and this and the other. But in the Latin field they never give it that real interest.

Loza: And of course this was the problem, and I can attest to that because for all these years I've been sitting on those screening committees for NARAS, and this is the problem. I can remember three or four years your Latin jazz format would get thrown out of the three categories for Latin. Your Latin jazz formats would get thrown over into jazz fusion, which was an impossibility, and all of a sudden you were competing with the Yellow Jackets, with Miles Davis.

Puente: I wouldn't want to win. It's like if I saw Dizzy Gillespie involved in the Latin field, I'll tell him, "What are you doin' here? You belong over there!" You know, that kind of thing.

Loza: It was futile. Of course the Latin Jazz category now exists. Ironically it's going to be in the jazz field.

Puente: Yes. As soon as it's in the jazz category, they call it Latin jazz; it has nothing to do with Latin, see? But why not? What we're playing is jazz, really.

Loza: It's all right. It'll work.

Puente: We play jazz with the Latin touch, that's all, you know.

Loza: At least it's a movement, but it took a lot to get that category, didn't it?

Puente: Oh, yeah it took a lot, sure. It took a lot.

Loza: You can attest to it. I can attest to it, and others, but let's get into this other thing. The idea that your music has not only penetrated jazz, you can even talk about things that you've done in symphonic formats, because you were trained, and you're able to orchestrate for a full symphonic orchestra also. But another area that certainly was one of great influence all over the world was the development of something that's now referred to as Latin rock. Now your music and the music of other Latin artists was probably entering rock, whether it was Ritchie Valens's "La Bamba," or "Louie Louie," or even the Beatles, or rather the original people who recorded "Twist and Shout" (the Isley Brothers). All of these tunes have been considered as outgrowths of or influenced by Latin rhythms and Latin music—certainly Carlos Santana, when he recorded your tune "Oye como va," which was originally a very basic cha-cha that you wrote and had recorded. This turned the rock world, the pop world, upside down. How did that happen? What was your reaction to it, and how did that affect your life?

Puente: Well it affected me both ways, you know. First of all, he utilizes the guitar, and the drum had to be heavy rock with the organ. That was the sound of Latin rock at the time he recorded "Oye como va." I had done it twelve years prior to that, but naturally his was the hit record. He was a big name, and he still is around the world, so a lot of people used to come up to me and ask me, "Tito, could you please play Santana's tune, you know 'Oye como va'?" See because people don't give credit to composers. They give credit to the interpreter of the music. They don't know who wrote this or that tune, "I Love You," or whatever. They don't know. They don't care. They only know of the guy who sings it, you know. "Oh, you know the tune by so and so," and that's what was happening, see? He surely helped a lot to bring the music and the Latin rock up to a very high standard. Today he's still doing it with that beautiful *Abraxas* album that he did, and he's into Latin music a lot, but naturally that's not his main field. His main field is rock—great guitar player and friend. He's an interpreter and he has a lot of Latin influence. He's Mexican, and a lot of people around him are also good percussionists, and all that. So he's hip with what's happening, and he plays a nice guitar, so that goes to the rock people. They love that because he has that beat for them. I can't play that kind of music, because I'm not into it. If I got into that I would lose my audience too. I'm in between. I'm into Latin jazz, which is far enough, but I still have my Latin rhythm going.

Loza: Now this did take your name into a whole new audience of people. All of a sudden rock fans were hearing the name Tito Puente. Santana then went on to record another tune of yours, "Pa' los rumberos."

Puente: Yes, "Pa' los rumberos." Yes, he really helped me a lot to get that recognition with the people, because when he does his interviews, you know he mentions it, and his interviews are twenty times bigger than mine. All over the world, and the people that he caters to, they're twenty, thirty, forty thousand people in a stadium. I cater to a few hundred people in a ballroom. It's quite different than the music that I play.

Loza: But it's true, in his interviews he attributes his early influences to when he came to San Francisco—he got into blues and then he got into Tito Puente and the cha-cha and the rumba.

Puente: Well, he had some people that were working with him, the Escovedo brothers and all that. They really got him into me, and that's where he got hip to the Latin.

Loza: Now young pop artists, even like Sheila E, who came out of that school, you might say she was greatly influenced by her father [Pete Escovedo] and yourself.

Puente: Yeah, but she's a young pop artist and a rock artist. She played with Prince. She's a great drummer, a rock and roll drummer, and also a great percussionist, and beautiful. I've known her since she was nine years old. I've done concerts with her, videos together playing the timbales, and she's a very good percussion player.

Loza: "Oye como va," of course, became almost an anthem for Latinos all over the world, from here down to the tip of Chile, where I've heard it. It's played in Europe and Asia and everywhere. It's an anthem, an international anthem. Now even the young rapper Gerardo took it and made it into a rap song.

Puente: Wow. Yeah, terrific, and Julio Iglesias just recorded it too. See, it's a theme. It's a happy theme, and it's very easy. Everybody that hears it, right from the beginning they want to get up and dance to it. When I play places and I see people may not be into Latin music, I say, "Hit 'em with 'Oye como va.' That'll get 'em," and they do. They always do.

Loza: In the area of popular culture, of course, Gloria Estefan and her husband have gotten interested in your services. How did that come about?

Puente: Oh, well, Gloria Estefan is a very talented young lady, and her husband too. I was on their last album, the Grammy Award album *Mi tierra*. I've done a lot of personal appearances. I was on the Grammy Awards television show with her too, but people don't know that, because she was not really involved with the Latin people. All her life, her big records were with the Americans and the rock people, the heavy [industry] people. So she decided to do this type of album, and she calls all the best Latin musicians from different countries—from Cuba, from Puerto Rico, Dominican Republic, Luis Enrique from Nicaragua, Cachao on bass, Paquito D'Rivera on alto. She took a group of good musicians and we all went there and we did it, and she did the Grammy Awards. It's a platinum record. It's still swinging all over the world. It's a very good record. She sings beautifully on it, but I don't think she'll stay in that idiom because she's already a big rock and roll recording artist around the world, and she's gonna stay with that kind of music.

Loza: But it's still interesting to see all these generations of pop artists, you know, continually reverting to the music of Tito Puente or Tito Puente himself. Putting him on their albums, like she's done.

Puente: Well, like Linda Ronstadt is one. She did the Mexican music, and Vikki Carr. A lot of the American singers sing in Spanish or sing Latin tunes in English, and the main singers too. Naturally the music is becoming popular. Vikki Carr is very popular in Mexico and all over Latin America. She gets Grammys and all that. Her influence is very big in the Latin field, more than in the American field, in fact.

Loza: Well, she's another one who went both ways. She started as an English only. People didn't even know she was Mexican, and now of course she's bigger in Latin America.

Puente: I could see that in the future a lot of them are gonna be doing that . . . like Gloria.

Loza: So it's interesting, the concept of two worlds—how you have lived them and how other Latin artists have. Whether it's going from rock to jazz, pure Latin music, English to Spanish, it's interesting how Latin musicians end up living, in a way, in two worlds.

Puente: Yeah, you have to know the other world too. This is my livelihood. I've been a professional musician all my life. I don't know how to do anything else. I mean, I've devoted myself to developing music—keeping it up there, trying to give it the worldwide recognition it deserves—like the rest of the other music in the world. I don't believe in the word *crossover*. A lot of people ask me what I think about crossover; I say, "What crossover? I'm on my way back. What, are you kiddin'? I don't believe in crossover." If you like some sort of music, you don't have to wait until it becomes crossover for you to like it. You like Chinese music? You like Japanese music? You like Russian music? You like German music? Whatever music you like . . . French music. I don't wait until it becomes crossover. I dig the French music. I dig the Italian music. I travel all over the world.

Loza: Do you accept this role that has sort of been given to you as spokesperson for Latin music? I mean, even Julio Iglesias and, from what I understand, even Frank Sinatra have wanted to record with you, and they still plan on doing that. Why are you the one that all these people, even the pop artists, look at?

Puente: Well, I've been around a lot . . . around their field, you know what I mean? That's where they know me—naturally, the newspapers, all the magazines, the American jazz mags. I win a lot of polls, and I'm always involved with the music, and I didn't stay only with my Latin crowd. In other words, I expanded more into all kinds of people around the world, and they hear about us. Whenever my name is mentioned, when they want to hear something the best, like *The Mambo Kings* movie. When they want movies with some authentic, exciting mambo music, my name always comes up there because I've been involved with these people all my life.

Loza: The movie *Mambo Kings* brought you together with one of your longest-standing colleagues, Celia Cruz. Do you feel that that was an important attainment? That at least put you and Celia out there on the big screen. Do you feel that was an important thing to exemplify for Latin musicians?

Puente: Well, the movie had nothing to do with the music. First of all, I got put down by a lot of the Cuban newspapers in Miami, all those press conferences asking, "Why did our queen, who is Celia Cruz, why did she sing in English?"—you know, that kind of thing. So I tried to explain to them that this movie had nothing to do with music. It's a story of two brothers that come up from Cuba, and it's based on a Pulitzer Prize–winning book by Oscar Hijuelos, and they made a movie out of that story. The only reason why they used me in the movie was for my music, which at first they wanted to commercialize, and I told them, "No, this is the way that it was played in the fifties"; if they wanted something else then forget about it. But then evidently they had their conferences and said, "Leave him alone. Let him play what he wants." That's the exciting part in the movie. The same with Celia, of course. But that movie has opened for me a lot of doors around the world, because of the different languages. I've been sent to play in Winnipeg, Canada. I didn't know where Winnipeg was. All I know is that they have a hockey team that plays in New York. I went to Cheyenne, Wyoming; I never played with the cowboys out there. A guy asked me for salsa because he saw [*The*] *Mambo Kings* and liked it, and a lot of people saw it on TV. It's been shown all over, so a lot of people like the movie. The music that I put in there really got on the map because I worked with Armand Assante and Antonio Banderas. Enough mambo just to show that segment of the Palladium era, but the rest, it was a story, that's all. So I explained that to the press, and they chilled out a little bit on the movie.

Loza: It did bring you and Celia Cruz together, and that was an important aspect of the film, because certainly you have been considered with Celia Cruz as the two progenitors, as the two icons, of Latin music—the godfather and the godmother. Certainly it's an interesting relationship, you being of Puerto Rican heritage, she of Cuban heritage. You being a man, she being a woman, and yet you came together in common with a particular musical style, and your relationship with her goes back many years.

Puente: Well, first of all, she's not the godmother, and I'm not the godfather. She's the queen, and I'm the king of the music. She is our queen—beautiful lady, lovely lady. I met her many, many years ago. When she first came to this country I recorded her, about nine albums I did with her in the sixties. She's the queen of our music all over Latin America. I try to play for her—I take her to Japan, and sometimes I do the jazz concerts, like the JVC Jazz Festival and Carnegie Hall. Last year I brought her to Carnegie Hall with me. The American people love her when she starts singing, because she's so beautiful, and she's becoming a big name in the American field and around the world. She has her big name anyway. She doesn't stop working. She did a lot of films, more than I have, in the Latin vein. She's our queen without a doubt, and I love her. I've played for her over 587 times already. I accompany her, and I have some beautiful albums with her.

Loza: Tito, on a final note . . . what are the things in life that really hold your spirit together, in terms of your family, your personal sentiments, your personal feelings, your politics, your religion, your spirituality, whatever it is? What is it that has enabled you, on a more personal note, to survive and to continue this life of beautiful music?

Puente: Well, I don't know if it's my Taurus sign. I'm a Taurus. Tauruses are supposed to be very creative people. That's what I read, anyway. I have a beautiful homelife—my wife, Margie. I have my daughter and my two sons. I have peace of mind in my house.

I'm a very creative, positive-thinking person. I have good vibes for the people, like Celia. When we perform for the audience, we give them good vibrations and happiness. They forget their problems because they see that we're giving it from our hearts. And when I compose and I write, I have an incentive to do that, to become creative as long as I can do it. I know it's not gonna last forever, but while I'm performing still, let me do as much as I can, and I'll bow to another young person—I know they're coming up now, like other people left the scene to me. They left it in good hands, so I got the right education. I was brought up in a beautiful home. Education I have, so why not go out and bring this music as far as I can, so I could become a role model for the young people? And no to drugs and all that. Teach them that they can become big in this field too if they dedicate themselves to studying the music.

Tito Puente at the age of twelve with his sister, Anna, seven years old (1935). (Max Salazar Collection.)

Photo taken in 1935 at La Milagrosa Catholic Church in Spanish Harlem. At top center-right, dressed in a soldier's uniform and hat, is twelve-year-old Tito Puente. His younger sister, Anna (center left), was crowned queen for the occasion. Future Hollywood actress Olga San Juan appears five places to the right of Tito. (Max Salazar Collection.)

Tito Puente with one of his early mentors, bandleader José Curbelo, in Miami, Florida, 1939. (José Curbelo Archive. Max Salazar Collection.)

Chino Pozo and Tito Puente (left background) performing with the Jack Cole Dancers (1942). The two percussionists had taken a temporary leave from Machito's orchestra to tour with Cole's company. (Photo by Maurice Seymour. Max Salazar Collection.)

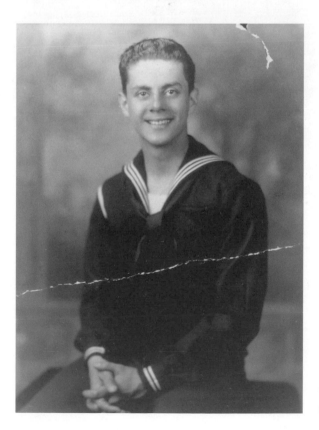

Tito Puente, U.S. Navy, 1944. (Max Salazar Collection.)

Tito Puente's Picadilly Boys in 1948 at the Palladium Ballroom. *From left to right:* Tito Puente, Angel Rosa (vocals), Jimmy Frisaura (trumpet), Chino Pozo (bongos), Al De Risi (trumpet). (Max Salazar Collection.)

Condensed score to "Picadillo," one of Puente's watershed hits, recorded in 1949. (Tito Puente Orchestra book.)

The Tito Puente Orchestra (circa 1951) at the Palladium Ballroom. *From left to right:* Al Escobar (piano), Tony Reyes (bass), Puente, Vicentico Valdés (vocals), Frank LoPinto (trumpet), Frankie Colón (congas), Jimmy Frisaura (trumpet), Harold Negbriet (trumpet), Manny Oquendo (bongos). (Photo by Harry Fine. Max Salazar Collection.)

The young *timbalero* fronting his orchestra during the early fifties. Behind Puente performing on maracas is *sonero* Vicentico Valdés. (Max Salazar Collection.)

Puente listens to the studio tracks just recorded for the LP *Top Percussion* in 1957, along with Francisco Aguabella (standing at left). Also featured on the recording were Mongo Santamaría, Willie Bobo, Julito Collazo, and others. (Courtesy of Bear Family Records.)

Mambo U.S.A. concert tour, Symphony Hall, Boston, 1954. Singing *coro* for the Tito Puente Orchestra are (from left to right) Puente, Luis Kant, and Willie Bobo. (Photo by Ralph Norman. Max Salazar Collection.)

Publicity still, 1957. (Photo by Bruno. Max Salazar Collection.)

Tito Puente is presented with an award by Mexican actress María Félix in 1963. Second from left is bandleader Xavier Cugat. The award was given in recognition of Puente as most popular artist in the Latin American community. (Photo by Villamil. Max Salazar Collection.)

Puente performing, circa 1965. (Max Salazar Collection.)

Publicity still, circa 1970.
(Photo by Martin Cohen.)

Classic publicity still by
Martin Cohen, 1978. (LP
Percussion.)

3

The Salazar Perspective

MAX Salazar is considered by many musicians, critics, and readers to be the most important Latin music journalist and historian to date. He has written over 200 articles on assorted topics, largely focusing on historical points of the major artists who have characterized Latin music, for example, Arsenio Rodríguez, Beny Moré, Antonio Arcaño, Miguelito Valdés, Chano Pozo, Machito, Tito Rodríguez, Charlie Palmieri, and Tito Puente. Salazar's articles have appeared since the sixties in magazines including *Latin Beat, Latin New York, Nuestro,* and *Billboard.* Salazar has also played an instrumental role in radio, hosting a Latin music program for fifteen years (1974–89) on WKCR-FM in New York City.

I have constructed this chapter from an interview that I conducted with Salazar in New York in November 1994. As a native of the New York barrio in which Tito Puente was raised, Max Salazar possesses an essential perspective and understanding of Tito Puente's role in the historical and cultural progression of Latin music. At the time of the interview, he was sixty-two years of age and had lived or witnessed all that he shared with me. His opinions are solid and candid and are based on a firsthand and sincere knowledge of events. I have the greatest respect not only for his insight but also for his ethical standards and analytical savvy.

I have attempted to leave the interview intact, including my own questions, which are sometimes involved and specific; that specificity was my aim, however, and I feel that the questions became an important part of the context of the interview and dialogue—an exchange of ideas at a particular moment concerning particular issues that were important to both of us. I have edited out portions that digressed significantly or that were merely points of clarification. The bulk of the interview is left intact, however, and its presentation here is chronologically faithful to our discussion.

❖❖

Salazar: Let me make an opening statement. Music has been part of my life ever since I can remember. It's helped me so many ways psychologically, helped me get through the day, through periods. Because when I hear a recording, the mambos or *son montuno*, it does something to me. It arouses me and I think it's one of the reasons why I was married for a long time. For forty years the same woman. My wife passed away three years ago. Now she was an Irish lady. I married her when she was fifteen, this Irish lady; I "Puerto Ricanized" her, and she danced the mambo like a native Latino. So the mambo I can say has played a very important part in my life because when I came out of the service I was in the Eighty-second Airborne down in North Carolina. That's where I met her; she was from the south. At that time, or even today, to make a marriage last you have to be lucky. You've got to be lucky, and I think music was one of the things that got us through. Listening to it day in and day out and, you know, different things and that.

Music is always in my life, and when I got that deejay job, that was an accident because this fellow, Carlos DeJesús, who happens to be on AM radio today, he was a college kid, he was a freshman at Columbia University, he had two shows, one on WBAI and one on WKCR, and he says, "Look, I can't cover both of them. How would you like to do it?" And I say, "Yeah, sure," but you know, I was afraid because I couldn't talk extemporaneously. Well, I did like I told you, only I didn't have nobody to talk like Machito, so I would say, "Well on September 3, 1943, blah-blah-blah." I would give them a piece of history that I learned from Machito, something like that, and that this was the tune that was popular then when we were playing Machito and Miguelito Valdés, and a few letters came into the station—they loved it. So they told me, "Hey, keep that guy on the air." That's how it started on October 25, 1974.

In 1989 I was very popular. Here I am on noncommercial radio from the college station, but yet I used to get mentioned in the newspapers—*Max Salazar Show,* the Saturday show, the one for two hours called the *Latin Musicians' Show.* It would be in the *New York Times* and my Sunday show, it would say "Max is going to interview Mongo Santamaría, Cal Tjader," whoever I was going to have, so I had a very important show, and a lot of people wanted me out because they wanted my spot, the one that I had developed. I was so popular people would send tons of money in. They loved it—there was no other show like mine. [Presently I'm] just writing. What I've done, Steve, is—even before 1974, when I went on radio—some people collect stamps or other memorabilia, [but] I collect records and conversation. You could say I was like a groupie, you know? And I would put information about Noro Morales, I would hear you singing it, I would write all of that down 'cause you were an eyewitness, and then I would put it in this file. Well, this file became voluminous. And here I have enough. All that information on Noro Morales, Spanish Harlem, Cuba, *la charanga,* and I had me like four files filled three drawers high with information—files, photographs, things I collected. I was like an addict. I would go and buy old recordings. I would buy photographs, spend as much as twenty-five dollars for one photograph. I was addicted, you know?

So not realizing that this break would come, I was attending City College in 1967, and in one of my courses, I think it was English Literature 102 or English Comp, the professor told us to write an article no less than 1,500 words about something that we knew about, and I selected Latin music. She says, "Hey, this is good enough to be published." At that time there was a magazine that had just come out called *Latin New York* magazine. So I sent it to *Latin New York,* and they said "Hey, we want to see you." And that's how it started in 1967. Since then there's been over 200 articles for different magazines, not only *Latin New York*. I'm talking about *Nuestro,* I'm talking about *Latin Beat,* there's been so many others too. And my reputation started to spread. They heard about it in Europe. People from *Melody Maker* heard about it and *Latin New York* had a very wide circulation. They were in business for thirteen years, and now *Latin Beat* is reaching Colombia, Venezuela, Holland, Germany, even Cuba.

And the people love the history. I knew about it because that's what got me the steady thing at WKCR. They loved it. To hear Miguelito Valdés say something and then go into a recording of his. Then he would talk about Cugat and how Cugat tried to pull a fast one on him and we'd segue—that's the history of those old radio days no one often heard. So I use these same things. I collected all these taped conversations and started using it for *Latin Beat* magazine.

◆◇◆

Loza: The idea here, Max, is that of Tito Puente and the making of Latin music. There's about ten books on Miles Davis. Finally he did an autobiography [with Quincy Troupe] that I thought was excellent because he got into even the negative stuff. When you're talking about any kind of expression, any kind of life, [any] job that you do, you can't just talk about all the nice, pretty stuff. In the case of Tito's thing, it's going to have to come down to some of that, including the negative—in other words, [to] what I call issues of conflict, and that goes for everything from politics, discrimination, [and] racism to religious convictions, to things in one's personal life. Now he may not want to get into a lot of that, but the whole issue of conflict in the Latino community is based on many things. There has been a thing about him, whether it was the record industry, the Fania thing, the little labels, the management syndrome, or communication in terms of business. I don't look at it as all bad or all good. As Latinos, a lot of times we're unorganized, but that's because they say we're unorganized. But they have as many wars as we do, if not more; we just tend to be very uninhibited about arguing with each other. Sometimes I think that's a positive factor. Anyway, what I'm trying to say is, let's look at it that way.

What I'd like to do is maybe write something—it might be just a compilation of chapters or articles or ideas. Let's look at this man Tito Puente, and let's look at the making of Latin music. What happened? How does he personify or represent a community? I would say the community he represents is the New York, Puerto Rican, *Nuevo Riqueño* community. That is what he represents. He's also one of the people in the Latin community, period, whether its talking about music, actors, writers, who has become an icon of Latino identity. Now that's very interesting, especially when it comes to musicians. In other words, Tito's not just looked upon within the Latin community as Puerto Rican. He's able to transcend that, yet everybody knows he's Puerto Rican, and his experience is that Puerto Rican experience. He internationalizes it. What is that community? Who is Max Salazar? What is the Puerto Rican community? A lot of us know why it happened here, but what makes someone like Tito or others like Eddie Palmieri, Charlie Palmieri, Ray Barretto; what is it that makes that community, and what is your experience with that and the reasons why the music came out of that, the reasons why music became so important? Like you—you married somebody, and your music became a thing that she adapted to and that side of it dominated. Why is it such a dominant thing in this community, and why is it maybe the most important thing in this community since this community evolved here in New York?

Salazar: Let me start by saying that Tito Puente is like our Bach, our Beethoven. The same way we heard about Mozart and we see a picture about his life 200 years ago. Tito Puente is that for the moment. However, it's not only him. Before him there was Machito. There was Noro Morales in the forties, and from what I've learned, this happened around the thirties, when the Latinos started to come here, when Puerto Rico became a commonwealth in 1919 after World War I. The first Puerto Ricans, the first wave, included Rafael Hernández, the famous Puerto Rican composer, him and his sister. They came here in 1919.

So ever since then they've come here; they started their life, but they had to learn the American way, the customs, the habits, get used to the cold weather and things like that. All this came with time. And the music was more like the ballad or the Puerto Rican *danza*. But that was only popular with Puerto Ricans. When the Cubans came, and the first musician was Vicente Sigler. It was here in 1926. That's the earliest I've been able to trace a Latin band here—Orquesta Vicente Sigler, a Cuban mulatto who played trumpet. He would not play in Harlem but in the downtown hotels, which were packed by people from Spain and the few political exiles from Cuba and Puerto Rico, whoever was trying to overthrow the country at the time and couldn't stay there.

So it built around the Cuban music because everybody, I don't care what your nationality was, gravitated toward the Cuban music, and in 1926, when Miguel Matamoros came out with "Son de la loma," I mean that exploded on the scene. Around that time there was "Siboney" and "Mama Inés," but none of them had the impact of "Son de la loma," and it just got all over. We heard about it here in New York. But in 1930 the Don Aspiazu Band came here to star, I think at an RKO Theater in midtown Manhattan. It was the first Cubans coming over to expose Cuban music.

Well, on that stage a man by the name of Antonio Machín, the vocalist for Aspiazu, came out with a pushcart and started to sing "Maní . . . ," "The Peanut Vendor," and started throwing peanuts out to the people in the audience sitting down. Well, it wasn't so much that they were getting a free peanut. It's just that it was a rich melody. I don't care what your ethnic background is, it grabbed you. It just heated your blood.

Loza: It still does.

Salazar: That's why everybody has recorded "The Peanut Vendor." Now you can say that, at that time, in 1930, when Don Aspiazu presented the Cuban Revue at the RKO Theater, that's when the beginning of salsa started. That is the genesis of salsa.

Of course Aspiazu went back to Cuba. Machín remained here, formed a group—Mario Bauzá became part of that group—and as other Cubans and Puerto Ricans started to come from the islands, the population just kept growing. First in Brooklyn, until it could no longer hold Latinos there. Then they started going up to Harlem, which was predominately a wealthy, Jewish area. In fact, I interviewed Victoria Hernández, the sister of Rafael Hernández, and she said that the first Puerto Ricans in Harlem were on Ninety-ninth Street. She was one of them. On the corner of Second Avenue, between Second and First, and from there it mushroomed out all over Harlem, which was a Jewish area. As the Puerto Ricans were hired as superintendents, they started moving into buildings, taking care of them; then, when someone would move out, the Puerto Ricans would notify a Puerto Rican, or a Latino, and say "Hey, there's an apartment available," and they would move into it. By 1935 there were Cubans, Puerto Ricans, Mexicans, people from South America that inhabited the Jewish area and it became predominately Spanish, I believe, with more Puerto Ricans than anything else.

By that time music was flourishing here. You had Machito coming over in 1937 because Mario Bauzá had told him, "Hey, over there the black man is left alone. They got their own businesses, they got their own nightlife, they don't have to put up with the same nonsense that you're putting up with in [Cuba]." So Machito wanted to come here and he did. One week later there was Las Estrellas Habaneras and Machito was singing. But then you had Caney, you had Enrique Madriguera, and you had all these other guys and then, of course, Mexico with Tito Guízar, Jorge Negrete, Toña La Negra, my God, you're just overwhelmed because here you have all these people in this area which is known as Harlem. They were just dying, they were thirsty for music.

Loza: And this was the beginning of the recording industry?

Salazar: Yes.

Loza: The film industry?

Salazar: Yes.

Loza: And sound in general, recorded sound?

Salazar: Yes, right. But then you had the theater where they showed Jewish movies only. It was called the Photoplay Theater. The new owners renamed it the San José. They would show Spanish moving pictures from Mexico, they would have a Spanish stage show; local kids who were talented played there. That's how they got their break. El Teatro Mount Morrison on 116th Street, which became Hispano. They changed all of that. They brought in people from different parts of Latin America; they exposed them there, like I said, Negrete, Tito Guízar—oh, so many others.

Loza: Sounds like the Million Dollar in L.A. The same kind of thing happened.

Salazar: Well, that was part of the New York Latino scene; [I know] because my grandmother used to take me to the shows, you know.

Loza: And they would do either movies or live shows, right?

Salazar: Yeah. They do both. I remember hearing "Jalisco no te rajes" for the first time at the Hispano Theater.

Loza: Jorge Negrete . . .

Salazar: Jorge Negrete. All those pictures there . . . María Félix. I remember the lights going on and hearing this piano, and it was Noro Morales. The place went berserk because there were mostly Puerto Ricans there. There were so many musicians that came at that time. But something happened around 1940 and what had happened was that the sound was changing not only here in New York but in Cuba.

In Cuba the Antonio Arcaño *charanga* through Cachao and his brother introduced a new sound of mambo they called *nuevo ritmo,* and over here you had a guy that was like light-years ahead, Miguelito Valdés, doing things with his vocal cords that no one else ever heard before. And he had been doing that in Cuba with Casino de la Playa. So when he came here, Cugat grabbed him right away, and no one [had] ever heard these things. And I, as a kid in Spanish Harlem, I was not interested in the Puerto Rican trios or my family's folkloric music. But when I heard Miguelito Valdés sing "Anna Boroco Tinde," I included Latin music, and so did all my Americanized friends. And then the following year we heard Machito's "Sopa de pichón."

Forget it, that was it. We were Latinos again, and that just made us proud. So that's how it started. But the big guys at the time were Caney and Noro Morales. You cannot single out Tito Puente, [except] maybe today. But Tito was a kid who was already learning his craft, learning how.

Loza: Like you, he was hearing this stuff. He was going to the same theaters.

Salazar: He was into jazz. He was into Latin music. You got to remember he mastered seven instruments. He was a top-notch dancer. He became a music arranger. And he didn't do it all by himself. If there's anyone that I must give credit for, I would start with his parents, who, what do you call, gave him the incentive to continue. Tito Puente's mother was a natural Puerto Rican. His father was born in Puerto Rico, of Spanish heritage. Ernest Anthony Puente was born on April 20, 1923, in Harlem Hospital.

From the things that I learned, 'cause I was very close to Tito at one time, the guy was destined for stardom for being a Bach or Beethoven because he had the feeling for music. Not only Latin music but the pop things he could sing. The guy did everything musically well. And he was already working with Noro Morales's orchestra in 1940–41. Tito was fifteen or sixteen. You see, Tito had dropped out of school at age fifteen or sixteen, so he . . . went into Machito's band. While he was in Machito's band in 1942 he was drafted. He went into the navy. He served aboard an aircraft carrier. There he mastered the alto and tenor saxophones, getting tips from musicians who were flyers or other sailors. He took advantage of every second of his life by asking and learning about music.

When he got out of the service, he tried to get his job back with the Machito orchestra, but there was no way he could do it because Uba Nieto had become the drummer after Puente was drafted, and Uba had a family of six to support. So Puente understood that and said he could get a job, and he did, because he, René Hernández, and Joe Loco were music arrangers that everybody [respected], especially René Hernández—he was the pianist of Machito's orchestra—this guy could take a simple tune and write you a score and make it a hit. And [Puente and Loco] were both admirers of René Hernández. Anybody that knows anything about music will tell you probably that René Hernández was their favorite of the guys who started it all.

By the midforties Tito Puente is working with the José Curbelo Orchestra, with Pupi Campo, with Frank Martí at the Copa, he's taking private lessons with Juilliard professors on orchestrating percussion and things like that, where he picked up the vibes and things like that. What happens is that we had in New York at that time what they call dance academies. They were places where men would go and buy a ticket, and that ticket would get you a dance with a hostess.

Now you had about fifteen dance academies, but Roseland and the Arcadia were the two most popular, and everybody just forgot about the others. The Palladium Ballroom wanted to stay competitive, so they selected Machito and Mario Bauzá, because they had such a tremendous following, they were great record sellers, that big-band sound of Machito you can hear. Nobody ever played like Machito, not even in Cuba. The closest anyone came to the Machito sound was a band called Julio Cueva that came from . . . I think it was Santiago de Cuba.

Anyway, they want Machito because Machito can play foxtrots, he can play waltzes, he can play boleros, he can play rumbas, and instead of hiring a second band to play the jitterbug stuff, the Machito band, they'd just give them the music sheets and they would play it. They would play a tango, they would play a foxtrot, they would play polkas, they were very versatile. But that didn't work. The boss calls them into the office at the Palladium. He says, "Hey, you guys always fill up the Jewish resorts up in the mountains. Why aren't the Jewish people coming here to hear your band now?" Machito explained that the reason was because they go away to other places and they've got their resorts and they support their own people. Mario Bauzá then asked, "How do you feel about black people?" And the guy told them, "Look, I'm only interested in the color of green." This is the owner of the club. His name was Tommy Morton. Bauzá says, "Why don't you try a Latin dance here? Let me set this up for you and see what you think about it, okay?" Because the Latin people, the Latinos in Harlem, went no further than 110th Street.

So they set this thing in motion and engage Federico Pagani, who is a promoter. He's got all these weird ideas, and then he calls it the "Blen Blen Club." They print up little cards with a fifteen-cent discount, and they gave it away at the subway stations and at the bus stops. So the Latin music was finally going downtown to the Palladium Ballroom at Fifty-third and Broadway. On that Sunday when they started, they were going to start at 4 o'clock. Mario Bauzá got there because he and Machito are the guys who are hosting this thing. There was a mob of people like New Year's Eve Times Square, you know.

He thought that something had gone wrong, that there was going to be a riot. It was just that they'd never seen so many Latinos in midtown Manhattan. And it was that they were going to the Palladium to this dance extravaganza called the Subway Dance.

Loza: But specifically Latin?

Salazar: They had six Latin bands. It lasted from four until one or two in the morning. Machito was the last band to play. They had Noro Morales, they had José Curbelo, they had a merengue band, and one unknown guy.

Loza: Now the motive here was to compete with these dance bands?

Salazar: Yeah. But when the six Latin bands brought all the Latinos, the blacks, the whites, and the mulattos from Harlem and Brooklyn, the guy made more money on that one Sunday than he had done for the months since he had opened up.

Loza: 'Cause it wasn't the Latinos and blacks that were going to Roseland and Arcadia, in other words.

Salazar: Right.

Loza: They weren't frequenting them. Those were basically white clubs.

Salazar: Yeah. You see, the blacks had the Savoy Ballroom at 142d Street and Lenox Avenue and the Latinos had the Park Palace at 110th Street and Fifth. The Puerto Ricans, the Latinos, used to go up to the Savoy Ballroom in the afternoons—I think from one to five or something like that—pay a quarter, and jitterbug there. Then at a certain time when it ends they went down to 110th Street to the Park Palace, and a lot of Afro-Americans went down there with them. And I understand they could dance just as well as any Latino. But that's as far as they went. Until these other little places opened up and closed because they didn't have a license and that. But that Palladium, it was in 1947 when it happened, it was a success. I mean they cleaned up.

So then the guy says, "Look, what I want to do, I want to continue this. I want Latin music here. We're going to do it on Sundays," because the guy made a lot of money. He sold his liquor; he sold his sodas. He'd never done anything like that before. So fine. But then Machito had to go out of town. So they got other bands. They told Federico, the promoter, they said, "Look, get some *vente tú* groups." You know what *vente tú* is? *Vente tú*—you come here. All these guys [a "pickup" band]. One night it didn't make it. So he says no, get the best groups. If you can't get the good guys, the best there is to keep this thing going.

Well, Tito Puente was with either Frank Martí or Pupi Campo, and Federico wanted to talk to them and said, "Look, get me a pickup group, 'cause you're going to start at the Palladium." So he's sitting down, and Tito goes over to the pianist, who is Joe Loco, and says something to him, or sings something to him in his ear. And he hands out this music, something new that Tito wanted to try out, which probably Pupi Campo said it's all right. They did it and the guy says, "Wow you should have seen that! That was out of sight!" So he goes up to Tito and says, "Tito, what was the name of that tune there?" And he says, "I don't have any name yet. It's something that I pushed together mishmash. Es un picadillo." So Federico says, "Look, I want you to take this group, pick a group and go down there, and I'm going to introduce you as the Picadilly Boys." So the following Sunday Puente opens the Palladium for the Sunday matinee with the Picadilly Boys. And one of the tunes written there, you know like.

Loza: "Picadillo"—that became a big one, yeah?

Salazar: To this day. So that's how it started for him.

Loza: So that's actually how his orchestra started, right there.

Salazar: He started—the Picadilly Boys were mostly guys from Pupi Campo's band, some from José Curbelo, he had Luis Varona sit in one week on piano. When Luis was with someone else, Charlie Palmieri would come in or Al Escobar, a pianist. What happened was that Tito must have loved the adulation, the grabbing, the pawing [of] all these nice-looking ladies. So in March of '49 he tells, I think it's Pupi Campo, that he's leaving, and he takes half the guys with him from the band . . . the Picadilly Boys—that was the name that Federico Pagani gave them. So the Picadilly Boys started building their reputation in '48–'49.

Loza: Pagani, what was he?

Salazar: He was a promoter. Federico Pagani, he was of Puerto Rican descent. He's the guy that used to book the bands and shows for theaters, whatever happened in Harlem. And Tito Puente forms his band in March; he leaves, I think it was Pupi or Frank Martí, because he was with Frank Martí, but whenever they needed him, he would say he'd send a substitute to Frank Martí at the Copa. He says, "I'm going to do this gig." Because it probably paid more or because of arrangements and that. He was always sending substitutes if he got a better gig.

So he forms the group and he gets his first gig, which is going to be the July Fourth weekend 1949 at a place called Atlantic Beach. Now the band consists of seven guys who are going to appear there. According to Frankie Colón, the conga drummer, who sat in on the rehearsals, the rehearsals were held at Luis Varona's studio on 116th Street near Park Avenue. Luis Varona was a very well known pianist at the time, and his mother used to give lessons, so they held it in the studio there. There were only seven guys; Tito was the seventh. And they were playing not Latin music but American charts. And the only Latin things they did was that watered-down stuff, like "Perfidia" and things like that. Well, no matter what Puente did, even the American foxtrots, they sounded great, you know, because his pen is too much, man. He knows how to write for those things. So they do the Atlantic Beach, and Frankie is brought in, and . . . when they do the Latin tunes, he plays conga in there.

So after Labor Day, when the gig ends, they come back to New York and Tito adds another trumpet player, he adds Chino Pozo on bongos; he augments the band [to], I think, eight or nine pieces, and it becomes a trumpet *conjunto*. At that time Tico Records was in existence a few months already. They were just looking to record people, and Tito realized that for him to be known he had to have exposure. So he agrees to four sides with Tico Records.

In the interim, a Cuban vocalist comes in from California who knows Chino Pozo, the *bongósero* who performs with Puente, and they are having lunch at Local 802, where the musicians meet. It's a cafeteria called La Salle. And Chino introduces his friend to Tito

Puente as Vicentico Valdés. Now Vicentico, you know [*laughs*], there hasn't been nobody like that guy since Vicentico Valdés himself. So "Hello, how are you, blah-blah-blah," and he says, "Look, we're going to have a rehearsal. Why don't you come down?"—not knowing anything about the potential of Vicentico Valdés.

Well, Tito had a vocalist—I think his name was Angel Rosa—a good vocalist, but there were parts of a tune called "Tus ojos" that he couldn't do right. So Chino Pozo says, "Tito, let Vicentico sing it. He'll show the guy the transition and how to do it." Well, they go into "Tus ojos" from beginning to end—bye-bye Angel Rosa [*laughs*], because what Puente heard there, who's going to compare with that guy? And a legend starts there. They both complement each other.

Okay, so in October of that year, 1949, they go to the studio to record four sides for Tico, and one of the sides is a tune called "Abaniquito." Well, "Abaniquito" hit right off the bat. Tico Records had hired a man called Dick "Ricardo" Sugar to buy fifteen minutes of airtime just to promote Tico Records. Every night for those fifteen minutes you heard "Abaniquito." The people who heard "Abaniquito" on Dick Ricardo's show went nuts; they went looking for [the band and its recordings, asking], "Who is this guy Tito Puente?" And that's how it started. Then Dick Ricardo's show was so popular that it grew from fifteen minutes to a half hour to an hour to two hours to four hours throughout the fifties and that.

By 1950 Pérez Prado's "Mambo Number 5" exploded on the scene, and in comes the new sound of mambo. The *guaracha* up to that time and the rumba were the thing, and Noro Morales and Machito were the number-one bands. All of a sudden Tito Puente and Tito Rodríguez come on the scene with these new ideas, this new sound. The West Coast had its version of the mambo; it was a Pérez Prado grunt sound. New York had a different sound, which later became the Palladium mambo and the one that finally stayed.

At that time Tito Puente started recording for everybody—for the Spanish Music Center, for Seeco Records, for Verve, for RCA, just to get his name out there. With each recording—it sold. I mean, the orchestrations were hip, they were modern, they were jazz influenced, it was a new sound. Tito clicked right away. Then he did "Vibe Mambo." No one ever heard of vibes in mambo. He did it and it caught on. He influenced people like Les Baxter, George Shearing, Cal Tjader, all these guys and then people out on the coast like Tony Martínez, probably Bobby Montes, and all these other guys that followed later on and that. He got stronger and stronger until he believed one day that he could walk on top of water. He started with the "king of the timbales," the "king" of this and that, and it goes to his head.

Loza: [*Laughs*] This started back then, huh?

Salazar: But the truth is, the guy was great. You couldn't take it away from him. This excited people. I'm talking about people like movie stars. They used to go to the Palladium to hear him.

Loza: That's why it's funny; it could be [that] if you compared him to, let's say, Machito, Pérez Prado or Tito Rodríguez, one of the biggest differences is that this cat spoke English. The others spoke English, but Puente had assimilated the mainstream a lot more than these other guys. And that probably enabled him to promote himself as "the king," and the Latinos started calling him "king" and therefore the Anglos started too, probably. I mean, that's part of the equation of what was happening, what do you think?

Salazar: No—well, yes, because you see, he was in the service, where he had to interact in English with other guys who spoke the language, and at night just before the movie, he'd entertain the men there, and he'd be with a sax section or a pianist playing "How High the Moon" and all those tunes.

Loza: He played all this big-band stuff. Straight-ahead stuff.

Salazar: He played trap drums, he played sax, he played piano.

Loza: Now Bauzá did that, but Machito didn't. And neither did Pérez Prado or Tito Rodríguez.

Salazar: No, but more important, in 1939 he was introduced to a man called José Curbelo who has got a business mind, who's not only a great pianist, but he has a business mind. He would listen to Curbelo and Miguelito Valdés, who had business heads—don't do this, do that, this is what you should look for, watch out for this, watch out for that.

Loza: Valdés had penetrated Hollywood.

Salazar: Yeah, he knew. They knew how to get around like boxers who know how to move and duck punches, but Curbelo especially. A lot of Puente's success is not only in his music but what Curbelo taught him, how to deal with people, when it comes down to the money and things like that. And in 1959, when Curbelo disbanded, he formed the Alpha Agency. That became the strongest booking agency because by the mid-1960s Curbelo had everybody of importance under contract, and whoever did not hire his bands didn't get none of the bands. Whoever was not signed with Curbelo would not work.

Loza: So he kept going.

Salazar: More than that, he protected Tito Puente like he was his own son. Puente would get the best gigs, the best money, the best everything.

Loza: Was Curbelo Cuban or Puerto Rican?

Salazar: Cuban.

Loza: Tito Puente also bonded with the Cubans.

Salazar: With everybody. I never saw Tito wave a Puerto Rican flag. Other musicians or bandleaders did. Not Tito. Tito would crack jokes, things like that. The things that Curbelo and Miguelito Valdés taught him he did very well. . . . Tito, with each passing year, just got better and better. And then in the early fifties, when the mambo was reaching its peak, he would go to Havana, Cuba, and any music store had rows and rows of orchestrations for a dollar. For piano, three trumpets and that—new songs! For one dollar! Machito, Puente, Rodríguez, you name it, they went there and picked these things up for one dollar, and you just pass the sheets out to the musicians.

Now, those were called stock arrangements. Now, Puente changed a lot of the stock arrangements. He got a hold of Arsenio Rodríguez's "Lo dicen todos." He changed it here and there, and it came out different. He added the Puente touch, which made it like Puente's signature. It's Tito Puente, you can tell. He has his own sound, like Machito had his own sound. René Hernández gave the Machito sound its own personal sound. And they were just out-of-sight tunes.

In 1952 Tito makes thirty-seven recordings—all thirty-seven of them had the hit potential, and that's when he rises like he's the guy on top of the world. Every week I remember going to the Palladium in '52 and '53; you heard a different tune, a new one in the book. How the hell can you compete with that? You can't. Somebody then credited him as "king of los timbales." And they had a dance at the St. Nicholas Arena. A writer from *El Diario Prensa,* a guy called Bobby Quintero, created a contest between Tito Puente and Pérez Prado as to who was the "king" of Latin music—that'll make it official. Besides being king of the timbal, people started calling him the "king of Latin music." This was '55. It's the cha-cha era, and he's still the king [Prado had been referred to as the "king of mambo"].

Loza: And by that time Puente was really progressing with the new sounds.

Salazar: Puente was hot.

Loza: He just kept going to each new stylistic gimmick, whatever you want to call it.

Salazar: He always had something there because some of his mentors would tell him, "Try this, now try that." And then he [individually] had these new sounds.

Loza: There's a very interesting thing there, because I wonder if some musicians were saying also, "Look what they're doing to the music." Like they say now—like they've always said. I'd be very interested to know if, let's say, Mario Bauzá was reacting stylistically, philosophically, with what Tito was doing to the music. And even going back before that. When Machito came up and joined Bauzá, and they were doing this stuff like combining the big-band jazz swing stuff with the Cuban music, you most likely had the traditionalists back in Cuba saying, "What's Bauzá doing? What's Machito doing?" Plus the fact that you even refer to the issue that Bauzá had sort of been fed up with some of the racial stuff in Cuba. Were there resentments? In other words, were musicians like Arcaño in Cuba saying, "What are these guys doing?" And then on the other hand, as Tito Puente progresses, maybe Bauzá starts saying, "What is he doing to the music?" Have you ever thought about that?

Salazar: I thought about that. There was no question about what he had done to the music. What he did was take it light-years ahead.

Loza: So it was adulated by everybody. I mean, there was no resentment?

Salazar: There was resentment because of the jealousies.

Loza: The jealousies. But it wasn't questioned musically, was it?

Salazar: No, sir. If you hear what Puente did; I mean he would get cha-chas that had nothing, they were just dead, jumpy cha-chas without a *montuno*—right, he had his own *montuno* there, and people would wonder, "Where the hell does this guy get his ideas?" It might be "El Silver Star," but that's not the way Enrique Jorrín wrote it. Its the Puente arrangements that made the difference.

Loza: Maybe Bauzá was noticing the attention Puente was getting because Bauzá thought that he was the one that infused these things.

Salazar: Machito and Noro Morales had the top bands. Out of nowhere the two Titos come and just moved them out of the picture. And then you start getting rich, erotic melodies and a guy like Puente, who knows how to write, writing the Cuban *montuno*—oh man, it was a different tune altogether. The people would go nuts.

Loza: And I think you're right. Tito Puente was able to produce it fast. He was able to score fast.

Salazar: Every week he had a different chart, and it just went on like that. And then the cha-cha-chá era here, a stale moment there, because there were some very bad cha-cha-chás. Instead of having the Cuban *montuno* there, you had the jumpy cha-cha-chá that has no *montuno,* jumping back and forth. It really stunk up the era. There were a lot of bands playing that. . . . So Tito grew strong in the midfifties. He just got stronger and stronger with all these new charts and people. He was selling records, he was going here, he was going there.

Loza: Well, he started doing some really beautiful cha-chas.

Salazar: Yes.

Loza: That *Dance Mania* album!

Salazar: I was just going to get into that. That's his best-selling album. That exploded in 1958. It was done in the last two weeks of '57. Prior to that in '57, just prior to those November and December recordings of *Dance Mania,* Mongo Santamaría, Willie Bobo, Bobby Rodríguez, and Jerry Sanfino of the Puente Orchestra recorded *Más ritmo caliente* with Cal Tjader. When *Dance Mania* came out, that's all you heard for three years. That year, '58, when it was released, you had some great recordings out there. You had José Fajardo's "Ritmo de pollo," you had Rolando La Serie's debut album, in addition to *The Most from Beny Moré,* which sold thousands, and Shorty Rogers's Afro-Cuban influence on RCA. Nineteen fifty-eight was a great year for music, but that *Dance Mania* sticks out, and that's all you heard for the following three years. I could just imagine . . . Puente, hearing this, reading these things about him: he's this, he's that, he's Jesus. Back on the bandstand it probably [affected him].

Loza: To you, what were the major tunes from that album?

Salazar: "Hong Kong Mambo," "Cayuco," "Mambo gozón." Oh man, every one of them! In 1959 a new sound comes in—the New York *charanga,* and Puente begins to receive competition from Pacheco and Palmieri. No matter how great Tito Puente has always been, to me, he never lost it. In fact, he's gotten better. He sounds better today than he did in the fifties, and that was supposed to be his best years. But what happened, like I tell you, people tire of things, it's just human nature. Like you eat a filet mignon every day and you eat lobster; one day you say, "I just want a hot dog."

Loza: He's also very smart, though. He seems to know when not to jump on a thing that's going to die out. He never jumped on the *pachanga* thing.

Salazar: He did a recording—*Pachanga con Puente.*

Loza: But the *pachanga* did die out.

Salazar: It did die out. The new thing was the boogaloo, and Joe Cuba became the new king. He and Eddie Palmieri were the most popular musicians at the time. In 1969 the boogaloo died. They stopped playing boogaloos on the radio, and the rest of the world follows New York. All of a sudden L.A. stopped, Miami stopped, Puerto Rico stopped. That was it. The new sound. The sound of the modern *guaguancó,* Johnny Pacheco's *conjunto,* Larry Harlow, they came in and took over. By that time Fania became so strong they made a motion picture. Pacheco was strong, Larry Harlow was strong. You had Ray Barretto who was strong.

Loza: That was the salsa explosion.

Salazar: Yeah, Fania killed everybody.

Loza: And that's when the word *salsa* just started getting thrown around.

Salazar: Cal Tjader is the one who started it. I don't care what anybody says. I got it from good sources. His album *Soul Sauce,* which means "salsa del alma," 1964, all right? That worked its way from California here. Everybody has been taking credit for it ever since, but Cal Tjader.

Loza: I heard that Jerry Masucci . . .

Salazar: Yeah, him too. Izzy Sanabria—they all "coined the word."

Loza: Somebody told me it was in Venezuela first.

Salazar: Yeah, sure.

Loza: The stories are incredible. And it was actually a lot of those postboogaloo *conjunto* bands that you were talking about that were first called "salsa."

Salazar: Yeah, but you got to remember that Tjader's album came out in '64, *Soul Sauce.*

Loza: So it took a little time to travel.

Salazar: Yeah, do you remember on the cover? A bottle of Tabasco sauce?

Loza: Yeah, I remember.

Salazar: The first ones to start calling it that were the Mexicans out in California—salsa, and then it spread through Los Angeles.

Loza: That would make sense to me. But I never heard that because Tito would always say "tomato sauce," and I always feel like saying, "No, it's not tomato sauce; what are you talking about?" Salsa is made with chile . . . it's hot.

Salazar: And then they started calling Santana's music—when Santana did "Oye como va" and "Evil Ways"—they started calling that [salsa], and that wasn't salsa, but yet the Mexicans had that in their mind. This was the brand of music they loved to listen to, and it worked its way from the West Coast to the East, and it got here by the early seventies. So they started calling things here "salsa," using the word *salsa* in everything. And then everybody here wanted to take credit for it. "Yeah, I coined the word." Bullshit. Tjader's *Soul Sauce* started that whole thing.

Loza: And the idea was that it was a hot thing. Hot sauce, not just tomato sauce. Because in Spain and a lot of Latin American countries, salsa can be a cream sauce. Salsa was the idea of a hot, picante thing in there, man. Wherever it came from, man, it sure took hold. And eventually Tito jumped on that.

Salazar: He made some good recordings, but they never got that much airplay because the strong people were the Fania people, and Jerry Masucci bought airtime for three hours from Chico Sesma in L.A., three hours in Chicago. He bought airtime in Miami and Puerto Rico. He made these guys superstars in ten years. Three hours every day of just Fania artists. That's why they rose. By the seventies they were ready, and Tito Puente made a recording called *Unlimited*. Critics put it down. He was trying to do disco—the hustle. To me, I liked it . . . he was trying to cash in on the John Travolta *Saturday Night [Fever]* thing. But the people are so used to the "Babarabatiri" up-tempo swing. They expect even the hustles to be like that, and it wasn't. Boy did they tear that apart. And with that his reputation just sank. Guys not only blasted it on radio, one deejay said it was a "piece of shit" over the air. And they wrote about it in their magazines. "Oh, this is not Tito Puente. No king does this." And I'm saying to myself, "This is so unfair. These guys are not even musicians. How can you criticize something you don't understand?" I myself loved the album. It wasn't one of his best, but musically he had new ideas. He's always branching out in new directions where no one else goes. They put him down and you know something? He was dead at that moment.

Then, I don't know how it happened, but somebody contacted Jerry Masucci. Masucci produced all those other labels: Vaya, International, Cotique, Roulette—all of them, so he can shelve them. They wouldn't be in the market, and the only things that were selling were what you heard on the radio, which were Fania. So somebody whispers in Masucci's ear, and the next thing you know, Masucci lets Puente record. He records an album called *The Legend,* with Tito Puente pictured as a baby. In that album is a tune called "Fiesta a la King." That's what brought Puente back. But it wasn't that alone. It was his arrangements.

Puente ends up being awarded his first Grammy for a tribute to Beny Moré—1979 on the Tico label, by that time bought out by Fania—and he had this "Fiesta a la King" that just exploded. You see that's one thing. If it's good, even the jazz stations, the non-Latin stations, play it. They say this is a motherfucker, and they played it. And Puente's always had that kind of luck that brought him back. But the guys responsible for bringing Puente back from the dead in '78 included Jerry Masucci for giving him that chance and exposing him on national TV. David Maldonado of *Latin Times* magazine had done these stories on Puente. They did spreads with glossy photos of Puente—good stories. My show, the *Latin Musicians' Show* on WKCR, there was more of Puente on there than anything else. I would have him talking about everything. I had him every second week. He would come up alone or with Charlie Palmieri. We did shows like the question of top billing. We'd discuss that for an hour. We would discuss other topics about Puente and what he thought at the moment and what he was thinking. And a lot of things that I would bring up from the past with Machito, interesting things, just to get the people to hear Puente and hear his recordings to bring it back. But you can't say that one person did it.

Then there was Marty Cohen from Latin Percussion, who had a group he started in '79 called the Latin Jazz Ensemble. He had Johnny Rodríguez as the leader. They were the guys from Típica '73: Sonny Bravo was on piano, Joe Manozzi was on trumpet. And the Latin Jazz Ensemble all of a sudden came alive and people started saying, "Hey, who's that? Wow!" They invited Tito Puente to Montreux with them, and Puente took over the Latin Jazz Ensemble. So I got to give Marty Cohen credit for organizing it as a group.

After Puente won that Beny Moré Grammy, within months he was calling himself the king again. Let me tell you something. He sounded great. He sounded better than ever. And I couldn't argue; if he wasn't the best, he'd be the second best. But I'm the kind of guy that goes by whoever they chose as the Grammy winner; to me, that's the king for the year. We got to go by something that's regulated.

There were a lot of people responsible for bringing Puente back, and by the early eighties with the Latin Jazz Ensemble, which he still leads today, Puente was back on top, back at being the king. I still respect the man, I think he's great, but we've had different kings each year. In 1983 Conjunto Libre made a recording called *Little Sunflower,* and I said this is the best of the year. Manny Oquendo is the king for the year.

Loza: There were other things that came out. How about some of those things Celia Cruz recorded with Pacheco and Sonora Matancera that broke through? Quimbara, stuff like that that broke through.

Salazar: Sold thousands!

Loza: Of course, Tito says, "Well, she's the queen." So there's this spot reserved for her. You know, during the period that you're talking about—seventies into the early eighties—but especially the seventies, Eddie Palmieri started coming out with great material. Charlie Palmieri was always very good. These cats were progressive. These guys were talented—to me that was the richest period of inventiveness.

Salazar: How can you overlook that?

Loza: You can't, and I think it sparked Tito Puente in a way that maybe his new competitor became Eddie Palmieri.

Salazar: Yes, he did.

Loza: That's what I saw. Because by this time Tito Rodríguez was gone—had died [in 1972]. Eddie Palmieri and Tito even had a Grammy tradeoff. It's five to four right now. I think Tito wants to get back even. Anyway, the whole Grammy thing, that's an issue, but I guess what I'm trying to say is, don't you think that that period became a fermenting period even for Tito? Maybe because of Tito versus Palmieri, because look at that album *El rey*. Look what happened all of a sudden with that Latin Jazz Ensemble. That stuff became extremely high-quality stuff. *El rey* blew everybody out of the water.

Salazar: The new Latin Jazz Ensemble sound just breathed life into Puente. He was very lucky that he came along at the time that Marty Cohen had that. He took over and he's made it work. I caught his more current group, the Golden All Stars, about two months ago at the Beacon Theater. Dave Valentín and Giovanni Hidalgo stole the show that night. They did "Little Sunflower," they did "First Light." The place went berserk, so I can just imagine how they're gonna sound all over the world.

Loza: Then they started taking tunes like that. Those are both Freddie Hubbard tunes. They took Coltrane tunes—"Giant Steps," "Equinox," just started adapting them.

Salazar: You see, depending on who the arranger is, if he's a young guy like Oscar Hernández or Dave Valentín who grabs *montunos* like that, he's gonna transform that into something that's incredible.

Loza: Now about that same time that you had all those explosions happening, 'cause

Eddie Palmieri was listening to McCoy Tyner, so pretty soon you had Carlos Santana do "Oye como va." Now that tune was on some Puente album back in the early sixties, right?

Salazar: '63.

Loza: That was another thing that he was able to exploit. That thing really had a big effect. How much did that '63 recording sell? It got around, but it was not a major hit.

Salazar: No, it sold. In fact, that was his biggest seller since *Dance Mania*.

Loza: "Oye como va" certainly helped him internationally.

Salazar: In '63 he made a splash with that. But in 1970 when Santana recorded it for Columbia, it sold millions. And it was responsible for Anglo kids buying conga drums, 'cause Santana turned them on. And I understand that Puente's first royalty check from Santana's sales was $15,000, so you can imagine how much Santana sold worldwide. "Oye como va" made the explosion.

Loza: Can you imagine how many times that gets played on the radio? Different versions? So many people have recorded it. You know how many times I have played it? I played it last Sunday at the Gershwin Hotel. I don't play a gig without playing it.

Salazar: I talked to this musician from Sweden. He told me he started his band the year Santana recorded the tune. He patterned himself after Santana, but he couldn't play guitar, so he got this guy from Italy, an Italian guy who played just like Santana, and they did "Oye como va." And he had a gig, he had a gig at restaurants in Sweden.

Loza: Since I was nineteen years old I don't think I've played a song more often than that song. And to this day I still play it. Back when I was in an R&B band I played it because it was an R&B top-forty hit. Now it's because it's a Latin standard. I still have a Latin jazz group, and whenever I want something to soothe out the audience, make them happy, I use that. We also use Clare Fischer's "Morning"; that's become a big standard now, and Tito recorded it. It's a beautiful song, and Fischer got a Grammy for it.

Salazar: A lot of people recorded it.

Loza: Anyway, again Tito Puente gets another—I don't want to call it a break, but destiny goes his way.

Salazar: I think he deserves it because he's a unique musician.

Loza: Well, Carlos Santana sits there and he's inspired by Tito Puente to mix this stuff with rock and blues, and he creates this thing called Latin rock and . . . you know, boogaloo was sort of like that, it was R&B, but Santana took it into another dimension, and who was it that he used? It was Tito Puente, and it wasn't just "Oye como va," it was "Pa' los rumberos." He also did a Willie Bobo thing.

Salazar: "Evil Ways."

Loza: Yeah. And those were his two first hits. Right out of the Latin catalog.

Salazar: But you see, Santana had a way of coming across. He knew it, he did it, and that's why.

Loza: And he had the same thing Tito did. They had this . . . let's face it, Tito has a unique approach.

Salazar: Where Tito was typically Latin, Santana was not. Santana was more rock than Latin.

Loza: He was doing things different. Like Tito says, he turned the clave around on that "Para los rumberos," but it's like you said when talking about "Manisero"—"There's that tune." Why does that tune . . . what is it that arouses them? "Oye como va" did it. Santana, the way he played guitar, all these things combined.

Salazar: Tito's tunes, Tito's music. It does that to people. Even though he didn't write "Babarabatiri," people praise his "Babarabatiri."

Loza: Again back to Machito, Pérez Prado, Tito Rodríguez, Tito Puente. This is more than just *chisme* [gossip]; this is something that concerns me. This is something I want to bring up with you. If we look back to the late forties, early fifties bebop, Cubop, and Latin music, it's all happening at the same time in New York City, uptown, downtown. The same thing happened with jazz—it went down to Fifty-second Street from Harlem, and almost the same thing was happening with Latin music when it went to the Palladium. There's a lot of parallels. Dizzy Gillespie was bringing in Chano Pozo, et cetera, mixing, bringing the Latin in. Blacks were saying, "We will not play for segregated audiences anymore." Gillespie would not do that. Charlie Parker would not do that. There was a social thing with bebop. Now maybe that was also happening with Latin. Like you said when the guy from the Palladium said, "All I see is green." And the question they had, Machito or whoever it was, "Do you mind black people coming in here?" Right? Was that Machito?

Salazar: They all said it. Pagani, Machito, and Bauzá, at different times they told Morton.

Loza: And then Bauzá here had this relationship with Gillespie, had played with him in Cab Calloway's group, et cetera. Anyway, there's a parallel thing there. Race was an issue, even in terms of people coming from Cuba and Puerto Rico, coming here and saying, "Hey, it's more integrated, supposedly. This is the northeast." Do you ever feel that that was ever something of major consequence in Latin music—this race thing? I don't know that the Latin context can be compared at the same level to what happened in the jazz thing. In jazz there was a more defined dichotomy—black and white.

Salazar: Chano Pozo was as black as ebony, but it was Dizzy Gillespie's quoting him, "Me no American, me Cuban," meaning me, you see, Latino. I'm different. I'm not black; I'm Cuban. So why was it taboo for a black African American to play in Miami, and I'm talking about 1945? The Machito orchestra was down there, and they had no trouble. "Oh, no, they all spoke Spanish." They had one African American, Leslie Jonikens. They told Jonikens just to nod this head and say *sí* and *no* and things like that.

Loza: Now where was this?

Salazar: They were going to open up at a place called . . . I think it was called the Beachcomber, in Miami in 1945.

Loza: When things were strictly segregated.

Salazar: Segregated. Machito spoke to the guy in Spanish and told him, "Yo soy Cubano, no, sí"; "Yeah, okay, that's different." All of a sudden, he wasn't black anymore. He was Cuban. And it played there, and they joked about it because Machito told me, and he was laughing about it—how they got over that. And I understand other Cubans did the same thing too. They started speaking Spanish—"Okay, it's different now." Black as the ace of spades.

Loza: The thing to remember is that with someone like Machito, there were problems in Cuba that made these guys want to come here, right?

Salazar: The most segregated city in the United States now is Miami.

Loza: And L.A.

Salazar: I don't know much about L.A., but I know about Miami because I'm in touch. This is why I'm so informative, right? They send me newspapers from there because I cut out anything musical. I never saw one black face in all the years I was getting newspapers in the Miami community, not one black face. And this guy tells me "Nah, we don't want to mix La Raza and that, we don't want that." And I say, "It's the black Cuban that put you guys on the map. Not only in music but in sports and other things. What's wrong with you guys?" "Ah, we don't need that shit." I say, "Oh, you need it because this is what made you famous the world over."

Loza: This is a Cuban talking?

Salazar: This is a white Cuban giving me this shit. I don't even speak to the guy no more. To me, he's an asshole, I don't want to speak to people like that. It's the same thing that happened with a family that moved to Los Angeles, telling me how one night the guys that were in the neighborhood started beating up Chicanos and anybody Latin that was wearing a zoot suit. He escaped with his life, and that always stuck here, about the zoot suit. He said, "They said it wasn't because we were mulattoes or Chicano but because of the zoot suit," and I'm wondering was it really because of the zoot suit? Was that the excuse they were using?

Loza: It's because they were Mexicans dressed in a zoot suit. And they accused them of being draft dodgers. So the sailors would jump them and strip them, take their pants off.

Salazar: But this guy gave us a blow-by-blow . . .

Loza: Well, they beat them up. They beat them up bad.

Salazar: Unmercifully, man.

Loza: You know, in my book *Barrio Rhythm* there's a whole section on that. It's true. Eddie Cano, one of the case studies in the book, told me that in the late forties, maybe early fifties, he was in the army. He went to the Santa Monica Ballroom to the dance hall. They wouldn't let him in in uniform because he was Mexican. So there was a lot of that. So you know the issue of race is something that is important to me, and there's got to be some stuff on it because we can also go from that period, what I call the bebop period, because race was an issue, man. These cats wouldn't play for segregated audiences. It's just like the way I developed that book; something happened after the war. The Latinos were there in the war fighting. My father was in Iwo Jima, in a tank. He was a guy who happened to be born here, and he went back to Mexico and he came back. This happened a lot. In fact, Latinos were the highest-awarded people in the war even, medals and stuff, per capita.

It's a very important issue because Tito Puente also comes out of that thing. In fact,

I asked him about this. He was in the war, the military, World War II. And that has a lot to do with the Latinos becoming more outspoken musically. The market opened in certain ways. And the other thing when we get to the sixties and seventies, when the salsa explosion really happened, and Tito still managed to ride that thing, that was a very politically fermented period. And when you look at salsa of that period, even when I see the old pictures, and I remember that period, I remember going to those dances at the Hollywood Palladium when they were still doing dances in the seventies, and it was a very political thing to get into the music. So that there are these periods of what I call reclamation. You reaffirm it. You bring it back. This is where the cultural thing comes in. "I'm Latino and proud of it." And you've got something to relate to and, "Let's go out and dance." You reaffirm what you are. I feel that in a large part Tito jumped on that bandwagon.

Salazar: I don't know if I would label it that way. When you were just speaking now a lot of thoughts came to mind. I think about 1930. How something exotic just turned on an audience—the "Peanut Vendor"—and the love affair started in 1930. Then a strike at 1940—the musicians [struck] against the radio stations because they weren't getting a big enough royalty. There was no music. So the stations had to come up with some music. So they go to this publishing company, MCA, and in there they have this guy called Xavier Cugat. For the first time coast to coast you start hearing Latin music. He did movies. Latin music is in the movies with Betty Grable and César Romero and Carmen Miranda and all of these people. Dick Haymes starts singing boleros with English lyrics. They become more enamored with the music.

Loza: It was very mainstream.

Salazar: Well, not only because it was a new sound. It was an exotic sound. Something that turned on people in Nebraska—some of them, not all of them. They really loved it. And then to meet somebody that was actually Spanish. Hey, if you cut him he bleeds like me. Hey, he eats breakfast like I do. There wasn't that much difference. We're just the same except I spoke Spanish and you spoke English. There's a lot of things we have in common. We have fathers, we're husbands. Then in 1949 mambo explodes with Pérez Prado's "Mambo #5." The Palladium was the laboratory. The catalyst that brought Afro-Americans, Irish, Italians, Jews. God, they danced the mambo. And because of the mambo, race relations started to improve in that era. What social scientists couldn't do on purpose, the mambo was able to accomplish by error.

Loza: Through art.

Salazar: The music. Puente, Rodríguez, Macho—[they] turned these people on. Music started going to all the Jewish resorts up in the mountains. The mambo exploded in '52 where Kenton, Les Baxter, George Shearing, Cal Tjader, they got in—

Loza: White guys.

Salazar: —and "Wow, what is that?" And they loved it. And you know something? There wasn't a better person than Cal Tjader. Cal didn't care what color you were or anything. He went up to Harlem, to black Harlem to sit on the *los bembés* the Cubans had because he wanted to learn. So ever since that's been happening, the relationships keep improving, except some of these diehard white Latinos.

Loza: All this relates to my question on race, although during the forties and fifties it was possibly a less nationalistic thing. In the seventies, which is after a lot of the sixties militant stuff, it was the civil rights movement, the black movement, really, that a lot of the Latins imitated—the Chicano movement in California, Puerto Ricans here, I think, emulated that. And in the seventies, if you look at the themes of Eddie Palmieri's music and maybe some of Puente's, even the way they dress, and the relationship of the black and Latin communities. Don't you think there was a thing of nationalism that started? I'm not saying that it necessarily was good for the music, but it happened.

Salazar: You could hear it in the lyrics. In Puerto Rico, all those things. Eddie had that on his mind. He was a musician with a purpose. Tito was in a different direction. No politics, no nothing. He shied away from politics.

Loza: I would agree with you that the mambo did more for race relations than any other kind of legislation or amendments to the Constitution.

Salazar: Yeah, it brought these people together willingly just to dance, and then next thing you know, they're socializing, and the next thing you know there's marriages and things like that. And nobody's really getting hurt.

Loza: But that did ferment. It almost seems that it went to a point and then it started crumbling. Just like politics. We're going back to Jim Crow laws. Look at what's happening.

Salazar: Republicans.

Loza: They want to go back to Jim Crow. States' rights.

Salazar: They want to go back to the way things were. One of the greatest things that ever happened to this country was the immigrant and the illegal alien. How can you tell somebody, "Stay over there and die"? We didn't want to come here. We came here because we had no other choice. So what's wrong with trying to improve our livelihood, make it as easy as possible. And then you have these guys with this nonsense, you're not gonna let this person eat, you're not gonna get an inoculation. Come on, man.

Loza: You're not gonna let a woman have prenatal care? You can imagine what we've gone through in California on this.

Salazar: You know why, because their people are not involved.

Loza: It's a racist thing. And people still have heavy feelings against blacks and Latins, who are very discriminated against. The irony being that the whole Southwest was stolen from Mexico, who had kicked out the Europeans, so you can't say that that was Spain. Some dude I was talking to on the plane here actually thought that the U.S. took it from Spain. I said "Man, you better go home and study your history."

Salazar: Sometime history is perverted too, because right now a few "Latin music historians" are rewriting history. Well, Puente's music at the Palladium was the catalyst, because like I told you, all these different ethnic groups were there, and one of the most popular patrons was Millie Done, who happens to be of Italian descent, and she's on all these documentaries about the Palladium. She's a Brooklyn girl, Italian who married a black Puerto Rican, and they got a gorgeous daughter. The coloring of their daughter is beautiful. So you know, it's things like this that happen. I say, "Hey, what's wrong with that?"

Loza: Some of the most beautiful stuff comes out of this.

◈◈

At this point in our conversation, Max and I diverted to a number of issues involving politics, race, and the growth of Latin music throughout the world, and especially in the United States, Europe, Japan, and Latin America. Toward the end of our dialogue, Max responded to a remark I made concerning his early involvement with Latin music, the Palladium, and the art of dance.

Salazar: I was in the army for four years. I was the Eighty-second Airborne featherweight boxing champ. I was on the boxing team. So whenever they went and jumped into Korea, being that I was on the boxing team, I didn't get to go. I wanted to go, 'cause at that time I was a nut. I wanted medals and all that gung-ho nonsense, but I didn't get to go when they made the jump into Korea. So being six hundred miles away, I used to come here as often as I could. I went to Birdland, I went to the Palladium. My wife is an Irish girl from there [North Carolina], and we got married and came up here. The subway ride was a nickel. Plate of spaghetti and meatballs was thirty-five cents. Not only did we go out with five dollars, but we brought change back, and we went to the Palladium. We danced for hours. We had a great time. You could say we were weaned on the music at the Palladium. That's why I know so much, because I was there a lot. That was the place to escape away from the everyday problems of life.

4

Joe Conzo
Reevaluations

S INCE I began the major work on this book five years ago, Tito consistently advised me to seek the help and knowledge of his longtime associate and close friend Joe Conzo. As related in the following interview, Joe met Tito during the Palladium years. Since then, besides developing a very close personal friendship with Tito, Joe worked as his personal publicist, assisted in public relations and productions, and through the past eighteen years has acted as the chairperson of Tito's scholarship fund. Joe has conducted his work with Tito while simultaneously maintaining a professional career as a social worker in the Bronx, where he still resides.

To facilitate the following interview with Joe, UCLA had him flown out to Los Angeles and accommodated him at the Hollywood Roosevelt Hotel, where Joe and many of Tito's close friends and associates had stayed during his Hollywood Walk of Fame induction. Joe spent a significant amount of time during the trip critiquing my initial draft for the book. The interview was videotaped in Schoenberg Hall at UCLA on June 21, 1996.

❖❖

Loza: Joe, where I wanted to start off is to ask you how you became involved with Tito Puente.

Conzo: Basically I met Tito at the Palladium. I was a frustrated conga player, and I just took a liking to the man. He intrigued me, and we got to talking. Tito likes people but he doesn't trust people, and he took a liking to me. I guess the fact that his older son, Ronnie, went to school with my sister, and then Margie, his present wife, grew up with me. I think all of that helped a lot. I really started getting into Tito's career—the pros and cons of why he played this and why he played that. Tito's a proficient musician as far as saxophone and piano, vibes, of course timbales and trap drums, too. It's interesting to see how this man thinks. Basically that was it. The rest is history. We've been together ever since.

Loza: Did you develop a business relationship with Tito, because you read all these articles, Joe Conzo the publicist, Joe Conzo the historian . . .

Conzo: I am a historian, you know that, of course. Basically I am now, you might say, Tito Puente's "curator." I am considered the foremost authority on the man and his music—in the world, not in New York City. I have every record that Tito has ever recorded. Yes, at times I do handle Tito's public relations. I have a tendency to get to people in the media better than his agent, whoever that may be. As far as a producer, yes, I am the chairman of his scholarship fund, and I have produced numerous concerts involving Tito Puente with the scholarship. So I wear many hats with Tito Puente, but basically I'm just his curator, and Tito likes to work. It's public relations, what I do.

Loza: His feeling is that you are the person who should have the last word on these things because a lot of people have conflated stuff, exaggerated, in terms of writing. We've discussed this in the past day or so. I know that as soon as I met Tito Puente, I met Joe, because it was a "one-and-one" kind of thing. Now getting into some of the opinions, your opinions, but also what you think of others through the years because you lived in New York, you've seen the Palladium, Spanish Harlem. You see how Tito represents that particular cultural area, but at the same time he became a New York phenomenon throughout Manhattan, throughout the Bronx, the New York area. Then of course the major thing about Tito is the international effect—the world. Like you said, he's approaching the 113th album. So what in your estimation, Joe, are some of the main attributes that made Tito Puente punch into the international scene in terms of serious Latin music—as I would call it a very serious art form—more than anybody else?

Conzo: I would say Tito, the man himself, as an individual. Two: Tito the musician. As a musician he plays all types of music. Tito has that advantage as an arranger, as a composer. Also Tito's book—when I say "book," I'm talking about his music book for the band—Tito has that knack of taking . . . Tito can play from Jewish music to "Havah Nagilah" to Egyptian music—he has the knack—that ability. That's one of the things that attributes as to why Tito is sold internationally. Tito has played all over the world, and he knows when to play straight Latin music, when to play straight Latin jazz, and when to play the "Tea for Two" cha-cha for the Jewish or Italian crowd or whatever the case may be. I would say that that is one of his greatest gifts, his biggest attributes. His personality—Tito is a funny person. You know that as well as I do, and he gets along with everybody. And he takes his music very seriously. When he goes into a studio and he records, it takes him two or three days to record. He doesn't do an album in one year.

Loza: He definitely has this quality. What you're talking about is charisma. A lot like people like Duke Ellington, Dizzy Gillespie, Basie, Pavarotti—all these people have it, and it helps them. It's the ability to communicate. If you can communicate with somebody talking, you can probably do it playing, and he is a consummate artist. How about that aspect of him, the fact that he was so versatile and played all these instruments; do you think that people—especially Latinos—recognize this as something special? Like we said at the end of the manuscript, Tito is sort of like the Bach or Beethoven of the Latin world. What do you think about that?

Conzo: Well, I agree with you. Tito's music will leave a legacy. We're still playing Mozart after 200 years. We still consider Mozart a genius, Beethoven, Bach. I think the same will be said for Tito's music. He *is* there. People recognize that. First of all, they recognize it more so when they look at Tito's history. Tito was a child prodigy at the age of thirteen. And Tito has the knowledge. He can play. He projects that to the crowd. He's a showman, which is the most important thing than anything else. Ellington had that, and so did Basie. They would play that piano, and they would direct in that certain style. I think people look to Tito for that—either for that timbale solo or for that little dancing he would do. Machito had that same knack, and so did Tito Rodríguez. They played a certain way. They projected to the public, and I think the public understands.

Loza: What in your estimation were some of the most important watersheds—particular tunes, recordings, or albums, or performances, for that matter? Or musical projects that he did that were watersheds, in other words, special moments in his career that sort of catapulted him further?

Conzo: I think the 1967 Metropolitan Opera that he did at CUNY University, where he conducted a symphony orchestra and he brought out Celia Cruz and Ruth Fernández from either stage, I think that put him in another sphere. That put him in another ball game. I think the scholarship concerts—not because I'm the chairman—but I think that has helped because it's benefiting students. I would also say things that he's done. He played for President Carter, the first president a Latin music artist played for. They say Cugat and they say Desi Arnaz. They may have; I don't remember the history. Tito was the first Latino to play for a president of the United States. They actually commissioned his band to play for President Carter. I think that catapulted him into a different ball game to other people. In his career, as far as albums are concerned, *Dance Mania,* everybody talks about that. The public went bananas on that. There are so many, numerous things. I think Carlos Santana also helped with "Oye como va." I think much more than anything else, "Oye como va" now is like the national anthem for Tito and Carlos when he plays. That is known the world over. Everybody happens to know "Oye como va." Tito used to tell the story—he told you the story?—"Play Santana's tune!" Turns out it's his hero's tune. He used to get pissed off about it, and then they told him, "Tito, play it! I don't care if it's Mozart's tune—play it!"

Loza: But it has definitely become the most played Latin tune in the world.

Conzo: Steve, I remember "Bang-Bang," I remember "Watermelon Man." They were all the watusi. They were an overnight success with the English audiences, but nothing like "Oye como va."

Loza: Tito's also made some attempts to go into other areas of the art world. We were talking about working with the opera. Doing things like scholarships. He is a trained musician. He went to Juilliard. He studied with great composers, arrangers, which I think is what people start realizing. That's part of him being the king. It's not just a pop thing. "The king" also refers to his abilities, the technical, the musical. I was listening to that album you played me yesterday with La India [*Jazzin'*]. I'm still amazed at what he's doing on marimba, on vibraphone. These are not easy lines he's playing. These are bebop, complicated melodies, structures.

Conzo: I think you know it as well as anybody. He's told me that you've got to know what you're hitting. You're a musician, and I've seen Tito . . . it's unbelievable.

Loza: The fact that he's able to put his money where his mouth is, because when you're up there on the timbales—he told me this one time—you've got to keep up with all these young *timbaleros* and still beat them, which amazingly at the age of seventy-three he's still doing.

Conzo: I don't think it's a question of Tito beating young *timbaleros*—he admires young *timbaleros*. I think it's a question of them respecting him and giving him that respect. I mean one day Tito is going to have to give up his sticks, and you and I discussed this yesterday. There are *timbaleros*—there was Willie Bobo, there was Orestes, there's numerous *timbaleros,* but they—well, Willie's no longer with us, but Orestes is not a kid anymore, but you've got young *timbaleros*. I think Tito admires that, yes. It's not a person kicking their ass; it's a question of respecting, respecting your elder.

Loza: Another thing I wanted to bring up was this industry thing. There's a couple of issues about it. Number one, your feelings and his feelings about the penetration of Latin music into the mainstream. It has been a constant challenge. Number two, Tito's attempt to get into other areas of the art world: entertainment, movies, television. Could you comment on those two items?

Conzo: As far as Tito's career, Tito has been lucky. I wish he did more. I could tell you numerous things. I could see Tito playing a complete score. It's unfortunate. And you live out here. This is California, this is Hollywood, and you as a Hispanic, as a Chicano, me as a Puerto Rican, I constantly read about it. I read about how this industry—we're talking about the movie industry—how it shuns away the minorities. They'll throw us crumbs, and it is an uphill battle. I know you guys have an organization that deals with, as far as the media is concerned, the TV and the movies, and they monitor things. Even the blacks have the same thing, and the Hispanics—there's a Hispanic organization out here; they're constantly monitoring the industry. Now as far as the music industry, that's a whole other ball game in itself. When you talk about the Grammys . . . you showed me something yesterday which was very interesting [a statement by Willie Colón concerning the Grammys; see chapter 7]. It's true. It's all politics. Tito hits the roof. I was on the Grammy committee, you were on the Grammy committee years ago, and you see it. We're still the low man on the totem pole. I'm not taking away from Mozart or Beethoven, classic symphonies, but we've been in this industry for the last sixty-seven years, and here comes the hip-hop music, and they create all kinds of categories for them. Why? Because it's politics. It's money. And as far as Tito's concerned, it's another organization. At this stage of the game in his life, he doesn't need them. I told Tito, "Be a Bill Cosby." The only award [program] Bill Cosby attends is the People's [Choice] Award because it's voted for by the people. He doesn't have anything to do with the Grammys, the Emmys, the Academy Awards. It's all politics.

Loza: He's turned them down.

Conzo: Yes. I told him, and Tito looks at me and says, "You're right." I said, "You don't need them." At this stage of his career at seventy-three years old, 113 albums under his belt, give me a break.

Loza: Now you mentioned Bill Cosby and Tito had mentioned something some months ago. Bill Cosby was very instrumental in recognizing Dizzy Gillespie, another great jazz artist, and he seems to have also identified Tito as one of these people.

Conzo: Yes.

Loza: What is your take on that?

Conzo: I think it's good, and I wish more of our people who are in the same type of position as a Bill Cosby—I'm not talking about monetarily; I'm talking about a position of power—would do that. Can you take another—and I hate to use the word *ethnic,* but we're all one, and God created everybody equal—but Bill, with all the money he's got, the highest-paid entertainer in America, he recognizes talent, he's a good friend of Tito's, he's a good friend of mine, and he's that way. He recognizes talent. He can also put you down too. Bill is not afraid to speak his mind. But it is unfortunate—and I think you and I discussed it yesterday—how a person like Ricardo Montalbán tried to do this here and how an organization fell by the wayside because it became politics, it became ego. It's a shame. At least you guys had something here in L.A., in California. We didn't have anything in New York. As far as comparison to somebody like Bill Cosby, to this day people call me and say, "Joe, you think I can get Tito if he's available? But I don't want to pay." This is the attitude, and these are your people. These are big politicians. I say, "What do you mean, you don't want to pay? You've got to call the office. It's going to cost you a lot of money." They say, "Tito's a good friend of mine." I say, "He may be a good friend of yours, but you still have to feed those musicians." This is what hurts us, the people in power. Instead of pushing like you've done with this book, and you just told me how we're pushing for NEA [National Endowment for the Arts], the award, the Kennedy medal for Tito, but you and I are small potatoes. We have other people trying to do it which is lower-level politicians, but yet we have to go to other politicians who know of Tito Puente that don't even reside in New York City, or they're of other ethnic backgrounds, and they do what they have to do, when your own people don't do it. They're always trying to get over.

Loza: Yes, and there has been more movement in the political side than there has in the entertainment side. A lot of people think it's because of the bilingual nature of it, which is another point. Talking about Bill Cosby, Dizzy Gillespie, Duke Ellington, the big people who represent their areas, which in my estimation is what Tito is. He's a Bill Cosby of Latin music, he's a Dizzy Gillespie of Latin music. But let's face it, I think those guys ended up getting—in the so-called mainstream of United States industries, whether the entertainment industry, or politics—recognition a little easier, wouldn't you say?

Conzo: Yes, I would say easier, but you've got to understand like a Duke Ellington, like a Count Basie, you had a Sinatra, a Sinatra that would play with these bands: Sinatra, who is of Italian descent and known the world over—he's "chairman of the board." Hey, it was a great honor. He was supposed to do an album with Tito—it never happened.

Loza: There's an example.

Conzo: Sure, that would probably have put Tito in a whole other ball game with Sinatra. It goes back to what I just finished saying. Bill Cosby took Tito Puente and put him on his show. The first Latin dude to appear on a major show like that. All I'm trying to say is that you need that. All God-given talent, like what a person like Tito has, could be corrupted. You need to go out there and prove yourself, but by the same token, it's nice to get that little push from [stars like] a Bill Cosby or Frank Sinatra or [an academician like] a Steve Loza or somebody within power.

Loza: Well, it puts your name on that, I would say to a good portion of people in the world, the United States especially. I talk to young people and they know. We're talking about these people halfway in the know, who listen to music—hip-hop, rock—I'd say among the other people—I'm talking about Anglos, blacks, Latinos, obviously—a lot of these young people *do* know who Tito Puente is. They know about him more than any other Latin artist, I would say, besides Julio Iglesias and that kind of stuff. So that's amazing. Now this thing about Latin America, he's also become an icon there, and that is one area where there is sort of a barrier, Joe, just like with the television stuff. Two percent Latinos on TV; there were three percent in the fifties, so we're doing worse now than we were before. A lot of people go into the Spanish-language thing and about all the English-speaking people who don't understand what Tito's doing. Are there really two separate markets that Tito Puente and Latin music have to deal with? How much of a problem is that, the Latin market and Latin America?

Conzo: When I think in terms of the mambo era, the Palladium era, one, we don't have the dance halls that we used to have, so it has become two divided markets. The Tito in the English way sings, "I'll always love you" with a Latin beat to it, and the Tito on the other side sings the Spanish, so I think it goes back to the politics again, it goes back to greed. Years ago you had the Hollywood Palladium; you had the Palladium in New York. The media was there, [and] you had more ethnic people dancing to our music. The mambo did more than anything else. The mambo and the rumba integrated. They call Tito "crossover." Tito says, "Cross over what? I've been doing this for the last fifty years." Tito could play. He did the boogaloo, he did the *pachanga,* he did the shingaling. He'll play something in English. When Twiggy was famous, the famous model, he did Twiggy's shingaling. When Petula Clark did "Downtown," Tito did "Downtown" in a Latin version. When Miriam Makeba did "Pata Pata," an African tune, Tito did it also. I think you don't have that today. You don't have the media, the radio stations playing; everything is a playlist now. You've got some a&r guy, or a program director, deciding, "Well, we're going to hear Gloria Estefan." I mean, every day you want to hear Gloria

Estefan? Those are the first forty tunes. Gloria Estefan I think has helped when she did *Mi tierra*. When she went back to her roots. I think it has a lot to do with the younger generation, people like Gloria Estefan; they created these two markets. Even Carlos Santana. Santana doesn't play straight Latin music. He plays Latin rock.

Loza: He's got big crowds all over the world. So I think that's another thing that people don't focus on adequately. They look at a Latin artist like Tito, and they say he should be bigger. Well, you've got to remember he's got a whole other world looking at him, all of Latin America, that even the Ellingtons didn't have, even the Dizzy Gillespies didn't have. Even the Bill Cosbys don't have. Bill Cosby is not bilingual. Bilingual, bicultural: that's the big difference.

Conzo: Tito, he can go to Latin America and play *joropo* or *cumbia* and then go to Manhattan to a Jewish crowd and play "Havah Nagilah." Tito has the best of two worlds in that sense.

Loza: Now Andy García came out and started helping Cachao a few years ago and did a documentary. Here was basically a man who had reached obscurity. None of the young people knew who he was; *we* knew who he was, how important he was. People like Tito knew who he was, and here he is eighty years old. But what that has done is that Andy García comes up with this, and Cachao gets Grammy Awards.

Conzo: It's like I said about Frank Sinatra. You need a person . . .

Loza: I'm thinking somebody should have done that with Tito.

Conzo: First of all, Tito had the push. The push that Tito had was *The Mambo Kings*. When they approached me and said they wanted to do a movie and I read the book, I told them you have to change certain things in the book, which they did in the hard copy, from soft copy. Also, when they wanted somebody to play Tito Puente, I said he's got to play himself. There's nobody out there. Me, as a consultant to the movie, I told them, "There's nobody to play Tito Puente." The closest person I could think of would be his son, Ronnie, who plays timbales and looks like him. They used Tito. Tito has told me that in his travels in Australia and places like that, *The Mambo Kings* has put him in another ballpark. For that fifteen minutes of fame, that two minutes he was on the stage there, it's . . .

Loza: That's really unfortunately one of the only movies in either language in the past twenty or thirty years that has come out focusing on the Latin music of New York, how the Cubans and the Puerto Ricans went up there and did this thing based around Machito and then Tito Puente and Tito Rodríguez and all this incredible stuff. You had Pérez Prado coming around the other way. First of all, how do you think that movement really reflected or personified the Latin music culture? Number two, why only that movie?

Conzo: There was another movie called *Salsa*. There we go back to the same thing all over again. We go back to Hollywood not listening to you. They think we're a bunch of dumb Puerto Ricans, dumb Chicanos, and all this stuff. No, this is what we're going to do. We're going to talk in those stupid accents and play "Babalú" or something like that and that's it. Everybody thinks that every Hispanic is a Desi Arnaz. Hollywood thinks that. We were fortunate. *Salsa* was the first movie, and they put that kid from

Menudo in there. The music was horrid; it wasn't even synched right. If you remember it, Tito was playing, and the sticks are going this way and the music is going that way. It was not even synched right. Also I think Arnie Glimpshaw had the foresight. He did a good job even though there's a lot to be desired as far as *The Mambo Kings* was concerned. He had the foresight to do a movie about the music itself. Robert Craft would come to my house and Pacheco's, and we would look for specific tunes of that period. Arnie Glimpshaw, the director, he wanted everything as authentic as possible. I think that helped. It was a good movie. It garnered four stars in the ratings, which is one of the highest, depending upon what paper you read. Everybody talks about it and Tito, Armand Assante, and Antonio Banderas. That was Antonio's first movie in the U.S. Unfortunately, I would then say, "Come on." I'd knock on your door, Steve, and say, "All right, let's call this guy Steve Loza and see what we can do." Let's do another movie. *The Perez Family* was the biggest joke. Marisa Tomei, that she comes from Cuba, biggest joke. They took an Indian director who did *Mississippi Masala* to direct a movie about a Cuban, a boat person coming over here. Give me a break. And then they have Marisa Tomei. There's so many actresses out there, from Maria Conchita to Rosie Pérez. Anyway, this is what Hollywood does, and this is the powers that be. It's become greed. It's nothing but greed. I wish they would do a "Mambo Kings Two." There's so many stories, not only the Puentes. Even here, the Lalo Guerreros—there's so much music.

Loza: That's right. *Zoot Suit.*

Conzo: *Zoot Suit* was another example. I worked very closely with Eddie Olmos, Luis [Valdez], and Danny Valdez when they came to New York, and Tito . . .

Loza: Tito's on the soundtrack. Beautiful stuff. But you know, in Latin America there might have been even more interest to do a movie, but Tito's not down there. He's based here. So sometimes it can work against you. Between a rock and a hard place. Lalo Guerrero used to say he'd go to Mexico, he was a *pocho,* and then up here he was a *spic.* It's not easy, because your mentality is here.

Conzo: What I'm saying is that there's so much talent out there, and there's so many stories that New York City has eight million people and there's eight million stories. Like they always say here, there's always that cliché. In the music business, from California to Cuba to Mexico to Puerto Rico, you have such talent. Years ago they *made* musicals: *Down Argentine Way, Fly Me Out to Rio.* There's no musicals now, so you make a love story like they did with *The Mambo Kings.* You showcase our music.

Loza: It's a whole different way. It also seems like it's hard to make movies about musicians like they used to. They used to make movies about jazz artists. *The Glenn Miller Story, The Benny Goodman Story, The Gene Krupa Story.*

Conzo: We were fortunate with *La Bamba. La Bamba* became one of the few successful . . .

Loza: Again, Luis Valdez does another one. Did *Zoot Suit, La Bamba.* . . . You mention stories, Joe, and that's one thing so far I don't think I have enough of in the book about Tito. Are there any particular stories that come to mind, inspiring stories, funny stories, political stories, important stories that in your estimation are important memories to you, that say something about Tito?

Conzo: As I think about them, a perfect example, as I was telling you yesterday, was one that came to mind how Tito is well respected among his peers. When I say his peers, not just musicians, I'm talking about anybody in the entertainment business. Tito was being honored about five weeks ago in Queens. From there we had to go to a big AIDS benefit, and Cristina, who is known now, she has a big show on TV. She was on channel 2, I think, and she's known as one of the top talk show hosts. When she saw me, she said, "You look familiar," and I said, "I'm Joe Conzo; I did the movie" and so forth, and I said, "Tito's here." She said "Tito Puente?" and I said "Yeah, I'll bring him over." She said "No, I'll come to him." I felt, wow, this girl ain't got no ego. Not only that, this woman, who is equally as famous—she's well known in Latin America—she could have taken the attitude, you know, "Bring him to me." She's a good friend of Tito's anyway. She went out of her way. That felt good to me. Other stories I could tell you are when Bill Cosby has come to Tito's restaurant, you could see the camaraderie there. You're not looking at Bill Cosby; you're looking at another human being. He's a regular guy. So many stories as you start thinking how many musicians, Dizzy Gillespie in the same room with Willie Bobo, Tito, and myself, and how they would trade stories and talk about this and say "Hey, Tito, let's do this." These are icons, and to see one icon talk to another and the respect. They look at Tito and like "Wow." Sinatra—he's one of the few people in my life that I've always stayed in awe—and how he talked to Tito, "How are you," you know, that respect.

Loza: Mutual respect.

Conzo: Frank Sinatra talking to Tito Puente, Bill Cosby talking to Tito Puente, those things. The president of the United States, Clinton. Tito says, "I'm Tito Puente," and the president says, "I know who you are," and they started talking. It's things like that that make you feel good and make you say, "We've come a long way." I'm sure you feel that way when you read about one of your students. You say "Hey, that's my student. I've done a good job." There's so many stories. I got stories with you.

Loza: I've got a great story making a pair of vibe sticks on stage while we're playing with Tito. We headed downstairs and we made some out of tape. His solo on that came out on TV. I've got to give you some of these tapes that we have because I don't think you have copies of them.

Conzo: There's so many stories. You and I were eating and we were talking about how Tito takes things and he jokes and what he says about his timbales. To us it's a double meaning, like when he got the Hollywood star. We were embarrassed. He finally translated it into English, and he said "my testicles—balls."

Loza: When he got the star. How did that come about?

Conzo: That came about through Josie Powell, Carmen Rosado, and others. You guys out here were doing your end, and I was doing the New York end. They wanted letters from Bill Cosby, from the governor at the time, Cuomo, and other people. Charlie Rangel, I think, and Tito had mentioned the fact "I got them." David Dinkins at the time was the mayor, or Koch. Whoever was mayor, whoever was governor at the time, we managed to get, [and] we managed to get Bill Cosby. I think it goes back to the same thing again, Steve, as far as that push. You got to ask. And here we go back to the same thing. Not one Hispanic wrote a letter. I had a black, which was the mayor, that was '90, right?

Loza: Yes.

Conzo: Yeah, David Dinkins was the mayor. David Dinkins, who is black, and an Italian, Mario Cuomo, was the governor . . . Bill Cosby, who is black. And the top politicians you couldn't get from here to first base with. And we asked them. I'm talking about congressmen. And you had guys from over here.

Loza: We had Bradley, we had Gloria Molina, Richard Alatorre. One of the most amazing things about Tito is the man just keeps going. He's seventy-three years old, and he's still recording one or two albums a year in addition to other recording projects. I don't know how you would estimate his current road schedule. There's people who have said he was touring more a year ago than he was twenty years ago.

Conzo: He was. Now I wish Tito was twenty years younger, to be honest with you. He's traveling more now. I've advised him and his wife; it's starting to take its toll, and he's starting to cut down. But as far as twenty years ago, Tito's doing more now than he was twenty years ago.

Loza: About two years ago I was reading that he was averaging over 200 dates a year. And that's over half the year.

Conzo: He's not going to Europe this year, but in many ways I'm glad, because he'd come back from Europe and then in August back to Japan. Give me a break. One thing you can mention here, Tito's going to be at the Olympics. Tito is one of the few Hispanics who have been called to play for the Olympics, the closing ceremonies. Tito, Gloria [Estefan] and Sheila E. We're talking about three and a half billion people watching this Olympics and the closing ceremony.

Loza: Two women who are leaders in the Latin community that Tito had a lot to do with, especially Sheila, in terms of teaching her stuff.

Conzo: That [Olympic ceremony] will put him in a whole other ball game. He explained it to me, the way it's set up, the band is downstairs, the Paul Schaffer band. Paul Schaffer from David Letterman picked all these musicians, I think Wynton Marsalis, and they put Tito and Sheila E and Gloria in a separate entity.

Loza: Estefan, Sheila E, Linda Ronstadt, Jimmy Smits—these people get a lot of attention in the media. But I would say that Tito Puente is not just *one* of the major Hispanic musicians, because there are very few Latin musicians that have the name that he does. He was on the Letterman show a couple of weeks ago, with Cosby, right? Everybody knows who he is, and at seventy-three years old he's competing still in terms of media name with these young icons like Smits, Estefan.

Conzo: I see what you're saying. They're in a whole other ball game. I learned from Pete Hammill and A. J. Benza; these are gossip columnists and writers, journalists. Tito doesn't have to be in the media. Only when it's necessary. Tito is not screwing some girl on the corner that they constantly put in the papers. I think the people that are behind these people, this is how they're making their money. They want to say something about Gloria. They want to say something about Jimmy Smits. Jimmy Smits is paying the publicist to put his name in the paper. Now with Tito, the way I do it, I do it if it's necessary. I spoke to Tito this morning, and he says, "Joe, I'm going on David Letterman and

I'm going to——," and that's important, so when I get back in New York, I can call A. J. Benza or Liz Smith and say, "Oh, by the way, Tito's going to be on David Letterman. He just did his 112th album." They'll say, "So what?" and I'll say, "Yeah, but it's his 112th album." They say, "What?" That's something to write about. Media is funny. I know dealing with the media in New York is funny. They'll do you a solid, but then when you really need something and you've run out of favors, then you're in trouble.

Loza: One more thing, regarding this scholarship program.

Conzo: Since 1980: sixteen years.

Loza: Since 1980. You've had a fundraiser every year, right?

Conzo: Every year.

Loza: So you haven't skipped any.

Conzo: In fact, we've done two in one year. At one time we used to try to do two. We've been very fortunate that Tito has been at each one of them. He's also said a couple of times he doesn't want to be in it. But I said, "No, as long as you're alive and you're kicking, you're going to be in it." That's another thing. Tito would like to give other artists a chance, which we do. Putting on a concert or a dinner dance fundraiser is not easy. There we go back to the politics again of your people. When I tell you, "Steve, take a page [an ad in the fundraiser program]," you don't flinch. No problem. I tell people, "Take a page—a hundred dollars." These are your people. These are people who supposedly love Tito Puente. Or it's 125 dollars [to attend the fundraiser], open bar all night, it's on a boat. Dinner. . . . But there it goes back to the same thing that you talk about, that I talk about. It's about our people not backing us up. But yet I can go to an Anglo, I can go to a Bill Cosby, Al Pacino, Armand Assante, Paul Simon—these are icons. I'm trying to get one from Jimmy Smits. Tito said we were going to get one from Celia. He's getting one from Lionel Hampton. You're buying a page, Josie's buying a page, only $100, half a page is $50. And they give me a hard time about that too. We've been very fortunate. We created it. We started with Juilliard, and Tito is an alumnus of Juilliard. Juilliard is a very prestigious school, but we started getting flak from the community. We wanted Hispanics, but you can't really, unless you get a grant specifically created for scholarships for Hispanic students. We couldn't do that. You lose your tax status. So we've been fortunate in that Juilliard understood and accommodated us. We took it away from Juilliard, in that respect, because we started getting into the Third World, into Spanish Harlem and the ballet, things like that. It's better off. We feel more comfortable and we get—well, you've been to Boys Harbor—and we get to little kids and Third World youths. It helps that way.

Loza: In other words, they don't have to be at Juilliard, which opens it up.

Conzo: We did it at Juilliard at the time I guess for the prestige and the fact that Tito went there, but now we go to Harbor for the Performing Arts, Ballet Hispánico, the New School for Social Research.

Loza: I know that one of his concerns also was the problem of just giving a scholarship for somebody to go to Juilliard. A lot of times you have a musician who just doesn't fit the Juilliard mold, later on going somewhere else.

Conzo: That was a problem there, too. Not only that; it made Tito more accessible by giving to other students. We were fortunate to use a couple of our students in the concerts, so we were watching the finished product, and Tito practices and rehearses a lot at Boys Harbor, so he actually could see the money being spent, where at Juilliard you can't.

Loza: It's like you just give it, and then they use the money the way they want. You don't have control. They have their standards, and they're not going to change them.

Conzo: Oh, no.

Loza: Like you say, they're probably not going to be as specifically geared toward the Hispanic students. Because that is important. Now there has been over a hundred scholarships given out.

Conzo: This year we're doing it in August, and by November we give the scholarships out. We put our heads together and we decide. Not only do we give money; we buy instruments for the public school system. Last year we gave to six schools. We worked something out with Martin Cohen at Latin Percussion, and we bought instruments from him, which we can get wholesale, and we managed to buy instruments and give to six schools. Plus we gave money to a seventh school. Because there's no money. There's no instruments in schools like when we were growing up.

Loza: And this kind of music is not normally taught by a lot of schoolteachers. Well, I think we're about wrapped up, Joe. Any final thoughts, Joe?

Conzo: I wish you success on the book. I hope that this book will be the first of many in which you and I discuss Tito Puente and the making of Latin music. I hope next year once this gets off the ground we have another one—Machito and the making of Latin music.

Loza: It should be just the beginning because I look at this area. I look at Ellington, Louis Armstrong, Miles Davis—there's twenty books on each of them. We got to get this thing off the ground.

Conzo: I wish you success. The most important thing is that this book becomes a guide, a beginning, a launching pad of other books.

Loza: What's going to happen is that this will do a lot for Tito. We're hoping for the NEA, the Presidential Commendation. The reason we've put this all on videotape is that what has got to happen eventually is a major documentary. That should be done soon.

Conzo: There's so much footage on Tito that there should be a documentary.

Loza: Some years ago I talked to Tito about the Guggenheim. That stuff should be happening.

Conzo: You know as well as I do that Tito will yes you to death. Or he'll turn around and say no. Then I come along and have to convince him, maybe you, then he starts realizing. I think now Tito is starting to realize, "Thank God there's a Joe Conzo, or a Max Salazar." And there's other historians who have taken the time, such as Steve Loza, who have actually documented this.

Loza: It's nice to be able to collaborate and cross-reference all this stuff and end up with something a little closer to the truth.

Conzo: I don't believe in this "I'm going to work with Max," or "I'm going to work with Joe." If you're a historian, which we all are, then I agree with you. "While Max says this, Joe says this." Sooner or later the truth is going to come out. You have to do things like that. You can't go by this "Joe Conzo is known as an authority on Tito Puente's music throughout the world blah-blah." I don't have the final word. I learn every day. Last night when I bet that guy. I called his bluff. I knew the picture. He says he's got the tape. There ain't no such animal.

Loza: At first he was saying there was a studio and by the end of the night he wasn't sure.

Conzo: It was a studio session "you were at." Tito Puente's not there. I think I caught him when he said Chano Pozo. Chano was dead. But you see, it's people like that.

Loza: They're the ones that say it and everybody believes it. I remember years ago a Puerto Rican guy here in L.A. told me that La Lupe and Tito used to be married. I might have asked Tito, "Well, you were married to La Lupe," which would have been embarrassing because it's not true. About a hundred years from now a lot of this will become clear. Especially the political, financial stuff that is a struggle for an artist. I remember Ray Santos saying that was what impressed him about Tito, that in the very early years he knew how to market himself.

Conzo: Tito's always been that way. He's been fortunate. Like we talked about yesterday, Tito is bilingual. He speaks Spanish perfectly and he speaks English perfectly. Thank God his mother said, "You speak English in school, you speak Spanish here." It's that bilingual thing we talked about. And you can put it in there. I'll argue with any bilingual educator. I don't care what you're telling me. I am totally against it. You're not helping our culture. You have to speak English and let them speak Spanish in the house. Schools are not teaching you culture. When they teach them in Spanish, they're teaching them about the United States. Yet they're teaching them in their language.

Loza: [In that particular case] it's almost irrelevant [although I think that there are more positive than negative aspects to bilingual education]. You know, you can't play Latin music unless you speak Spanish anyway. You're not going to play with the right inflection. If you can't pronounce *la música,* how are you going to say it? That's why English doesn't work for salsa.

Conzo: It never has.

Loza: Linguistically it doesn't work. That's a whole book right there.

Conzo: We could argue about that, too.

5

Reflections on the King
Ray Santos, Chico Sesma, Jerry González, Poncho Sanchez, and Hilton Ruiz

SINCE this book is a composite representation of reflections and conversations on the life and music of Tito Puente, I have included the present chapter: profiles of five artists who in very different ways have become aware of the Puente legacy and who shared their thoughts on him.

Three of these artists, Ray Santos, Jerry González, and Hilton Ruiz, have based the majority of their musical careers in New York City. The other two, Chico Sesma and Poncho Sanchez, have been based in Los Angeles. The bicoastal perspective lends itself well to the manner in which Tito Puente has penetrated so many significant sectors of both a national and a global cultural matrix.

Ray Santos

Ray Santos is considered one of the major musical arrangers and musicians in the field of Latin music. He has done arrangements for and performed with Machito, Tito Puente, and Tito Rodríguez, among many other major artists. He was one of the principal arrangers for Puente's 100th album and the film *Mambo Kings* and the sole arranger for Linda Ronstadt's Grammy Award–winning album *Frenesí*. I interviewed Ray in December 1994 at Victor's Cafe in Manhattan.

Loza: Who is Ray Santos, the musician?

Santos: I'm born and raised in New York City of Puerto Rican parents. My mother and father migrated here from Puerto Rico in the mid-1920s, so you could say they were one of the first wave of Puerto Rican migrants to New York City, and I was born here in 1928. I'm just about two weeks away from my sixty-sixth birthday. I went to all the public schools here in New York City, and by the time I was in my teens, my ears were picking up all the great sounds of the swing bands on the radio. You'd hear Glenn Miller, Benny Goodman, Count Basie, Duke Ellington, so that big-band swing music caught my ear. Hanging around the neighborhood you find friends that are interested in the same sounds as you are listening to the music, and we collect records, go out and buy records, discuss them: "That's a great solo, this guy's." I demonstrated an interest in big-band jazz and small-band jazz; bebop was just starting to come into existence, and on the smaller radio stations you would hear things like Thelonious Monk, Dizzy Gillespie, Charlie Parker, because they wouldn't get on the big stations, but there were smaller stations that would cater to that type of progressive jazz that was just starting to be heard in late 1945 to '46. My interest in music started to expand into the more progressive jazz as opposed to the big-band swing, which I've always liked anyway. And at the same time [as] in the living room in my house we'd have the American [English-language] radio stations on, my mother in the kitchen would have the Spanish radio going. Ethnic Spanish radio stations here in New York state would cater to lots of Puerto Rican sounds and Cuban sounds. That's why I was exposed to Machito, Miguelito Valdés, [and] Noro Morales, who played a lot on the Spanish radio. At home I kind of get the two sides of the music scene, the ethnic Puerto Rican, Cuban sounds, as well as the big-band jazz sounds or progressive sounds on the American side. All through this period my mind was being programmed with all types of music, and probably the first time they came together, big-band progressive sounds mixed with bebop and the Afro-Cuban mixture, was when I first heard the Charlie Parker sessions with Machito. That was very impressive to me, the way that Charlie Parker sounded with Machito's band on the recording date, doing his thing over the Afro-Cuban rhythm. It kind of opened up a whole new thing. You could say that was the beginning of Latin jazz.

Loza: It probably really captivated you because you had heard both of these things, then all of a sudden you heard them together.

Santos: Right, and it was really impressive.

Loza: So that it hit home.

Santos: There was a whole new music there—like jazz soloists. Machito's band was the first band to really get into that. Mario Bauzá was a product of the big bands, Cab Calloway, Chick Webb. He had the big-band swing concept, and he adapted it to Afro-Cuban music to get the same type of orchestration and some kind of a big-band feel over the Afro-Cuban music. He understood the Afro-Cuban rhythms very well, being a Cuban. I always had Mario Bauzá and Machito's band as kind of a role model. Anything that I tried to do after I started playing professionally and writing for bands, everything was kind of based on the path they were taking.

Loza: And you were playing mainly as a saxophonist?

Santos: I was a saxophone player. I was also always interested in writing music, writing arrangements. The saxophone was more or less a way of getting into the bands, to be able to do so writing.

Loza: Who were some of the first bands you played with? You've actually played with Machito.

Santos: After I got out of school and went out to work professionally . . .

Loza: Where were you going to school?

Santos: I went to Juilliard School of Music. I graduated in 1952. I got a job with Noro Morales. I played with him for a couple of years. My first trip out to Los Angeles was with Noro Morales in 1953. Went out to the Zenda Ballroom. I still remember: Seventh and Figueroa, right?

Loza: I don't think it exists anymore.

Santos: I don't think so. I heard it burned down or something like that.

Loza: I think Chico was doing those gigs too.

Santos: Chico Sesma. He's still there. He was a deejay also.

Loza: He had a group back in the days of Eddie Cano.

Santos: Eddie used to come over to the apartment house we were staying at and visit with us a lot because he was a very big Noro Morales fan.

Loza: Oh yeah. That was his main early influence. So you were playing with Noro Morales, that's when you started arranging?

Santos: He was like the first really big professional orchestra that I got to arrange for. I had been doing some arrangements before here in New York, but Noro was the first band that I had arrangements recorded with. I moved to Puerto Rico for a while with an orchestra called César Concepción. I played with him for a while, then I came back to New York and about 1956 I joined Machito's band. There was an opening there. I think I had applied for that job six years before, but there were no openings then. The personnel changes were very rare, especially in the saxophone section. No saxophone players left. So finally one of the original founders of Machito's band, Freddie Skerit, left, and they called me up to see if I wanted to come in. I stayed there about four years with Machito's orchestra, which I think was the longest I ever played with an orchestra for any period of time. It was like a real musical education. Great charts by René Hernández, Chico O'Farrill. Just sitting there and absorbing those sounds into your ears is an education in itself.

Loza: Especially for an arranger.

Santos: You're hearing everything, you're hearing the voicings, you can analyze them as you play along.

Loza: A lot of these arrangers like René Hernández were also arrangers for Tito Puente, Tito Rodríguez. That was interesting that these bands shared arrangers; there were some common arrangers for all of them. Like Chico O'Farrill.

Santos: He arranged for Machito, he arranged for Puente. Miguelito Valdés had a band out in L.A. for a while, and he came with that band from L.A. to New York, very hot for a while.

Loza: Like Eddie. I think he played with that band for about two years. As an arranger, I guess you eventually started doing stuff for different people, including Tito Puente.

Santos: I moved to Puerto Rico after I left Machito. I went back with Noro Morales to Puerto Rico. By this time Noro was suffering from ill health. Glaucoma had taken over his eyes. He was legally blind. Anyway, he got this gig in La Concha Hotel in Puerto Rico on the Condado strip, so he took a band from New York to Puerto Rico. He hired some guys from Puerto Rico also, but the nucleus came from New York. José Madera Sr. was on saxophone, Jorge López on trumpet, and I went as a saxophone player. He stayed at that gig until his death. He stayed there around four years. I just stayed there around a year with him, then I went up to another gig at the Hotel San Juan with the show band there, Charlie Fisk. I was really not doing too much writing, but I was absorbing all the Puerto Rican sounds, like the typical Puerto Rican music like *bomba, plena,* Cortijo's [band. I was] very friendly with Cortijo in Puerto Rico and with the singer Ismael Rivera, the big musical people down there at that time, 1960 or so. I stayed there around two years, then I came back to New York. After my return to New York in 1962, in '63, I joined Tito Puente's band. I was there around a year and a half with Tito Puente. On the trip we took to Puerto Rico I met a girl down there that I married and brought back to New York. From Puente I went to Tito Rodríguez's band and I stayed with his band until he broke up the band, his permanent orchestra. He'd have pickup orchestras for recordings. He stopped working as a bandleader and went to work as a single. In 1965 he broke up his band. I moved to Puerto Rico in 1966. Shortly after that Tito Rodríguez moved to Puerto Rico. He built himself a house down there. I stayed in Puerto Rico eighteen years.

Loza: So you knew Tito Rodríguez pretty well.

Santos: Oh yeah. I was very friendly with him. We kept on collaborating throughout his stay in Puerto Rico. He had a TV show. René Hernández also had moved to Puerto Rico. We collaborated with him [Rodríguez] on a TV show that he did. He did around thirty TV shows that he produced himself. Tito Rodríguez was in Puerto Rico for a while, 1971–72. By this time he was suffering from leukemia. He left Puerto Rico and moved to Miami, Coral Gables. After that he passed away in 1973; I stayed in Puerto Rico until 1983 or '84. I've been back in New York about ten years.

Loza: Since you've come back to New York you've been mainly freelancing as an arranger with different people?

Santos: Freelancing as an arranger. Whatever is happening out there. I was involved with that *Mambo Kings* movie. After that a lot of stuff with Mario Bauzá's band.

Loza: I heard that band about two years ago at the Village Gate. Were you involved with that?

Santos: Oh yeah. I did some writing for his dates. I didn't play with the band. I played with the band on his first recording around 1984 when I had just come back. And then he stopped doing anything with his band for a while until he got his contract with Messidor records, a German label. I was involved with him for those three albums with Messidor. . . .

Loza: The arranging aspect is probably one of the most important things about Tito Puente. This is what he basically had to live off of. That was your bread and butter right there: arrangements, gigs, and recordings. What were some of the differences in the kinds of arrangements that had to be prepared for, let's say, a Tito Puente versus a Machito or a Tito Rodríguez? What was Tito Puente doing different, even though he had learned so much from Mario Bauzá and Machito? Was he doing something significantly different? I think so, but I'm curious to know if you think so. How did you have to think of things differently when you wrote for Tito Puente than when you wrote for those other people?

Santos: Tito's approach to the music is one that concentrates a lot on the percussion, on his timbal playing. Whenever I would write anything for him, I would think about a timbales approach: lots of opportunities for him to do hits with his timbales with the band when he is playing as part of the arrangement, which is something that he does very well. Take a thing like "Ran Kan Kan," which is an arrangement built around the timbales solo or a timbales solo synchronized with an arrangement.

Loza: Were the horn riffs actually the same phrases as the timbales at certain parts that he accented?

Santos: The arrangement is an integral part of his timbal playing.

Loza: What were some of the arrangements that you did for him that you can think of?

Santos: I did around four originals: "Caribe," another was called "Cochise," a bossa nova called "Carminova," and "Flamenco Moods." He had a style of voicing of his own . . . closer. His style of rhythm is a straight-pushy. He wants to be exciting. That's one of his fortes, exciting. The way, technically speaking, a wide voicing tends to drag the orchestra, but close voicings, everybody huddled together—when you get into those ensembles, that type of voicings pushes, kind of synchronizes into that pushy beat that he favors.

Loza: Is this something you noticed just from listening and playing in the band, or did you discuss it with him also?

Santos: I noticed it playing with the band and listening to his recordings. I never really discussed it with him. I kind of felt that was the way to go when arranging for him.

Loza: That's interesting. In "Ran Kan Kan" those are very dense chords going on, and it's close. Do you think that he harmonically extended more than others, like ninths and elevenths?

Santos: Harmonically he demonstrates great sophistication. His harmonic concept is very based on the bebop era. Another big influence on the bands, on Machito and also in Mario Bauzá's concept, was Stan Kenton's West Coast band. Kenton was a big fan of Machito. I think they wrote a tune called "Machito." In return Mario Bauzá and Puente got into a lot of those Kenton big-band voicings, screaming high brass. It was a mutual admiration thing going on there.

Loza: In a way Tito was doing a lot of stuff like Machito, but maybe he was starting this percussion thing, close voicings, this exciting thing. Even harmonically he wanted the excitement. Machito kept the form [more traditional].

Santos: Machito used to have a lot of Arsenio Rodríguez influence: vocal emphasis, a lot of Cuban *son* going on there.

Loza: Tito's use of the vibraphone certainly proved to be an innovation in Latin music.

Santos: "Cuban Cutie" was heavy on the vibes. There's another one with vibes called "The Vibe Mambo." Tito was the first one to come out with the vibes. Although he played very good, I always thought that Cal Tjader's jazz concept was really out there. I would say he was like a spin-off when it came to Latin jazz; he was a spin-off of Puente. But Tjader was very technical, very schooled in the vibes; he was a very good vibe player. A clean player. The first one to really do the vibes was Puente. He was a keyboard player. He understands keyboards.

Loza: Do you think the fact that he did the keyboards made him a little different from the other bands: Rodríguez, Machito, Bauzá?

Santos: Tito had a great knowledge of how to write piano parts and to get those great jazz harmonies.

Loza: He was also, unlike Machito, Bauzá, or Rodríguez, not only able to deal with the piano concept in context on vibes as part of the rhythm section, but he was a percussionist. This had to have a whole different relationship in writing, or in using arrangers, or even working with his musicians. Did you ever feel that? You played with him.

Santos: He was always first, last, and always a first-class percussionist. Everything to this day that he does with his band has got to go with his percussion playing.

Loza: There is always going to be a solo somewhere.

Santos: Exactly. And parts of the arrangements always synchronize with certain beats that he does.

Loza: He featured great soloists like Mongo Santamaría, Willie Bobo.

Santos: Right. Always great rhythm sections . . . heavy percussion players.

Loza: Did the *charanga* style of playing and orchestration penetrate Puente's concept?

Santos: It had been in Havana, but it started to break here in New York in '55–'56. So the bands approached it still with that big-band feel as opposed to the Orquestas Aragón and América and their strings and flute, good rhythm but not as heavy and loud, more relaxed, a lighter type of rhythm section as compared to the big-band rhythm sections that they needed here to propel those big saxophone and trumpet sections. But Aragón was the original concept. They didn't do the heavy breaks back then. That's Puente's thing. He likes breaks because naturally they give him a chance to do his thing with the band on timbales. He also approached the cha-cha differently. The New York style of cha-cha was different. The *charangas* didn't catch on here until the sixties.

Loza: The Cubans would have coffee playing the *charanga* and then Broadway would play and they were sweating. That seems to be the constant metaphor—that musicians here would always play it up, hard, and faster. Did you ever think of that looking at these different guys: Puente versus others, for example?

Santos: I guess it's a reflection of the New York pace.

Loza: The urban life, that's what I would connotate it with.

Santos: Pushing, rushing ahead, everything. With the Cubans, it's their music, so naturally they're the first ones to get into it and that's a certain style they have. They created it. The New York approach has always been . . . I'm looking for the words.

Loza: Well, it's a hard edge, and it's more up-tempo. It's just like living here, life.

Santos: You take a group like Conjunto Clásico. To me the first time I heard them, that's Arsenio Rodríguez at a faster tempo. Really pushing ahead. I guess the city life has something to do with it, that New York pace.

Loza: I'll hear a group like Sonora Ponceña, which is from Puerto Rico, and they're back there in the groove; they know how to relax. Actually I like that sound better.

Santos: That's my favorite Puerto Rican group, Sonora Ponceña. Papo Lucca has it really together. He's a great writer. I like the sound of the group, the productions, the singers, and the choice of material is good. They stuck to their guns; they didn't go for the romantic, pornographic things. A funny something about Papo Lucca. I first saw him when Tito's band went down to Puerto Rico in 1957 and played a place called the Escondrón Beach Club, I don't know if it exists anymore; it was right next to the Hilton. Anyway, we played some gigs alternating with Sonora Ponceña, and they were relatively a new group at the time. The pianist was Papo Lucca, but he was around ten years old. His father used to put telephone books on the piano bench so he could reach up to the keys.

Loza: Did Tito do arranging for other people in his early days?

Santos: He did some things for Machito and Curbelo. I think he got his roots in writing while he was in the service. He was with Machito in the early forties. At the beginning of World War II he went into the service.

Loza: In the film *Mambo Kings,* did you do quite a bit of the arrangements?

Santos: I did all of the rhythmic things, except for the ones that Tito did himself, such as "Ran Kan Kan." Besides [using] his band, we made a separate orchestra, like a house band, to do those instrumental tracks that we used in synchronized scenes in the film. A band here in New York. The nucleus was out of Mario Bauzá's band and a lot of studio players.

Loza: Another aspect of the development of Latin music in New York was the emergence of many instrumental arrangements, not depending therefore on a constant vocal verse.

Santos: That especially started in the late forties with Machito's first recordings with Charlie Parker. Puente's band took that same path, lots of instrumentals. In the fifties a dance set would consist of maybe a bolero, maybe one or two instrumentals in the set, plus whatever Santitos Colón would sing with Puente, or Machito with his band with Mario Bauzá as director. But there would always be at least one instrumental tune per set, which doesn't happen today on a dance stage. You go to the jazz clubs and it becomes instrumental.

Loza: Nor do they have the long *montuno* sections, the solos.

Santos: Of course. The instrumentals were an integral part of that instrumental arrangement.

Loza: So comparing those eras, another thing you could comment on is the *sonero* [vocalist] tradition. How did that change?

Santos: Well, the type of tune has changed. The lyrics are more into sexy-type lyrics, whereas before the lyrics would be talking about the drums, food, party, some *santería* religion, Changó. That would all get into the popular tunes and arrangements: "Changó ta vení" by Machito and things like that. "Elegua Changó" by Puente, an instrumental. The religious connection was there. Talking about food, *las tumbadoras, los timbales, los cueros,* things like that. All those things would be in the lyrics: the festival, the party, the dancing.

Loza: The dancing itself was part of the performance.

Santos: The reason the mambo was so popular, the dance was very popular. The mambo was big, and the cha-cha also.

Loza: In a way the music of that era, the late forties to the late fifties, at times it's almost as if the music is secondary. We have to remember that the main focus of that culture is that people went to dance.

Santos: The dance. The dancing caught on big. It caught on big with non-Latinos. That's why you have these nice ethnic mixtures in the clubs where you would play. One needed the other. The dances needed that type of music, and the music needed those dancers.

Loza: The dancing used to be more intricate.

Santos: I used to love to memorize my parts so I could just play and watch. That kind of energy fed . . . you'd feed off of the dancers. You see them swinging so much; you try to get into their groove and their getting into your groove.

Loza: Whereas with a lot of the new pop stars with the new salsa—Tito Nieves, Eddie Santiago—a lot of people are going to listen to them in concert settings. They aren't even dancing.

Santos: I've gone to a lot of those clubs and watched the dancers. I'm not saying the old days were better than this, but I can't really compare it technically as far as steps and energy. It's not happening.

Loza: All of that was part of the improvisation aspect of this music. You had percussion soloists, you had instrumental soloists, you had *el sonero sonando.* That also is not improvised today.

Santos: The *soneros* I hear on recordings today, they have a tendency to be preplanned, memorized. Some guy comes along and writes the *soneos* out. There is no improvisation there.

Loza: You have this *típico* period, then you have the heavy salsa period of the seventies, with Eddie Palmieri, ending somewhat with Rubén Blades. It was sort of a social movement.

Santos: The lyrics started to change. The words started to be more important than the music itself.

Loza: A lot of politics of race. That sort of died and we ended up with the *salsa erótica.* It went from A to Z.

Santos: That's where I think the music suffers the most because the rhythm sections can't really let go. I've been on some dates in Puerto Rico where the producers were actually trying to tone down the rhythm so it wouldn't get in the way of the words.

Loza: Who were your major models as an arranger?

Santos: As far as my arranging concept, Tito was always one of my role models. When I first started arranging, you have to listen to somebody, so the people I listened to were René Hernández, Tito Puente, and Chico O'Farrill. They're the ones that got that sound and approach that I was interested in doing. And I more or less have stayed with it. Every once in a while I have to deviate from it when somebody wants to get away from the typical thing and go into something more salsa. I'll make my attempts at doing salsa, more for commercial reasons than anything else. Whenever I had the opportunity to write for a Puente or Mario Bauzá when he was around, I just stuck to the old concept: big-band voicings, nice saxophone writing, jazzy harmonies, and generally jazzy sound.

Loza: Now Puente sometimes seemed to do some very nontypical things with breaks.

Santos: He has his own style of breaks. He has good technique, he's very flashy, so he'll take advantage of that rapidity, that looseness he has in his wrists. He can do things that the average timbale player can't do.

Loza: When *Dance Mania* came out, it was a big hit with the people. It was like '58.

Santos: I went to some of those dates.

Loza: Did any of that stuff surprise you harmonically? Was he really going ahead?

Santos: He did some more jazzy things on his *Night Beat* album. It is strictly an instrumental album. He really went jazzy there, Latin jazz. Heavy with lots of jazz solos. He brought in Doc Severinson.

Loza: He did a lot of that in *Dance Mania,* [especially on your own] "3-D Mambo." It was a mambo jazz instrumental. I heard a lot of bop lines myself, flatted fifths.

Santos: That was more my bebop influence. When jazz and Afro-Cuban music first came together, the jazz that was happening was bebop, so that's why bebop harmonies became part of the genre.

Loza: On this album the vocal thing is not what I would call the dominant thing.

Santos: There was an era when Puente actually went out without singers for a period of around four years until he brought Santitos Colón. He never let Santitos take a dominant part. He'd use him a lot, but the band was the thing. In Machito's band, the funny thing was Machito's name and Machito singing, but the band got so powerful it tended to overshadow him. Of those three bands, the only one where the singer was dominant was Tito Rodríguez, because he was a great singer and he made sure everything was billed around him. And even then he played a lot of instrumentals also. His style of rhythm section was a little different. It was like a cross between Machito's rhythm section and Puente's. Puente was like hard-driving straight ahead, pushing the beat, and Machito was more laid back, and Rodríguez was in the middle. That's how I felt when I played with the band. Rodríguez could sing great melodies. He was a good *sonero.* Nothing was preplanned. He'd make up things as he went along.

Loza: On the earlier Puente stuff with Vicentico Valdés that old Cuban style was still a heavy part of the singing. He was doing the *soneo.* By the time we get to *Dance Mania,* you're not hearing that kind of singer anymore in the late fifties. A lot of *coro* [chorus]. Half the tunes were largely instrumental, with some *coro.* Take "Pa' los rumberos" or "Cuban Nightmare."

Santos: In the fifties the Latin big-band instrumental was right there in front. Now the producers won't even let you record an instrumental on a commercial album, unless it's a jazz album.

Loza: On Puente's 100th album there's not one instrumental. And here he's the one that made that happen: mambo jazz instrumental.

Santos: In that era, even Rodríguez, who was a singer, would record instrumentals. That was the thing at that time.

Loza: These days they don't even put the genre of the tune on the notes anyway. Were you ever involved in any of the lyrics, having to adapt them to arrangements?

Santos: Very little. As a producer sometimes I suggest a change in lyrics, maybe there are too many syllables getting in the way of the song. The tune might have too many syllables in the lyrics. It rhythmically detracts from the swing of the music. That's about the only time I get involved. I'll make a suggestion.

Loza: How integrated was the listening public?

Santos: I found that in the fifties and sixties there was more diversity of clientele. It was very intercultural. It was amazing because this was the 1950s, pre–civil rights, pre–Little Rock, Arkansas, with the integration of the high schools. Way before all this. It was a very integrated scene at all the places we used to play.

Loza: And the music was integrated?

Santos: The bands were very integrated: Jewish guys, Italian guys, African Americans. Now I see the makeup of the clientele is very polarized. You don't get Italian kids and Jewish kids from Brooklyn going to Club Broadway to dance, whereas in the 1950s in the Palladium that's what we used to get.

Loza: Music to me represents society. In other words, the fabric of music relates to the fabric of society. If you have divisions in society, you have divisions in music. The new music we have is also more polarized; it's limited.

Santos: White clientele are afraid to go to a Latino club. They feel hostility.

Chico Sesma

Lionel "Chico" Sesma is a major figure in the history and development of Latin music, especially so in the city of Los Angeles and especially with respect to Tito Puente's initial exposure on the West Coast. A trained musician and trombonist with many big bands in his early career, he eventually emerged in Los Angeles as a dominant radio personality and producer of Latin music and concerts featuring major contemporary artists during the fifties through the seventies. I interviewed Chico at his home in East Los Angeles in September 1995.

◈◈

Loza: How were you exposed to Latin music, and how did you develop your own appreciation for it?

Sesma: Los Angeles is my home. My musical background stems from my early teens, when I started to study trombone and went through high school as a music major and also to Los Angeles City College. During my teen years I played with all of the local bands during that period, the mid- to late thirties. There were a number of bands here locally, and they were all big bands like [Sal] Cervantes, Phil Carreón, Fred Rubio. Their repertoire was comprised for the most part of many of the recorded big-band successes of that period, like Artie Shaw, [Benny] Goodman, [Jimmy] Lunceford, [Duke] Ellington. The few Latin things that were in the book were mostly boleros, a few little polkas, and things like that. Primarily the music scene of that period, the mid- and late thirties, was as I've just described it to you. As I began to improve my own skills, I went on into mainstream big-band environments, having played with the bands of Johnny Richards, with whom I traveled all the way to the East Coast and toured with him for a number of years, in addition to the bands of Boyd Rayburn, Floyd Ray, Jimmy Zito, and Russ Morgan. By this time I'm still in my early twenties; though I was not conscious of it, what in fact was happening at that time to the big-band activity nationwide was a slow decline. Though rock and roll had not made its entrance as of yet, there was certainly evidence of it, and the economies of that period just were not sustaining the cost of the big bands, which in numbers could range anywhere from fifteen to twenty musicians.

In the late forties there was an opening at a radio station (owned by Gene Autry and Arthur Krogan) for a Mexican American to do a bilingual half-hour program. One of the account executives there had been a childhood friend of mine and was aware of my musical background. He thought that I would be a likely candidate, so he capsulized a two-year course in broadcasting with me in about two weeks. I auditioned and was accepted. I started in February 1949 for what was then KOWL at the foot of Pico Boulevard in Santa Monica. They engaged me for a short term. They wanted to see how this thing would be received by the community, "this thing" being a bilingual program of both popular music and a few little Latin records. The program was aimed at the Mexican American community, particularly since nothing had been formulated for this section of Los Angeles, which at that time compared to now was primarily Mexican American as opposed to Mexican nationals. Most of us were English speaking, and we spoke some Spanish in varying degrees from poor to very good. The program was such an innovation that it was immediately embraced by the community. What was a half-hour program inside of three months became an hour program and by the second year was already a three-hour broadcast. Radio was much different at that time. The major networks were KFI, KABC, KHJ, KNX. The independents such as KOWL were into what at that time was referred to as specialized radio programming: disc jockeys, or personalities, staging a program designed for a special segment of the community. Before me this particular station had enjoyed great success with Joe Adams, who was geared to reach the Negro market. The program was very well received at that time, but the inclination was that there should be more Latin music on the show. It tickled me pink. What I did even before the show started, though I would only be playing one or two Latin records during the course of the program. . . . The extent of my familiarity with Latin music didn't go beyond Carmen Cavallero and Xavier Cugat and Enrique Madriguera and the like. It didn't impress me much; it may as well have been a hotel band. I did a considerable amount of research, and I had plenty of time to do so. I went to different record stores downtown and found what the public was buying. For the most part they were buying *rancheras* and boleros. All of the rock and roll groups, such as Los Bukis of today, didn't exist then. There were *rancheras,* mariachis, and *boleristas* and the like back then. I noticed there were little bins here and there where there were some names that I had never heard of, like Puente, Machito, Rodríguez, Pacheco, Miguelito Valdés. So I thought I would give them a listen, and oh, I went wild. I know the reason I appreciated this was because of my musical background. How else could I have possibly recognized something of this quality? So I started interspersing my program with these artists that I've just mentioned and a lot of others. Vicentico Valdés was Tito Puente's featured vocalist. I came to regard Tito Puente as one of the principal star makers of his time because it was not only Vicentico Valdés, but Santitos Colón, Gilberto Monroig, and probably a number of others which reached varying degrees of fame in their own right. So the program was very well received. People were hearing artists and music that were never heard here, throughout Los Angeles. Sad commentary: we're only 3,000 miles apart, and communication was pretty good back then. The few radio stations that we had that were Spanish speaking were in the very early hours of the morn. All they played were *rancheras,* and I'd heard that since I was a little tot and I'd had it with that. I was saturated with that just as we are for the most part saturated today with rock and roll—which I detest.

Going into my second year, the young man responsible for my having started a rather long-term career in radio had the idea of staging an event of Latin music. Those Latin Holidays that became a byword here locally was his idea. He prodded me on. These artists whom I'd become familiar with on record, I now became familiar with live, in order to contract them for what was to become the first Latin Holiday ever in Los Angeles. I had been discouraged, particularly with the impresarios of that period. They don't let Mexicans into the Hollywood Palladium. But by that time—1953 or 1954—I had already committed myself to the VP. . . . I rented the Hollywood Palladium. At that time the Palladium operated on a seven-night-a-week basis with all of the name bands—I mean Les Brown, Tommy Dorsey, Jimmy Dorsey, Goodman. There was a big crossover at that time for someone who had really made it big, and was to make it even bigger, namely Pérez Prado, with "Qué rico el mambo." He was appearing there at the time. . . . For my first Latin Holiday the entire cost of the Hollywood Palladium, plus the orchestra of Pérez Prado, was $800. The other artists for that first event were Joe Loco, Tony Martínez, and Manny López. Two-fifty [$2.50] plus tax was the admission at the door. It was a very revolutionary event. They thought it was going to be a bomb, but I believed in it.

Loza: It was always interesting to me that you started these Latin Holidays at the Hollywood Palladium, and of course, three thousand miles away in New York you have the Palladium. Did that ever cross your mind? Were you trying to emulate what was going on in New York? Were you aware of it?

Sesma: You've got to remember that when I was in New York with Johnny Richards's orchestra, I was a struggling musician. I was not aware of the Palladium. We're talking the early to midforties. That it was or was not a Latin dancing music center, I don't even know. I isolated the Palladium not because it had any relationship with the Palladium in New York; I wanted to get our community to move out of . . .

Loza: The barrios.

Sesma: Yeah. There's nothing wrong with the barrio. I would live in the barrio all over again myself. That challenge was also a sociological challenge; would our people go? And they went! So what was an annual event for a couple of years became a semiannual event, and after that it became a monthly event. . . . The Hollywood Palladium was the place. We had arrived en masse. . . . That we had moved our community into a mainstream social area was very rewarding for me. . . . Tito Puente had already been here once or twice at the Zenda Ballroom on Seventh Street and Figueroa. Joe García had been the entrepreneur of that period, and back in the early thirties he started "El Club Alegrías Black and White Ball," which he used to stage at various places like the Los Angeles Breakfast Club, the Royal Palms Hotel, and moved on to the Zenda Ballroom. He brought Puente for the first time out here, and Pérez Prado as well. For the most part he had American pop music bands entertaining there.

Loza: Now your dances were like sellouts. I mean, you packed them in?

Sesma: Hey, some of them were tremendous successes, but some of them were tremendous bombs. . . . In the midfifties the Palladium was no longer what it was. That was the official ending of the big-band period here locally. . . . The last event I staged there was in late '73. The cost was something like $5,000. What a difference twenty years make. It must cost eight or ten grand now. Not only did we have our monthly events at the Palladium, but there were at least maybe a dozen different nightclubs. They were all mainstream—by that I mean they had pop American music. But one night of the week it was a mambo night. It could have been any night of the week—however, not a weekend; a Sunday yes, but not a Saturday. It was almost as if they were all coordinating with one another. They were not in competition with each other. For example, there was a mambo Monday night at the Malabar on West Pico Boulevard. There was a period there for a number of years when . . . I joined the then very popular local orchestra of Tito Rivera and his Havana Mambo Orchestra. We were working seven nights a week. The people wanted to dance. Back then the mambo was the big deal. Later on the cha-chachá and then the *pachanga*.

Loza: Pérez Prado had become popular all over the world really, but he really hit it big here in the U.S. He had a big hit here in Los Angeles and almost made it on the West Coast before the East Coast. Then people started looking at the mambo of Pérez Prado versus Puente and Rodríguez and Machito. What was your feeling?

Sesma: I must say I'm not very complimentary about Prado. I considered him a kind of noisemaker. Forgive me. I don't mean that literally; I mean it metaphorically. He was very far away from what I preferred musically. Yet he was a very accomplished musician, but I can't dispute the success which he enjoyed with his style, which was very individualized. He's the one that went to the bank with all the bread like no other Latin artist before him. "Cherry Pink and Apple Blossom White," forget it. Worldwide. That will never happen again. When you think of Latin music of that period, Pérez Prado is over here, the rest of them are over here. . . . I was speaking musically. You couldn't compare him with Puente or Machito. Apples and oranges.

Loza: Do you think the people here in Los Angeles gravitated more toward Pérez Prado?

Sesma: I'd have to say that they did, sure.

Loza: Why was that?

Sesma: You have to bow to the idiosyncrasies of the public. Back then, as now, how do you account for rock and roll being so successful? There isn't anything as far as trends are concerned that could be less musical than rock and roll, yet it has been the most successful musical entity that has ever occurred, worldwide. . . . I'm making these analogies in a very exaggerated form, but I want to make that point.

Loza: The other possibility is that, of course, Prado was based in Mexico City, and you have this large Mexican population here which probably was familiar with his sound. In other words, Mexicans were partly brought up on his sound. It was more of a western continental phenomenon, whereas the other Cubans had gone to New York, such as Arsenio Rodríguez, Machito, Miguelito Valdés, and developed a harder style of the mambo.

Sesma: The individuals that came out of Cuba in the same generation as Prado were far more traditional. You mentioned Arsenio Rodríguez and the Orquesta Aragón. Of course, they never came out of Cuba, but for those exiled into Spain. They, like some of the others like Mariano Mercerón, went to Mexico. [Singer] Beny Moré came out to Los Angeles one time, and I feel very proud that I was able to contract him. When I went to contract him again at the Palladium, I couldn't because that sugar curtain had already come down. I remember during my early years in radio before Prado had made it, I was very much, as I still am, a Beny Moré admirer. All of those early RCA Victor recordings with Beny Moré's big name; down in very fine print is the La Orquesta de Pérez Prado. That's part of his beginnings with the RCA Victor people. His orchestra used to accompany a number of the artists, including Beny Moré. You could hear that Prado stamp then, but it became more defined when he himself sprung forward on his own.

Loza: Of course, Tito Puente, in '79, his first Grammy was [awarded for his] tribute to Beny Moré.

Sesma: His roots are not Cuban, but that will give you an idea of the great regard Puente had for Cuban music.

Loza: What started being the differences stylistically that earmarked Puente from these other people? What did you start noticing about it, and did Puente's band come on different to you?

Sesma: Yes, like none of the other bands. He was much more modern. He broke the traditional barrier. Machito did also, but not to the degree Puente did. I can't account for the why. When I say "broke that traditional barrier," [I mean that] he used [the band] not only harmonically but took some liberties rhythmically as well. But mostly harmonically, the chord changes.

Loza: A lot of these people were hitting the jazz structures. Maybe Puente was really experimenting.

Sesma: You hit it. That's what made Puente and Machito different from all of the other bands, Puente much more so than Machito. René Hernández, I think, was Machito's pianist and arranger at that time. I think Mario Bauzá did some arranging as well. And Bauzá's background was very jazz oriented.

Loza: Puente was edging out there. In many of those early recordings he started, for example, using the vibraphone. That was a big change from the other groups, and yet he was still up there in front of people who were dancing. He was coming up with these modern ideas, and yet he was still in a very commercial venue of people dancing. You had used the word *avant-garde* to describe his music. He had some early—his "Picadillo," which is a unique little tune, "Abaniquito."

Sesma: Speaking of "Abaniquito," that was Vicentico Valdés on the vocal. He was not the greatest *inspirador;* he was primarily a *bolerista*. But he did the best he could with the improvisational segments with some of the things he did with Puente, including "Abaniquito." That's when Tito was on the black label Tico Records. George Goldman was at the fore of the Tico recording company at that time. There is an irony in Tito's career that must have galled him. Tito enjoyed many recorded successes, but I don't think any of them were on a par with, let's say, what Prado enjoyed. The one experience in his career he enjoyed some success with was a thing called "Oye como va." The irony is some group out of San Francisco, Santana, whom I had never heard of at that time, comes out with the same recording, which was inferior, both in terms of the musicality and the engineering, but why was it a success? That was the one recording that Puente could have retired on. He probably made more money off the royalties of that Santana recorded success than he had made in his entire life before that. That must have galled him to no end.

Loza: His agent for much of his career was José Curbelo, and he had played with Curbelo's band. Did the agents send you Puente's recordings?

Sesma: No, I was serviced in the main by either the recording companies themselves directly or the local distributors, of which there were quite a number. The whole Pico Boulevard was lined with distributorships. They used to send me all the releases and some prereleases. Curbelo had nothing to do with supplying me with Puente's records. . . . All the record companies at that time had their PR people, their a&r people, allotted *x* number of new copies of albums to supply the deejays at that time. It is certainly not what happens now.

Loza: They always talk about the old "payola."

Sesma: That was very commonplace. More so than not. I prized my freedom of programming to such a degree that to this day I am yet to receive my first nickel for playing a record for anybody. I only played what I thought our listenership would enjoy and what I myself appreciated. I had been approached by a number of various artists' representatives that would offer me ten dollars or twenty dollars to play a recording, but I thanked them, I told them I was well salaried, and I didn't accept any money for playing records. It wasn't long before no one approached me with money. I'm not going to say that all of the disc jockeys accepted money, but it was common practice.

Loza: The first time you brought Puente here was in what year? Fifty-eight?

Sesma: Right.

Loza: And that was also the [Hollywood] Palladium?

Sesma: Right.

Loza: I think it was in that year that he recorded his *Dance Mania* album. It became his top-selling album, the one with RCA Victor.

Sesma: To this day that's my favorite Puente album.

Loza: It's certainly the one that cut through.

Sesma: Did not cross over but it cut through. I think Puente has never crossed over, but for the effect of Santana's thing.

Loza: Even at that time he was doing stuff that they would call crossover today. There was an old jazz tune on that album—which of course he did on another record, I think on RCA, *Puente Goes Jazz,* he did about the same time, '56, I think. He had also done the albums with all percussionists, Mongo Santamaría, Willie Bobo. He always had these interesting percussion sections. A lot of people have said that his band was more percussive than, let's say, Rodríguez's band because of the fact that Puente was a percussionist. He had these strong affinities toward bringing these . . .

Sesma: Well, not exclusively. He did a lot of things that were very percussive, but that was the context of the album. You made a comparison of Puente with Rodríguez. Once again I just don't think the two organizations should be compared. When I think of Rodríguez, I think of him as a single artist, though I trace him back to his bandleading days. His bands were always very good, but they didn't have the same instrumentation as Puente. Puente's things were a full reed section, full brass. Rodríguez always had a small group, never had a big group. When he stemmed out as a single soloist and he gave up his band, he had full André Kostelanetz string sections. You know the albums I'm talking about. All boleros, gorgeous things. The matter of Rodríguez and Puente, I don't think of them in the same . . .

Loza: I see what you're saying. In other words, Rodríguez was a singer who relied on people doing this behind him, whereas Puente was actually the arranger. By 1962 Puente had come on pretty strong. Puente just kept producing records. I think Tito Rodríguez, in the early fifties, had actually outdone Puente on a few gigs in New York. Puente rolled right back by hacking out all these records. Of course, *Dance Mania* in 1958, with all those dance hits on there, probably brought Puente into the stardom thing. And of course eventually Tito Rodríguez died. Also the life of a bandleader sometimes can go longer than a singer. Of course, Machito kept singing until he was older, but certainly not like in his younger days. There was also a transition period in the early and late sixties and early seventies when this whole salsa thing becomes the rage. You, of course, went through that transition when you went to the other station, when you went to KALI. You were actually contracted by Fania, right?

Sesma: My last year in radio was in '67. At that time KALI had been sold. They terminated all of the deejays then. Aside from my entrepreneurial efforts, I was unemployed, off the air. In about a year I set upon a different career with the state of California that lasted for well over seventeen years. To get back to your topic, immediately following my termination at KALI I was banging on doors, but there were just no openings. Even with all of my experience that I had had, zero. So I applied for a position with the state of California, and I was engaged. In late '78 I noticed that KALI had started a salsa program with one of their staff announcers, Salvador Solís, Luis Hernández, at the helm. I didn't think it was going to work because Salvador, very Mexican music oriented, despised salsa to the core. Hey, this can't happen. This was just the observation of an outsider, me being the outsider. November, December of '78. In early April of the following year, '79, the vice president of KALI, Phil Malken, whom I had known during my late days at KALI— he was the new owner's right-hand man, hatchet man—he called me. I had maintained a relationship with him because I was purchasing a lot of time on all of the Spanish-language radio stations to promote my Palladium events. Anyway, he called me. "How would you like to go on the air?" I said, "Great, when do I start?" He said, "This is what's happening. There's a program we have in late evening that's sponsored by the Fania recording company—namely, Jerry Masucci—and he wants to make a change, so he'll probably be calling you." . . . They accepted my request for scale, and I worked there for three years. I enjoyed it. My hat was off to Jerry Masucci. There was never anyone during my twenty years on the air that had done so much with and for Latin music. These Fania all-stars were out of this world. . . . All of the artists I knew on a personal level. I was home again.

Loza: What was your impression of people like Tito Puente who were trying to keep up with these younger *salseros* at the time? Were you still playing a lot of Tito Puente on the show there?

Sesma: This was the first time in my radio career that I was not programming my own show. I had a playlist. I was just announcing. They were exclusively the Fania artists. Puente was not a dominant figure on the Masucci playlist. People like Larry Harlow, the Palmieris, Rubén Blades, Willie Colón, those guys from Puerto Rico. Rarely was Puente on the program . . . typical of the recording company impresarios of that period, and even today. It hurts me inside. Puente enjoyed great success saleswise with a certain composition, I don't know what it was right now. George Goldner received the composer credits and as such was receiving the royalties. . . . It was Puente's work. At that time George Goldner was in Africa. Puente had to go to Africa and find George to claim his rightful royalties. You believe that?

Loza: It was about 1980 that Tito Puente takes on this contract with Concord Records, largely on the recommendation of Cal Tjader. And the Latin jazz thing, which had never really died. . . . Willie Bobo and Mongo Santamaría were going in a different direction than Tito Puente when they went with Cal Tjader in the late fifties.

Sesma: They didn't have much say because they were with Cal Tjader. If anything, Puente may have taken a page out of Cal's book by emphasizing his vibe work in that period to a greater degree because of the successes Tjader was enjoying with the Fantasy label. Cal engaged Mongo and Willie because of their Latin music backgrounds, which would lend authenticity to his works, and they sure did.

Loza: In a way Puente followed that up, and it wasn't too long after that Cal Tjader died.

Sesma: Long before then both Mongo and Willie had gone their separate directions and enjoyed a considerable amount of success. Can you imagine Willie became a highly regarded singer? He was a great song stylist. I loved his work. What a talent.

Loza: It seemed to me Puente was able to keep the incredible dynamic in his playing, and Bobo had adapted more to the pop music.

Sesma: Willie by design didn't strive to achieve the excitement levels that Puente always reached. That wasn't his thing. He was a kind of Mr. Cool. A difference in personalities. He became much more Americanized. Talk about crossing over, he sure did. He was yet to reach his peak, but someone else had different plans.

Loza: Tito Puente ended up going into this Latin jazz thing, which some people think saved his ongoing career. Here you have Tito Puente, now seventy-three years old.

Sesma: He's about the same age that I am. Celia wouldn't appreciate this either, but we're all about the same age. Puente has gone in the direction of the economics. The economics would not now and has not been able to sustain his *conjunto* that we all loved so much. He has gone into Latin jazz exclusively. That was dictated both by the economics and I'm sure his representation [management].

Loza: Of his four Grammys, three are for that format. Would you agree with the fact that it was the thing that kept him going, those Concord records.

Sesma: Certainly. Aside from the money he has received from "Oye como va," I think he has achieved a far greater success in that field than he ever did in the Latin music field, which is the sad truth of it. I have a very strong feeling that Latin music has gone into a recess period.

Loza: Especially the dance music. It has become a sort of pop music. They call it "*salsa erótica.*" It's really watered-down stuff.

Sesma: It seems that the only traditionalist which has survived all of these changes is Celia Cruz. You can't find anyone more representative of the traditional genre of music.

Jerry González

Through the past twenty years, Jerry González has emerged as one of the major artists representing the Latin jazz idiom. A prolific trumpeter and conga drummer, he has for many years led his own ensemble, Fort Apache, cofounded (with Manny Oquendo) Conjunto Libre, and has recorded and toured with other major artists ranging from Tito Puente, Ray Barretto, and Eddie Palmieri to McCoy Tyner, Dizzy Gillespie, Tony Williams, Jackie McLean, and Cachao. He has most recently been under contract with Fantasy Records, which released his 1994 Grammy-nominated album. My conversation with Jerry took place at his apartment in Greenwich Village in the fall of 1994.

◈◈

Loza: First of all, tell me how you got into Latin music, the whole thing: where you came out of and then how you reacted to this thing of Tito Puente, and how he came out of it.

González: My father would sing in the old mambo era of the fifties, and he collected all the records and all the music. I grew up with Tito [Puente] and Tito Rodríguez, and Machito, Totico, Santos, La Sonora Matancera, later on the Palmieris, Joe Cuba, the whole thing. I grew up with that. But the stuff that really tickled me was the Cal Tjader–Mongo–Willie Bobo triad on Fantasy. That's what really got to me. I started hearing more rumba kind of percussion and jazz and I just naturally gravitated to that more so than typical shit. And Mongo with his Latin jazz band—I dug all the Mongo stuff, all the Tjader stuff. I prefer nonvocal stuff. I prefer instrumental stuff. I started playing trumpet. I picked up the drums in the street. I remember the first Tjader thing I heard was "Guachi Guara" with [Armando] Peraza [*sings tune*]—that shit blew my mind. When I was seventeen I met Peraza, and he encouraged me a lot, throughout the years just collecting all the latest music that was happening. Then we bumped into René López. Me and my brother [Andy González] and Nicky Marrero and Nelson González and Charlie Santiago and a whole bunch of people were hanging together at the same time. We used to go to René's house and we used to play us all the all-stars, Arsenio, Arcaño, Chapottín. We used to play all the older Cuban stuff from the thirties and forties, the whole deal, and I hooked up the history of it. Somehow the groove that was happening on those older Cuban things was the groove that I wanted, much more so than the New York Latin. We grew up studying, tried to hook up the old Cuban fifties feel.

Loza: Did you ever hear any of the stuff straight from Cuba, like Cachao's *descargas,* or was it the Mongo recording here that you heard?

González: No, I grew up studying Tata Güines. I studied those bongo solos like homework. But a little slow getting into it.

Loza: How do you think that thing started diverging there where you start having a New York thing happening via Cuban guys like Machito and Bauzá coming here in the late 1930s?

González: Machito, Bauzá were the first cats to use conga drum. They didn't use conga drum before that. They had little trios with a bongo and a maraca, something like that. So they were the first ones to bring in a conga. They were the first ones to turn Dizzy on to Chano.

Loza: In Cuba they had the *conjunto,* which had the congas and bongos.

González: Yeah, but in the thirties there were no conga drums around. Conga drums started jumping in around midforties with Arcaño in Cuba. I think they were the first ones to bring the conga drum into a *charanga.*

Loza: So how do you look at the thing—the Machito thing happened, Bauzá and then the Tito Puente kind of stuff coming out of that? Comparing that to the old stuff you're talking about?

González: Tito, he started playing with them, he came out of there. Went to Juilliard, took some music at Juilliard and studied. Studied some arranging and got his ideas together. Ideas that he was working with were really from the Cuban source. For instance, "Oye como va," that's from Arcaño.

Loza: Yeah, that was '63 or something. And then I guess it got around because then in the later sixties it went into the rock thing. What do you think he was doing different than Machito? Where did he take the music where Machito didn't? What was different?

González: To me it's the same parallel as Duke and the Basie band. Duke's band became more harmonically and symphonically expansive. Whereas the Basie band I would parallel to Puente, I would parallel the Duke Ellington band to Machito. Even the sound of Machito's saxophones and horns was coming out of the Duke Ellington sound, the way the saxophones were voiced and the chords that were written for the orchestra were voiced in the Duke Ellington way. But Puente was more like the Basie band, a riff band. They worked on riffs; they weren't as orchestral in the beginning as Macho. And it was more percussive: it was a riff band, man, working the band with drums.

Loza: That's a good analogy. These dudes, of course, such as Tito, had been affected by jazz, just like Bauzá.

González: Bauzá was much more profoundly affected and actually played in jazz bands, like Chick Webb, Cab Calloway. Before Machito's band was even formed, Bauzá had worked that whole black big-band jazz thing, whereas Tito didn't. Tito's experience in that is not as profound as Mario's . . . Tito played a little swing but not to the extent that Bauzá did.

Loza: Bauzá lived it. He roommated with Dizzy Gillespie, right?

González: No, they used to hang together, and he used to give Dizzy lessons.

Loza: But they never played together in one of those bands?

González: Probably Cab Calloway. But he gave up the gig to Dizzy, pretending to be sick so he could give Dizzy a place in the Cab Calloway band.

Loza: But I hear what you're talking about because in those Machito arrangements—those things are not just jazz-derived harmonies, they're jazz progressions. There's a lot of blues-derived progressions in there. Where the stuff is resolving, the I–V thing is also from a blues perspective. I don't think Tito got into that.

González: By the sixties Tito started getting a little more jazzier than his original stuff.

Loza: He started interpreting jazz tunes.

González: That's even much later.

Loza: I think at one point in the sixties he did a thing highlighting jazz . . .

González: That's with the alternating big bands.

Loza: This is related to an important point that I hadn't thought about that is a profound difference. His harmonies were almost like *típico;* harmonically maybe he was deriving more . . . what would you say he was doing harmonically?

González: Well, one of the prolific arrangers of that time was René Hernández, who was Machito's piano player and arranger. He would write arrangements for Tito Rodríguez and Puente. Puente might maybe change a little voicing here maybe, but René Hernández was the core of the New York sound at that time.

Loza: Although Puente did handle a lot of the arrangements himself.

González: He did. I'm sure he did.

Loza: Well, let's compare him and Tito Rodríguez. Sometimes I think I hear a bigger extended thing, like when Tito [Puente] would end on [*sings*], those breaks when he'd expand this chord. You think that he stretched it more?

González: Puente was listening to the big band as a rhythm player and interpreting the band as a drum. Tito Rodríguez is a singer interpreting the band as an accompaniment to his singing. That's the difference. And then Macho is coming from that old Duke Ellington school where they're doing a wider scope of a thing.

Loza: Did you find yourself—you said you started listening to more Cuban straight stuff, such as Mongo. Of those three bands, Rodríguez, Puente, Machito, did you find yourself listening more to any of them?

González: No, I dug them all. I dug all three of them.

Loza: Well, they were all heavy. René Hernández was doing arrangements for all three of them. He was really the secret figure behind the whole thing. It's a shame these guys—just like Strayhorn or Bauzá for many years, nobody knowing, the public not knowing. The musicians *do* know. Is he still alive, René Hernández?

González: No. Last thing he did was with Eddie Palmieri.

Loza: Did you ever listen to any of that José Curbelo stuff?

González: Yeah, that was almost in the same groove, same time as Macho. It came out after Macho.

Loza: . . . and Tito Puente played with Curbelo.

González: They all played together at one time.

Loza: . . . and Curbelo was maybe Tito's sort of mentor?

González: I never asked Tito who his mentor was. I don't think it would be Curbelo. Curbelo had a big band, sure. But it didn't last very long.

Loza: Tito seems to talk about Machito being his mentor. I think Tito played with Machito first before he went to the war. Then he came back and he couldn't get into Machito's band, so he went to Curbelo's band.

González: Yeah, Curbelo already had something happening.

Loza: When did that Latin percussion, that Latin ensemble start—that Martin Cohen project?

González: Around '80. I worked with him for about three years [during that period].

Loza: So you were there in the earlier years of it. So what made him go that way? Was it a musical choice, a commercial choice? Easier choice?

González: I don't know, but I think it was because he could travel with a smaller band that was playing jazz. Made more bread. To travel with the big band the way he had and make some money was impossible.

Loza: And also that old dance era of that time was dying.

González: Big bands are expensive. Just airfare alone to get a band from place to place is a killer. I had a fifteen-piece group, and I couldn't get the money I wanted to travel. I had to break it down to a sextet.

Loza: And it wasn't like the fifties, when you had the Palladium, or even the early seventies, when the salsa thing was still exploding, because these guys had big bands—

Eddie Palmieri, Tito Puente still had a big band. But by the late seventies that wasn't the case, right?

González: Well, Macho and Puente kept shit going in the big-band style. It wasn't until the eighties that Puente actually broke it down to a smaller group, and that was like making a band, making a small little Latin jazz ensemble. One of the advantages was that you don't have to pay that many cats. Traveling, airfare is costly, and you can make better money for yourself. That's the only logic behind that.

Loza: And he also broke into the jazz market at the same time, right?

González: Well, the jazz cats had always been checking Tito out because of the one time in Birdland. It used to be Art Blakey, Tito Puente, and John Coltrane, all night long. Alternating sets. That's the way the shit should be. It used to be like Miles Davis, then Machito, then Dexter Gordon, or Art Blakey. That kind of Latin and jazz combination was happening at Birdland. They were alternating with each other.

Loza: You played with that band for three years. Now you probably came up during the same time period I came up. I'm forty-two, you're . . .

González: Forty-five.

Loza: And so you obviously got into the jazz thing very heavy—Miles and . . .

González: All of it was the same.

Loza: You didn't divide it?

González: No.

Loza: That's a lot different than what the average jazz musician goes through. The average jazz musician is not playing *tumbao* and rumba.

González: Average jazz musician? They don't know nothing about clave or anything like that. Maybe they might think about emulating some Latin shit, but they don't really know.

Loza: How much of that was an opportunity, to you personally, to play with a Latin jazz band in terms of really exploiting your two sides? Did you feel that was a great, fulfilling opportunity?

González: I always wanted to play with Tito. I knew him since I was a kid and watched the band before I ever even started playing. I used to stand in front of the band watching and daydream like "I wish I do that shit, I wish I could play like that," you know? And then it happened. The dream came true. Same thing happened with Palmieri. I used to stand in front of that band wishing that I was playing in that band. Ten years pass by and I'm sitting there pinching myself. I had a good time checking out Tito. He was a trooper. He was a beautiful cat.

Loza: Now did you do some of your own stuff with [Tito's] band, your own arrangements?

González: No, not really.

Loza: But you played congas and trumpet.

González: Yeah.

Loza: What do you think of his approach to adapting this jazz stuff, because he took tunes like "Equinox," "Giant Steps" . . .

González: Yeah, some of that shit started coming from stuff that we were doing.

Loza: So you had done that with Libre?

González: We had done that with Libre. . . . We were all searching, trying to prove ourselves, expand our vocabulary in the language. I was studying Trane and Diz and all those cats at the same time I'm studying Los Muñequitos de Matanzas to get the drum thing down.

Loza: Which is a very different thing than the straight jazz musician. It's like what Gillespie said, that Latin musicians learn more about jazz than jazz musicians learn about Latin. It's obvious.

González: If the Latin musicians open their heads up, because I know some Latin musicians that just listen to *charanga* forever. They don't put nothing else on. I know some other drummers who just listen to *santo*. They don't put nothing else on.

Loza: But a lot of guys your age did get into the jazz thing, because they were getting both. You were a very bicultural generation compared to Tito Puente or Machito.

González: Both of them, just by being in New York, they got it. Even if they weren't in it, they got it. And because they were big bands, they encountered each other. They crossed each other's paths. Palladium was right down the block from Birdland [Fifty-third Street and Broadway]. Cats would probably go downstairs on their break to go check out the jazz band and then go back upstairs and play their gig.

Loza: Now Tito used to say about that band, the one you played with, that that was like a band where he was trying to preserve what Cal Tjader, Mongo Santamaría, and other people had done with Latin jazz.

González: I think originally it was Marty Cohen running some promotion scam to promote his drums and since he had the connections to hook up concerts in Japan and Europe because of the distribution of his stuff. At the same time he's trying to distribute his congas internationally. And Tito was part of his roster of cats that he stole from.

Loza: Well, and Tito jumped on it.

González: Well, the money's offered, and Tito's gonna go for it. Tito's no fool.

Loza: He had an exclusive contract.

González: That was the catalyst for Tito to go that way. To make a small ensemble so they could go to Europe or Japan, where the expenses are not that expensive, and they could make a little taste and then come back. You couldn't take a big band, so that was the catalyst to make that idea a little more solid in Tito's reality, because Tito was just gonna deal with the big band. He wasn't gonna make a quintet.

Loza: It was right about that time, about '82–'83, also about the time that Cal Tjader died, and I remember feeling that Tito Puente's jumped the—I think he even said it one time: "Well, we're gonna try to fill the shoes of" . . .

González: Well, I put out *Ya yo me curé* in 1979 [or] 1980, my first album. And that one kind of shook everybody up because they didn't know I could do shit like that.

Loza: That was that experimental . . .

González: No, that was before that. That was '75, Folklórico . . . that was started in our house in our basement. That was a combination of old cats and young cats trying to make some new shit happen, and it got usurped, the power of what we're gonna do, and taken over by other people.

Loza: Yeah, you were doing tunes like "Tune Up," "Milestones," all these Miles Davis things, and putting them to rumba, whatever, probably by the early seventies, right? I don't even think Cal Tjader was—Mongo Santamaría did not make it a habit to take jazz tunes and adapt it.

González: Yeah, but he was playing some shit already in that groove.

Loza: Well, Tito jumped on that. And also Cal Tjader died—Mongo Santamaría was already getting older.

González: And Tjader was an influence on Tito too, through his rhythm section. And the core of the inspiration for those two cats is Lionel Hampton. Hampton led a big band with vibes, Tjader played vibes, he went to go see Tito play because Tito plays with vibes, and checked out how deep that shit was and he said, "Wait a minute, we got" . . .

Loza: And he took Mongo and Willie Bobo, and that made Cal Tjader, those two guys, let's face it.

González: [*Agrees*] Uh-huh.

Loza: Basically he went around promoting them. Tito, he was getting older, and another interesting thing about that band you played with, the one that he still has; technically, even though he was getting older, he could still hang musically, very adeptly, wouldn't you say?

González: Oh yeah, Tito's bad, man. All he had to do was [wood]shed. Man, I remember playing gigs with Tito where you could tell he hadn't practiced his vibes. We play in a club for a whole week, and he starts playing his vibes. In the beginning he's hitting wrong notes and missing, mallets falling out of his hands; by the end of the week he starts 'shedding a little bit, he starts getting it together. I could see the power of musical intelligence shining right through man. And I go wow, if Tito's cats would 'shed every day for a little bit, they would have some monstrous shit happening.

Loza: And he keeps—he also adapts. He does new things, he's not playing the same chords.

González: He's got a very good harmonic sense. He knows what he's playing.

Loza: You think maybe that's what's helped him? Let's compare him to someone like Mongo, who had to depend on his hands so much; Tito was basically holding two small sticks and was able to jump on the vibes, had this harmonic concept, from the piano to the saxophone. You think that helped him hang on to this thing longer? Attract younger musicians like yourself? And progress, do an "Equinox," do a "First Light?"

González: Mongo's still attracting young cats to his band. He's still going strong. The quality of the music has ebbed a little bit on all of the older cats only because of the sidemen that they got. Sometimes they don't have the right sidemen to make the shit happen like it used to happen before. When you got the older cats playing with real young cats that are not too experienced, they can't—it's like Palmieri right now. Palmieri had a band, a kid's band.

Loza: Palmieri brought all that stuff, because it sounded like McCoy Tyner. Do you think Tito had as progressive a mentality or philosophy as Eddie Palmieri? Because now you compare Tito with Eddie Palmieri, for example.

González: Tito's gonna be progressive all the time. He's got a very youthful spirit and he's open-minded. You just gotta be around him to inspire it, and then if he's not gonna do it, you could set it up for him and he'll go right with it.

Loza: Now let me ask you another thing: the issue of politics. A lot of the older dudes say this has nothing to do with politics, people love the music, and back in the fifties everybody did the mambo: Italians, Jewish, whites, Irish. It's still like that. But in the sixties and especially by the early seventies, there was a heavy civil rights movement with the blacks and the Latinos all over the country. From California to here, things sort of emulated that. Chicano movement, Latino movement. It seems to me that you identify with that very heavily. How would you say that your political awareness—because that was a heavy, I don't want to call it nationalist, but an identity thing where Latinos were saying, "Hey we're proud of our music and we're gonna play it." It was like a rebirth. Now if you take a guy like Tito Puente, he sort of jumped on that too. But how is his thing different from your thing generationally, philosophically, or politically? It's very apparent to me in your approach.

González: I'm more radical. I'm more radical, period. They have no idea of how deep the oppressive factor is. They've been oblivious to it. It's like Lionel Hampton being a Republican.

Loza: Where has your group gone to play?

González: Oh, we been all over the place. We been to Japan, Yugoslavia, France, Italy, Switzerland, Belgium, Holland, Germany.

Loza: Things are starting to happen.

González: We've been to Bogotá, Colombia. We've been all over the States. I was shocked when we got to Bogotá. I thought we were gonna play for a bunch of *cumbia* hicks. I thought they were gonna throw vegetables at us on the first set because we weren't playing *cumbia*. But I was surprised, man. There is a jazz environment in Colombia. There was jazz after-hours clubs with cats sitting in and playing blues, playing out of the *Real Book,* you know. Everybody's interested in jazz down there. I was freaked out. First gig I ever played, two beautiful girls came on and brought this thing of roses and flowers, man. Gave it to us. I never was treated like that before in my life.

Loza: Your own group?

González: Fort Apache, yeah. I thought that our shit was gonna go over their heads.

Loza: The name of your group, Fort Apache. That was a name given to the Bronx. Were you raised in the Bronx?

González: Yeah. I was born in Manhattan; about four years old, we moved to the Bronx. I was raised there since. But Tito's been a very heavy influence in my life, and I'm grateful to even have the opportunity to know him and to play with him. I learned a great deal from him, and he's a beautiful human being. I played with Palmieri and that was a big influence in my life too, but he wasn't as progressive musically as Tito. Tito was a real person.

Loza: When did you play with Palmieri?

González: 1970, '71. I was there for about four years.

Loza: You were in the big group.

González: Me, Andy [González], Alfredo De La Fé, Harry Vigiano, Víctor Paz, Chocolate, José Rodríguez, Barry Rogers, Manny Cugat, Mario Rivera. Bad motherfuckers. Best band.

Loza: Which album did you record with Tito?

González: *On Broadway* [*sings the riff*]. I'm pretty sure that indirectly, I'm not claiming to be an influence on Tito, but I feel that what he's doing is going more into what I'm doing.

Loza: Yeah, in fact that album, *On Broadway,* I think sort of shifted him into a new direction with that band.

González: Small big band, the same group that he was doing.

Loza: But I think he just started opening up, like just doing "On Broadway." He also did that "First Light" on that album. You played the trumpet on that?

González: Yeah.

Loza: In other words, not just taking the old standards but taking something more contemporary and also a little bolder. Like "On Broadway"; I don't think he would have done that. Was that his idea?

González: No, it was probably Jorge Dalto's idea. Jorge played "On Broadway" with [George] Benson. Jorge was playing in Benson's band. Jorge was Benson's musical director. So Jorge got into Puente's band, and that was where the influence came from.

Poncho Sanchez

Within the past fifteen years, Poncho Sanchez has emerged as one of the most prolific artists in the medium of Latin jazz. He has recorded over fifteen albums as a leader, mostly on the Concord label, with which Tito Puente has recorded as well. Three of these albums have been nominated for Grammy Awards. Sanchez has been especially influenced by Mongo Santamaría and Puente; he has performed with both men, has featured them as guest artists on his own recordings, and has significantly attested to his respect and affection for them through the middle names of his two sons—Monguito and Tito. Sanchez, a Chicano (Mexican American) from Los Angeles, has maintained a progressive, stylistic blend while at the same time continuing with a traditional base of interpretation and performance practice. Prior to performing and recording with his own ensemble, he spent over seven years as the conga player for Cal Tjader (until the latter's death in 1982), one of the major constituents of Latin jazz. I interviewed Poncho during the winter of 1996, immediately after he had conducted a lecture (with pianist David Torres) at UCLA.

Loza: Why is Tito Puente such an important musician in Latin music? In your estimation, what has he done musically, historically, culturally? How has he affected your music? What are the things that he's done that you in a way have emulated?

Sanchez: Tito is a wonderful musician and arranger, composer, and conductor. He can play I don't know how many instruments. He's an accomplished vibes player, timbal player. I think he played saxophone also. He plays piano. Tito really does know music, which is number one in any great musician. Cal Tjader is the same way. Not only was he a great vibes player; he was not a bad piano player either, and a great drummer. Not only is Tito a great timbal player; he's a great musician—the fact that he knows composition, theory, all that stuff. In the early years Tito used to do almost all his own arranging and the charts and stuff. I think that is a very important fact figuring in Tito Puente's life. And especially coming from me, another musician who has respected him all my life, I know he's a great musician. In his younger years Tito was incredible. He was one of the first guys to use four timbales. He would use two timbales and the timbalitos. Not too many guys did that at the time. He would actually get some melodies out of them. That was fairly new at the time. Nobody was doing stuff like that.

I also think that Tito figured out early in his career that he was a great showman. He knows how to conduct a crowd or audience and deal with it. He knows when to be funny and when not. Tito is an accomplished musician all the way around. He has written so many tunes. Now they are putting out so many CDs, I'm getting all the old CDs, the classic stuff. And he has written so many tunes. I mean, some of them are pretty simple, a little cha-cha or a *guajira,* but some of them are a little bit more complicated too. He has done some pretty complicated stuff.

Loza: What were some of the differences stylistically with what Tito was doing and, let's say, Machito or Rodríguez? What made his sound unique?

Sanchez: When I really started listening to Tito's stuff, Santitos Colón was his lead vocalist. Santitos has a very unique voice, so I always knew Tito's band because Santitos was singing. A great singer, he had his own style—a real strong voice. I connected a lot with that because Santitos was his main singer for so many years. But at the same time Tito always had a powerful trumpet section. They were always hot, even in the mixing of the recordings; sometimes they were extra hot. But you know what? They were in tune, and they were blowing hard, man. The album that comes to mind is the twentieth anniversary album where they do "Mambo a la Tito" and all those tunes. Man, the trumpets are just burning . . . And then he had the big bottom with the baritone saxophone. So Tito had a very unique sound because he had trumpets and saxophones mainly, whereas some of the other bands had trombones—although Machito had a lot of trumpet players. Machito had a lot of jazz guys playing with him, a lot of the great jazz cats of that time—Doc Cheatham—and he even did an album with Charlie Parker and all of the great jazz players of that time. I liked Tito's band a lot at that time. Machito's band on some tunes sounded more dated when I first started listening.

Loza: There are two interesting musical points. Number one, you mentioned the incredible variety of tunes that he wrote, and second is the vibes thing. Tito was doing things like "Mambo Diablo" in the early fifties. What is the relationship between Tito and Cal Tjader . . . ?

Sanchez: Right around that time Tito had Mongo Santamaría and Willie Bobo in his band. Tito would let Willie come and play the bongos from time to time, and they say

Willie was getting so good that people would sometimes wait for Tito to go play the vibes so that Willie could play the timbales. They were waiting for that. Willie could really play, and I'm sure Tito knew that; and Willie played great bongos. That's where Cal Tjader, seeing Mongo and Willie in New York playing with Tito Puente's band, comes in. Cal said he used to take his jazz band to New York City and on the breaks he would run around the corner to one of the Latin spots there and go hear Tito's band play. He said, "I couldn't believe the feeling, the sound, the way the music made me feel." With Willie and Mongo playing with Tito, they sounded great together. They actually left Tito's band to move to California to join Cal Tjader's band. All these important people have played with Tito or through Tito's band have made something of themselves—as well as myself through Cal Tjader.

Loza: Puente certainly had a knack for wanting a good rhythm section. Barretto was in there soon after that in the late fifties.

Sanchez: He's had all the greatest guys play with him.

Loza: People like Patato Valdez, Manny Oquendo, Mongo Santamaría. One of the interesting things was that Tito was doing a variety of things; he'd go to the vibes, he'd do a bolero, a cha-cha. He's probably one of the guys that pushed the cha-cha in terms of a large orchestra.

Sanchez: At that time everyone was doing the mambo and the cha-cha-chá at the Palladium. It was such a big thing going on at that time in New York. Of course, I was just a little boy, and I knew nothing about that. However, I learned all this in my music studies and upbringing. Then it came out to California. Not too many people were hip to it right away, but it was here. My brothers and sisters, somehow they picked up on it. They used to go to the Hollywood Palladium when Chico Sesma used to have the Latin dances at the Hollywood Palladium. I was just a little boy, but my brothers and sisters would come in and say, "We've seen Tito Puente, we've seen this and that at the Palladium." The *pachanga* was a big thing also at that time. It was a hot dance for a while.

Loza: For some reason a lot of people—in fact, Chico Sesma and Jerry González said this, and I wanted your reaction to it—they described Tito's sound, especially of that period when he had his big orchestra in the fifties, as a . . . I call it an orchestrated percussive sound. Tito's approach was more like making the whole band into a percussion section if you compared it to Tito Rodríguez or even Machito. What is your reaction to that kind of description?

Sanchez: I somewhat agree with that. I remember when I was going to Cerritos College and Jack Wheaton was the musical director at the time, and he asked me if I had any Tito Puente records. I said I used to listen to them a while back but I hadn't heard any in many years. I remember I brought the album that has "Oye como va" and all those tunes on there. One of the first things he told me [was that Tito] wrote everything out like it was very percussive sounding. I said, "It's true." Yet it still had some very melodic texture to it and harmonically it was decent.

Loza: In fact, harmonically he used to go for very extended voicings.

Sanchez: I think he created his own sound, his own style of writing, his own style of playing, the sound of his band, whereas Tito Rodríguez was a little smoother—his voice was a little smoother sounding. A different approach, and his ranges were a little different than Tito's were.

Loza: The way I look at it, Tito [Puente] emphasized a lot of solo work, the *montuno* sections. Getting into Cal Tjader . . . Now Tito is one of the few living Latin jazz artists besides Mongo and a few others of the older generation. Where do you put Tito in the role of Latin jazz? Who was the leader in the Latin jazz thing?

Sanchez: Everybody was trying to outdo each other. There was a big competition going on back then. I think Tito was very much involved in that. I don't blame him. Cal knew jazz better than Tito, I think. Tito knows the Latin thing better, whereas Cal was a jazz musician. How could he know more than Cal about jazz? Tito wasn't quite the technician as Cal. I shouldn't say "technician," because Tito had some very good technique, but Cal made it flow better on the vibes. It swung better. More of a jazz approach, whereas when Tito plays vibes, its a little more [locked into the Latin rhythmic patterns].

Loza: It is. It's more Latin. When Tito was playing in the early fifties, it was mostly just dance halls. They were gigs. I mean he played one dance after another.

Sanchez: I think that's where it's at. It's not really a putdown; that's what was happening in all of their lives at the time. I think the Latin jazz thing started growing somewhat back in New York, because even Tito Rodríguez did an album at the Palladium where they did all the jazz standards like "Summertime" and "Bye Bye Blues" or something. One of my favorite Tito Rodríguez albums is called *Tito Tito Tito*. They do "Descarga malanga." They have a guy playing a jazz solo on there and somebody, probably like Víctor Paz, playing a *montuno* style, a Latin style. So you could hear the jazz and blues even going in Tito Rodríguez's music as well as Tito Puente's. They both, I think, started experimenting more with Latin jazz around that time.

Loza: In many ways Cal Tjader paved that Latin jazz as an independent movement. I mean he wasn't playing dances.

Sanchez: Even more than Tito or any of those bands. Cal Tjader—of course, he's not the one that invented Latin jazz, not at all—but he made the thing really come alive and grow. So many relate Latin jazz to Cal Tjader, especially the older people, older than us: "Cal Tjader was the guy that played the great Latin jazz sound and Tito Puente had a great dance band."

Loza: Tito picked up on the Latin jazz, especially around the time that Cal Tjader died. I think it was '78 or '79 when he started the little jazz group. Cal Tjader died in '83. Since Cal Tjader died, people like Tito and you have been the major proponents of the Latin jazz movement.

Sanchez: I would agree with that. I think at the time Tito realized how expensive it was getting to travel with a twenty-five-piece orchestra or even a sixteen piece. The airlines started just getting expensive. Everything started getting more expensive. You just can't do that anymore.

Loza: And the dances weren't as popular.

Sanchez: As a matter of fact, I remember Tito telling me that he really loved the Chicano people in Los Angeles. He would say, "I would come to play in San Francisco and Los Angeles because of the Chicanos, not the Puerto Ricans or the Cubans." It was very important. He had to thin out his band little by little because everything got so expensive to travel.

Loza: He had some rough years in the seventies. He was not at the top. That's when Eddie Palmieri and all those people . . . Barretto . . . Fania. And Tito wasn't [exclusively] with Fania.

Sanchez: But he hung in there all the time. He kept his pride and his sound and his style. Everybody still would be excited to come and see Tito take a timbal solo. I mean, all of the drummers I know [would say things like], "Ah, Tito, man. I'm seeing him to-morrow night." He still played.

Loza: Let me ask you something else, Poncho. The other thing about Tito—and I would put you in this category also—there's something about the old *típico* sound, the old Cuban sound. You know Dizzy mixed it with the jazz thing and it worked. There was still a *típico* sound. Cal Tjader had it. We have Miles Davis, Duke Ellington, Count Basie, and John Coltrane in jazz. Where would you place Tito in relation to these other people we've been talking about: Tito Rodríguez, Machito, Bauzá? Do you ever feel like you guys might be an end of an era, that old *típico* thing?

Sanchez: It could be a possibility that that could happen. I think it would be the worst thing that could ever happen to this music, to lose that authentic sound. I've always carried that with me. Even when I just play the drum by itself, I want it to sound like the way Mongo sounded and Chano Pozo and all that.

Loza: Tito in his younger days had the same attitude. I mean, "It's Cuban music and we have to do it authentically." Is that going to carry on?

Sanchez: I think so. I really do. I'm always surprised at how many young kids come up to me and tell me that they really love the music and they're starting a little Latin jazz band in places you never think that they would be doing that, places like Seattle or Arkansas. They're always going to put their new twist to it, but I think that with this music, Latin jazz, you can't go that far away. You're always going to have the authentic sound of the conga drum, the *cáscara* of the timbal, the cowbells. I think it's still going to carry on. I think there are some young people that will carry it on.

Loza: How do you feel about your relationship with Tito Puente in terms of him look-ing to you as one of these people to pass this tradition on?

Sanchez: First of all, I feel totally honored. That's like one of your heroes in life ask-ing you to help. I know Tito very well, and he really likes our band a lot. I'll tell him about a new club that we just worked in and it worked well for us. You know it's going to work well for Tito's band and vice versa. We both do that for each other.

Loza: I think Tito is looking at you to carry on the torch. I know in many ways you are doing that for Mongo. You are trying to bring Mongo back in a way.

Sanchez: Yeah, Mongo does not have his band anymore. He works with Tito's all-star band and he works with my band. Whenever we can get Mongo on a date with us, we do. We just did a tour in California and recorded the Poncho and Mongo album that will be out in September. At this point Mongo just doesn't have the energy to run a band and take it all over the country anymore, and I don't think he should have to. . . . Tito wants to keep on being on the road and keep his band going. In all sincerity, if Tito stops playing, I think that will be the end of his life. That will kill him. If he actually stops, it will probably kill him.

Loza: I think the playing has given him such longevity. You know, Max Salazar considers Tito Puente's playing on "Lover Come Back to Me" off your album *Chile con Soul* as the greatest timbal solo that he ever took.

Sanchez: Well, he took a good solo. As far as the best one he ever took . . . there are some recordings that I like a lot.

Loza: I don't think you could pick the best.

Sanchez: It's a great compliment to me. I feel flattered because of the fact that maybe we made Tito play his best. That's a compliment to me at the same time. Another thing that surprised me that Max also wrote—we did the twenty-five favorite albums on the *descarga* catalog thing. He did one, José Rizo did one, me and Ramón did one together. I noticed that he picked one of my albums; he says that of the twenty-five or thirty recordings of "Manteca" that are out there, that mine is his favorite version. I felt totally flattered. . . . If we made Tito play his best, and Max thinks that's his best solo, I'll take that as a feather in my cap. It's a good solo, it's a very good solo.

Loza: It is. He is hot on it. I very often feel that Tito did get better. I think that about five years ago he was still playing at an incredible peak. I don't know that he's still there, but in my estimation Tito did get better after he was sixty. On the other hand, on some of those early recordings he blows them away: *Cuban Carnival* . . .

Sanchez: *Top Percussion,* "Hot Timbal." First of all the tempos are incredible, and then he takes a solo on top of those fast tempos [*sings*]. Man, Tito!

Loza: Those albums were like '55 and '57, when he did those two percussion albums. That was pretty ahead of its time, the whole concept: no orchestra, no Latin group, just bass and percussion. That was pretty radical, wasn't it?

Sanchez: Absolutely! They were ahead of their times, and Tito has a lot to do with that.

Loza: Even today, that would be a gamble. That's what they told him too.

Sanchez: Those are classic solos and classic albums.

Hilton Ruiz

With the release of *Jazzin'*, one of Tito Puente's most recent albums (featuring the singer India), I began to realize the central role that the prolific pianist, composer, and arranger Hilton Ruiz has been playing in the current musical world of Maestro Puente. Although Ruiz has been for years working with major artists, including Puente as part of his Golden Latin All Stars, his work on *Jazzin'* seemed to have a special purpose and meaning in relation to the current state of Latin music and Puente's continuing legacy.

I met Ruiz during one of his club dates in the spring of 1996 at Catalina's in Los Angeles, where he was leading a trio including the legendary conga player Francisco Aguabella. The following interview took place the next day at the Hollywood Palms Hotel. Joining Ruiz and me for the interview was Bill Marín, a record executive for the RMM/Tropijazz label.

As is apparent through the interview, Ruiz has had a distinguished career as an artist, recording and performing extensively. Born in 1952 in midtown Manhattan, he represents another example of Puente's never-ending collaboration with artists of different generations and of the highest artistic integrity.

◈◈

Loza: Hilton, how did you get into this business and how did you learn your trade?

Ruiz: I started with Santiago Messorrama, who was from Puerto Rico, and he used to teach at 125th Street and Broadway. I was born in midtown Manhattan on Fiftieth Street and Eighth Avenue. My parents used to listen to Liberace and Duke Ellington—those are the two people they'd listen to. And also the radio. My mother had records by Libertad Lamarque and Ray Parker. That's the kind of music they listened to at home. We knew about Tito Puente way back then; he's been a household name for so long. I started by studying a method called "Eslava" method of solfeo, which is a sight-singing method before you go through harmony. I went through that, and then I went to Carnegie Hall. I was eight years old when I played my first recital at Carnegie Hall and another one at nine. I've got the reviews, got good reviews back then.

Loza: Classical music?

Ruiz: Yes, classical music. I was a conservatory-trained classical pianist. Then through my teenage years in high school I used to play organ in church. I was a church organist. When I was about sixteen or seventeen years old, I went with Ismael Rivera. I played with him for about a year. Then when I was about eighteen, I went to Mary Lou Williams, who was considered the first lady of jazz. She wrote music for Benny Goodman, Duke Ellington, and Andy Kirk, considered a pioneer. Her contemporaries were Thelonious Monk, Erroll Garner, Art Tatum, Fats Waller, Bud Powell; these guys used to go to her house and have piano collaborations. So Mary Lou heard me play, and she said, "I'll teach you free of charge," and I said, "Wow, that's great." So I used to go to her house every day, and she would tell me more or less what *not* to do. Because I was really playing, I had records, I listened to McCoy Tyner, I listened to Herbie Hancock, and I was doing my own work by listening to records. Mary Lou gave me insight on ragtime, blues, boogie-woogie, how to play authentically. I got it from a person who was really there. Then I studied with Cedar Walton and people like Roland Hanna, Barry Harris. I met Joe Newman and Frank Foster. Joe Newman and Frank Foster were from the Basie band. They had a workshop called the Jazz Interaction Workshop for Young Musicians, and that workshop was free of charge also. I used to go there, and somehow one night somebody got busy and couldn't make a gig and they said, "Who should we get?" "Hilton, that piano player. Let's get him out of the workshop." So these guys actually showed me what to do. My career has been a hands-on, on-the-job training type of thing. So when I was with Joe Newman and Frank Foster, Clark Terry heard me, and Clark Terry took me on the road for the first time. I wound up going to Europe with Clark and all over the country. Then after that I went with—let me just give you the biggest names—Rahsaan Roland Kirk, who was a saxophonist who played three saxophones at the same time and nonstop breathing. During Rahsaan's performance he would play the music of Fats Waller, then the next tune would be Charlie Parker, next tune would be something by Johnny Ace. He would do blues, real gut-bucket African American blues. I got five years of experience traveling all throughout the country, all throughout Europe; we went to Australia, we went to New Zealand, we went all over the place. I learned a lot with Rahsaan. I made five albums with him. During this time I was recorded by a guy named Nils Wefey for Steeplechase Records, which is a "beige" label. I made five albums for them. Then Columbia from Japan, I made an album for them, CBS Japan. Then I did an album out of France, Free Lance. Out of Munich, Germany, I did a trio. So I have like twenty-two albums now. That's what I have now, my twenty-second album as a leader. Also I recorded with other people as a sideman. Basically I got the hands-on experience from the originators of this music. I was familiar with Tito Puente all this time because everybody knew. If you didn't know who Tito Puente was, forget it. You won't understand it.

Then I met Tito. Jack Hooke and Ralph Mercado had a thing called "Salsa Meets Jazz" where they would have two big-name bands, like El Gran Combo, Ray Barretto, Eddie Palmieri, all these great bands, and then they would have a guest jazz soloist. I was the guest jazz soloist on a lot of these things. Charlie Palmieri, I met other guys through there. I had known them a little bit through the music before, but I was coming in there as a Puerto Rican jazz pianist. I was a jazz soloist. That's when Tito really first heard me. He knew about me because he was open-minded. I had friends who played in a band with him who had told him about me, you know, "You got to check out Hilton. This guy's a straight-ahead jazz pianist." So I was more of a jazz pianist than a Latin or salsa pianist. That's really how I came about to meet him. The first time I played with him there was a tune that I was playing, it was my arrangement—no, it was Tito's arrangement . . . actually I'm not sure who arranged it, but it was a thing called "Blue Bossa." We tried to play tunes that everybody could relate to. That's one of the most-played tunes ever, by Kenny Dorham [*sings the tune*]. Tito looked up at me as he's playing timbales and he gave me a look, and what I read in his eyes was, "Hey, man, I know everything that you're doing. I like what you're doing, but dig this." And he started playing some stuff and I say, "Wow, man." He was *on* it. He took me to a level I had never been on before. So we hit it off real good then. Then we made an album, *Live at the Village Gate*. He came out with this band called the Tito Puente Golden Latin Jazz All Stars. We did another album called *In Session*. From then on almost every album he made he had me there arranging and writing the tunes. I was contributing originals. As far as arrangements, he would tell me what he wanted. He'd say, "I want to make this kind of tune this way, I want the instrumentation to be like this." He knew that I could pull it off. That's how we came to do so much.

Just this year I've done twenty recorded arrangements. We have Mongo Santamaría, Charlie Sepúlveda, Dave Valentín, Juan Pablo Torres, [Long John Oliva], who came out from California to [join] Batacumbéle. All of a sudden I became an arranger.

Loza: Learning through Tito, then.

Ruiz: I was doing arrangements before. I was doing jazz arrangements. I did five albums for RCA on the Novus label on which I used Latin percussion. I noticed the audience was changing completely from the Latin rhythm. The same tunes I'd been playing all along, now using the drums, the people are jumping out of their chairs, going nuts about it. The reception was so hot.

Loza: Like a lot of other jazz artists would have problems, [but] you didn't have problems going back to the *guajeo*.

Ruiz: No, not at all.

Loza: You've done that. A lot of jazz players don't do that.

Ruiz: It's because of the clave. It's the guide of Latin music, which is like a different flavor. It's like getting two different chefs, a French chef and a Japanese chef, and try and put that together. You actually have to be there and live that to be able to relate it. The thing was that jazz was my real love. I wanted to become a jazz bebop piano player. I came before Michel Camilo. I was ten years before all these guys, like Chucho Valdés, Gonzalo Rubalcaba; these guys listened to my records. Jorge Dalto, I got him the job with Paquito D'Rivera because when Paquito came over from Cuba, they were looking for me. They said, "We want Hilton Ruiz. He's the guy we need to make this thing work." So I made two albums with them right away. So I was the original in my era. Because you had the Machito era, the Cal Tjader era, a lot of things involved there, people like Chick Corea and Vince Guaraldi, all these other piano players were doing that also. They were not necessarily *guajeo* piano players either. They were jazz pianists, but they had the feel for it. Armando Peraza and Willie Bobo—those guys told them, "Listen, with a rhythm like that, if you just have good feeling, those guys will make [and] play the right feeling because of what they're constantly putting under you." But Tito more or less, after Rahsaan Roland Kirk, has been the greatest point in my career. Because he got more out of me than I knew that I had. He had so much knowledge about the big band. He would say, "It would be better if you double these horns here, if you double the baritone with this chord, try this chord over here, don't do this like this, there's a better way to do things," and all of a sudden, within a year I had doubled my knowledge.

Loza: Basically at this point he doesn't have the time to be doing that, or the energy.

Ruiz: If it was energy, he did it. Nobody's got more energy than Tito Puente.

Loza: But orchestrating all the stuff he does by himself . . .

Ruiz: What he did for me was the flavor that I had, and the flavor that I had in my arrangements, he found that that was the true jazz flavor that he wanted to portray because his stuff is not watered down. It's got a lot of history behind it. He was around Thelonious Monk, he was around Charlie Parker, he played opposite sets at Birdland, they would have the Tito Puente band then they would have Charlie Parker. I have seen Tito on short notice make a big-band arrangement—it was fantastic—and have that thing here the next day, the whole thing written out with all the parts. People don't really know that about him. If you've got an artist who plays timbales so great—he's such a showman and carries himself so well and people love him so much that people who don't do the history might not realize the magnitude of what he encompasses as a musician.

Loza: His early recordings were all his arrangements. Some are 80 percent his arrangements.

Ruiz: He's a genius.

Loza: Little by little he started using some other people, which diversified his sound.

Ruiz: If he needs something special, he'll get somebody to do it. But he's the executive chief arranger. He oversees everything, so I'm what you would call a staff arranger. In other words, he'll give me a project—say, four or five tunes—and say, "I've got an album coming out next month. Go to work; this is what I want." Maybe he'll give me an idea, but I'm free to do anything I want because he's not making me do things out of my ordinary thing. He's using my talents as they are, but then he gets more out of me, you know: "I've never thought of doing it like that."

Loza: When you were coming up, what did he represent to you culturally, musically, in terms of what he was doing to the industry? In other words, people were going to see bands at the Palladium when all of this was happening. You probably remember some of that. What were particular events, pieces, things that really seemed to affect you that he did, that affected you as a musician and that you think affected the whole world of music?

Ruiz: I find that a lot of the arrangements that I heard were Latin, let's say, harmonic modes. They were great arrangements; they were fantastic the way they were put together. Quality stuff. But I heard Tito's "Jumpin' with Symphony Sid," that arrangement, and I said to myself, "Wow, this thing sounds like real jazz." 'Cause I was talking about chewing off African American jazz, so you would hear guys play *at* jazz solos. But the real flavor, the real thing, you could tell the difference. I noticed that in his band he had the soloists who were playing the real sound. That's when I knew right then. I was aware of his regular Latin mambo arrangements, which also had jazz flavor, but then he had these things that were like . . . I could play it next to John Coltrane as part of my listening thing. I did a lot of listening. I used to listen to jazz for enjoyment. I never realized that I was going to become one of the top jazz pianists in the world. This was never in my mind at all. I wanted to be a commercial artist. I was painting and drawing and things like that. Then all of a sudden I found myself in this career, so I realized it's all a matter of flavor or taste. That's the difference being a musician. A person who is a doctor, a lawyer, a plumber, a garbageman, or whatever, when they listen to this music they *know*. They don't know about the staff or the notes and everything, the theoretical aspects of the music, but they know it when they hear it. The mambo dancers—a lot of Jewish people were the greatest mambo dancers. Something totally outside of their thing, because they're Mediterranean people, but they would know by the flavor whether it was right or not. In other words, like my mother, your mother, you can't fool them, no matter what. They're not going to deal with the notes.

Loza: So he was passing the test with the public and with the professionals.

Ruiz: That's right.

Loza: What you're saying also seems to be that you were noticing that he was experimental.

Ruiz: Experimental but with quality. Because a lot of music is a matter of taste. Like the avant-garde movement that came in, playing a lot of free music, Albert Ayler and Pharoah Sanders. A lot of people loved it, but a lot of people didn't want to be bothered with it. They were like Louis Armstrong fans; if it wasn't Louis Armstrong, they didn't want anything to do with it. If it wasn't Dizzy Gillespie . . . 'cause they had their own personal taste. The end result is that the buying public goes by what they like and peer pressure. Sometimes they might not like it that much, but if their friends like it, that enables them to become part of "the set." Like the rap thing now. I don't think that everybody really likes rap that much, but because of the beat of it, it's tolerable, and the rhymes. . . . I like rap, but some of it I don't. I'm just like any other person. Just because I'm a musician doesn't mean I don't have my own personal taste. But I realize that a lot of it has to do with peer pressure. Oh, get this record, this guy has got this, this guy has got that. If a lot of these youngsters were exposed to other forms of music, they would probably say "Wow, I really like *that*." But because it's being put on the radio and that's all that they hear, it's all they have to choose from, they have to pick out their particular artist from that.

Loza: Speaking of dancing, when you heard Machito, Tito Rodríguez, Tito Puente, Pérez Prado, what did you sense musically that Tito was doing that Machito wasn't? Machito had actually started Latin jazz. He put the rhythms in the jazz. Where was Tito going to expand that? What did he do harmonically, rhythmically?

Ruiz: He chose the correct musicians to interpret the music that was going on. Like a person like myself. When he heard me, I believe that what he heard was . . . the reason that I'm there is because I was doing something fresh and a little bit different than what had already happened. Since he has a track record of fifty years and 110 albums recorded, he's heard it already. You can't just go up to this guy with any old thing and say it's new. He'd say, "No, no, I did this on this record, I did that on that record." Great guys came up through that band. I just happened to come at a different time because I was born in 1952. I'm forty-four years old. My experience came out of the baby-boomer generation. I was into the Temptations, the Four Tops, Aretha Franklin. It's the personnel that you choose that gives the music a freshness, fresh approaches. Now we have Internet, we have satellite communications, we have things that when I was a kid were unheard of.

Loza: He had Joe Loco, Eddie Palmieri, Charlie Palmieri, all of these people worked with him. He picked up Mongo Santamaría, Willie Bobo, all these percussionists. The fact that he was able to go to vibraphone, which was such an unusual thing also, with his big orchestra; he was a percussionist, a *timbalero,* but he would go to the vibraphone on things like "Hong Kong Mambo" or the arrangement he did of "Autumn Leaves." Even that early one he did called "Cuban Fantasy," that's 1950, how would you characterize what he was doing there musically? Was he "sophisticating" the music or was he harmonizing it?

Ruiz: He was innovating. He was taking it and making it fresher and making it just like the Ford Motor Company. You go out and get your Lincoln Towncar now, it talks to you and everything, tells you the temperature. It's like that. To make a comparison to Henry Ford, he started off making a car, then all of a sudden the new technology and computers came in, [so he] put a computer in the car, but not to mess up the car, because it has to enhance the car; it's got to be the right thing.

Loza: People feel he used the whole orchestra as a percussion instrument.

Ruiz: It is. The horn lines [*sings a syncopated pattern*], they're percussive. These lines are taken from the drum beats [*sings drum pattern*]. You just add a melody [*sings syncopated melody*], then the whole band becomes a drum.

Loza: That's why I call it orchestrated percussion.

Marín: At the time you met Tito, you were truly a jazz pianist compared to other guys who came out of Latin music?

Ruiz: Right. I was 100 percent uncut bebop. I knew the bebop repertoire, I knew stride piano, I knew boogie-woogie piano, I accompanied singers like Betty Carter, I've accompanied Joe Williams, Eddie Jefferson, who made up the words to those Miles Davis songs, I was his pianist too. I was pure jazz, and that's what Tito wanted. I was a jazz pianist who also played Latin, but I started first with Ismael Rivera. I used to go to the Cheetah, I used to go to Hunt's Point Palace, I used to go to the Colgate Gardens, I used to go to the Corso, St. George Hotel, they would have thirteen bands, the Lebrón brothers, TNT, Willie Colón. I was there. I was fifteen years old. I was with my girlfriend dancing to this music. I saw this movement. I was in there dancing. But I was a teenager. We used to go to hear these bands because we knew this was going to be hot and the scene was going to be happening. From the time I was eighteen I spent twenty years traveling through America, through the Midwest and the South, and meeting these original musicians. I kind of went away into that because that's what I wanted to do, that was my love. I heard John Coltrane and Charlie Parker and I said I want to play this music. In order to do that I had to separate myself and learn that and then come back again. I came full circle. I rediscovered my roots again, and Tito was the one who helped me rediscover my roots. He straightened me out from all the confusion. He said let's get you down to earth, this is how it goes. You need to do this, you need to do that, and that made me even stronger. So he's my feet firmly now. I can do jazz, but I also have a working knowledge of clave that took a long time. It took a long time to learn how to play clave. Some people can't figure it out.

Loza: Did you ever find yourself going back to study his arrangements?

Ruiz: Yes. When I did the arrangements for [one of his albums], if you read the liner notes, it says, "original arrangement by Hilton Ruiz inspired by original arrangement by Tito Puente." I listened to the original arrangement. Charlie Sepúlveda wanted a nice arrangement for the trumpet, so I listened to Tito's arrangement, the rich textures he had in the baritones. I said, "Wow, this is so good I'm going to use it in my arrangement."

But I gave the credit to Tito because if I hadn't heard that arrangement, I would have gone in twenty different directions. So 50 percent of it is research. If you want to do a thing on, let's say, "In the Mood," you should listen to the original arrangement.

Marín: Tito was a pianist also. Nobody talks about that.

Ruiz: You see, Tito was in the navy. He was in a lot of battles on an aircraft carrier. He was fighting in the war on an aircraft carrier. He's seen bombs and the Zeroes coming down; he was putting out fires on the boat. He has a decoration from the president of the United States. He got a citation from the president for action during World War II. Back then he was also a bugler. He played the bugle. So when he came out, there was the G.I. Bill. A lot of people became dentists, doctors, et cetera. Tito went to Juilliard and he studied formal music. Carnegie Hall and Juilliard were the two greatest schools of music in America—period. That's where he [continued to use and] learned to play piano. So he can play you a *comparsa*. He used to play opposite Charlie Palmieri, playing piano in a trio. There's been situations where he's sat down at the piano to play, and I say, "Man, that sounds like Art Tatum." I didn't know. I knew him from his timbales, his vibes, his arranging.

Loza: The man is just immersed in musical ability.

Ruiz: He's an authentic musician. He can write in any key signature, he can arrange. So anyway, he did this stuff on the piano, and I said, "Do that again. I want to use this in my style." He did this thing that was in double octaves that made the whole thing sound bigger. All the years that I had been playing I had heard this sound and I had never been able to . . . see, a lot of things are visual. You can try to hear it, but if you just sit next to a guy and watch how he does it, it might be totally different than what you thought was happening with your ear. These things happen in music because of the way it was recorded, the time it was recorded, the quality of the recording, certain things happening harmonically, certain overtones that come out, and you're hearing notes that are not really there. Most of them are being produced by other notes being played. When you actually see the visual thing, you say, "Wow, that's how it's done." Now whenever I want to do that, I call it the "Tito sound," because it makes my whole thing even bigger.

Loza: Most really excellent arrangers have a knowledge. First of all, they are usually studied. They have studied some kind of musical concept in terms of how harmony is put together, and if you can deal with the keyboard, it really helps. And Tito had that.

Ruiz: Of course. Now I won't mention any names, but one day a guy brought an arrangement in, and it was quite a difficult arrangement. It was about twenty pages of music. Tito had just got off the plane from somewhere, maybe Australia, a twenty-four-hour plane trip. He comes in, he's the first one at the rehearsal, he's sitting there. The guy brings in the arrangement. All of a sudden he [Tito] says, "Wait a minute. This arrangement doesn't have the right feeling. It's not what I need." Not to belittle the person, but he's not going to take any garbage. He has a very high standard. So he gets his glasses out, he sits up there at the stool, he puts out the music, and he sight-reads the whole thing with all the breaks, perfect the first time. I saw this. Then he told the guy it needs this, it needs that. I took the arrangement home, brought it back, and the arrangement was better because of that. But he's not the kind of person who just stands up in front of a band just because he has a big name, who doesn't know each line of the music. He can actually sit down and read it for you and show you the application. I would say the proof is in the pudding. You can say everything you want to say, but when it comes time to sit down in front of people, put the music in front of you, that's when you're going to find out if you can do it.

Loza: And he can do it. I remember the first time I brought him to UCLA, we were doing arrangements that were newly written. And he sight-read on stage.

Ruiz: You've got to realize this man has been doing this with thousands, maybe five or ten thousand arrangements.

Loza: He sees ten bars ahead.

Ruiz: Like Frank Wess, from the Basie band, and these studio guys, Jon Faddis. These guys have done it so much that they read pages ahead to see what's coming. They also have intuition. You can tell more or less by the pattern of what's happening now what is going to come later. Actually doing it, that's when you find out how good a person is.

Loza: Francisco [Aguabella] was doing some of that last night with no music.

Ruiz: He has that insight. He was playing one of my tunes last night, and this tune has a section that is jazz and not a mambo type of section, and he played it as if he wrote the thing. I say, "Maybe you wrote this then. It's my tune but it sounds like you wrote it." I was very impressed with that. That is musicianship and experience. You can do it by ear. I always say that it's the blind musicians you've really got to look at, like Ray Charles and Rahsaan Roland Kirk and José Feliciano. Their world, their sight, is a sonic sight. They see in audio color.

Loza: They're almost better off. They're not inhibited by the notation. They're seeing some other notation.

Ruiz: We who have all our functioning senses need to learn from them. We have all these advantages that they don't have. But in this world, the creator gives us certain gifts for certain things. But if you have all your functions and you can see, you're going to be playing in the studio. Now I have gone with Tito to do shows, like at Kennedy Center— we played for the president of the United States; we played for President Clinton. Any situation that you're in you're going to be presented with music, and you're in front of people at the rehearsal, you've got to either do it or not. If you can't do, then we have to get somebody who can.

Loza: Did Bill Clinton sit in with you guys on that date?

Ruiz: No. He wasn't sitting in. He was there with the first lady, sitting right there, about from here to where that lamp is over there. I was so proud. He looked good, man. Better than he does on television.

Loza: Now you just did this album *Jazzin'*. I don't know how it's doing, but I would imagine it's going to do good.

Marín: It's already charted.

Loza: Now this woman, India, I really wasn't making it a point to listen to her, 'cause she was doing some commercial, some sort of new salsa, but I was really amazed by what she was doing.

Ruiz: We were all impressed.

Loza: It's a mind blower. "Jazzin'," which you wrote, is the name of the album. You got two tunes on that thing?

Ruiz: I wrote "Jazzin'" and I did the arrangements for "Wave" and "Love for Sale."

Loza: Well, let's talk about those three tunes. "Jazzin'" is a really Monkish thing. You're very Monkish; you've got a lot of Monk in your playing. It's a very bebopish line, a very difficult line, that main theme, and there's about two of them, really, which you bridge, and Tito's doing it on marimba and then she's singing it, and I guess you're also doing the lead on the piano, right?

Ruiz: Right.

Loza: Now, tell me about that. How long did it take Tito to learn that? Did he just jump on it? You know, it's not an easy tune to play.

Ruiz: With the amount of experience that he has and since he's familiar with that kind of music, he just had to do it like everybody else had to do it. He just had to sit down and play through the arrangement and learn. And he solos on it.

Loza: It seems to me that he is soloing better on the vibraphone than he was thirty years ago, when he did "Hong Kong Mambo."

Ruiz: He's supposed to be better. The man is better. He's seventy-three years old.

Loza: But he takes a hell of a solo, and then he plays that line. Now, we're talking about crazy intervals. And then she sings it right on. Did that take a while to formulate? Did they jump on it?

Ruiz: They did just what they did on the other pieces on the album.

Loza: What about India? Did you rehearse with her on the piano?

Ruiz: No, India had never done that before. She was a freestyle singer. This girl has an instrument of music that is unbelievable. I'm telling you that she is one of the greatest singers of our day right now. What happened with her was that she needed the right people to really hook her up. So what we did with her was a lot of rehearsing, and we got together and found out the right keys, and I would just work with her, as far as "Wave" and things like that, and the intervals, how to sing the intervals, things she had never encountered. She's only twenty-six years old. She was a freestyle artist and she made it big at Warner Brothers when she was sixteen years old with Louis Vega. From the time she was sixteen she already didn't need anybody. She had money. She had everything already. The woman is very beautiful, she's got a great personality, and she's fun to be with, but she knows what she wants. Tito was really the one who showed her. I would do something like "Love for Sale," and he would call in from California and say, "Let me hear it." We thought it was good, but he said, "No, no, do it again. It's got to be better than that. I want her to sing higher. I want her to do this and that." In other words, when we get it to where we think it's there, he takes it a second step.

Loza: The writing or the recording?

Ruiz: The arrangement was fine. But her singing on it. She sang it fine. It was beautiful, it was great. But he said, "No, hold it, she's got to go higher at the end. When the part comes [*sings*] 'follow me and climb the stairs,' you've got to make it seem like 'follow me and climb the stairs.' It has to have that raise." He knew she had that.

Loza: So he was teaching her.

Ruiz: Yeah, he taught her what to do. I also helped with my experience, because a lot of times Dave Valentín was not there and he was on the road, so I was the one who finished the project off. Dave was coproducer. Tito was producer, and Ralph Mercado and Jack Hooke were the executive producers. But I had to be there a lot of hours. I was spending eighteen-hour days in the studio. One thing you learn about the studio is every eight hours you've got to get out of there for a half an hour, because there's a magnetic or electronic field that you're saturated in that makes you tired and drains you. I had to be on top of the entire chorus; I had to be on top of the mixing. To me, it made me more tired than arranging or playing. I never knew this. I had to produce a record for George Adams, the saxophone player, years ago. We got five stars for that record. It came out real good. It's called *Paradise Space Station*. That was an easy production because all I had to do was make sure that the sound was right, because the musicians knew exactly what to do. But for this project, I had to really be on top of everything by the time I was there, because Tito was out and Dave was out at the same time. So I was in contact with them on the telephone all the time making sure that all the directions I got from them were carried out so that when they got back, everything would be fine. I think it was probably one of the greatest projects I have ever been on. But to see this girl do this and people listened to this tape up at Tito's restaurant—he played it for some of his friends—and they said, "That sounds like Ella Fitzgerald."

Loza: She died almost the same day it came out.

Ruiz: To me it sounded like Dinah Washington at times. But also I got feelings of Liza Minnelli, I got feelings of Barbra Streisand.

Loza: There's a little Broadway in there too. And she sounds like Nancy Wilson.

Marín: Nobody talks about that album like the people in the industry. People that don't know anything about it say, "This is a pop album, not a jazz album."

Loza: But it will be put in jazz.

Ruiz: But who could define "Jazzin'," the title tune, as a pop tune?

Marín: I'm talking about the album itself.

Ruiz: That's good because that's marketability. In other words, Tito's music and some of this music that I'm playing, tunes that I've written like "Home Cooking" and "Miami Girl," I have got kids listening to this record who listen to heavy metal. This is the *Beavis and Butthead* crowd. And they told me it was the greatest thing they ever heard.

Loza: They're hungry because nobody's giving it to them. And they will buy it. They will learn it. Just like how she's learning this stuff. She's got musical ability. It doesn't matter if she did hip-hop or whatever. If she's got the ability she can do it, but somebody's got to teach her.

Ruiz: So Tito and I guided her through that whole thing. He took her to places she never knew she could go.

Loza: I just hope she stays on it. Now did you write that tune specifically for the album *Jazzin'*?

Ruiz: Yes, I did. That tune was a tune that I used to . . . what I do when I'm sitting at home four or five o'clock in the morning, I might get up and go to the piano and just start off with something [*sings a short phrase*], like that, and I'll file that. I'll put it in the file cabinet because at that moment it won't go any further right there. There's no use in me prodding myself. It could go a hundred different directions, but it's not going where I want it to go, so I just say hold it, just sit there for a while and let's see what happens with you. Then all of a sudden I say now I could use this because it's good for the voice, you can sing this. Then [*sings another phrase*], I wrote that whole thing after that, from that one line.

Loza: You themed it, you developed it.

Ruiz: That was what got me into it. That was the first idea. From that automatic idea you could have gone any kind of direction, but it had to be bebop.

Loza: So that's a motif that you put away and then you go back to take from it.

Ruiz: Right. I've got a bunch of those at home now. Sometimes it has to come out of the clear blue sky.

Loza: So he wanted you to write something. He said, "I want you to write," so you worked it out.

Ruiz: I had to make sure that it was jazz, because when I presented that in front of the jazz community, my integrity and his integrity were held up—so that anybody who is not a bebop player that doesn't have the command of the instrument would not be able to play that song.

Loza: What made him decide to make that the title track?

Ruiz: He liked it the most.

Loza: "Love for Sale" was with the Basie band, right?

Ruiz: That sounds like a big band the way I arranged it, but it's the Latin Jazz Ensemble.

Loza: The same with "Wave?"

Ruiz: That's also the Latin Jazz Ensemble. I do that kind of arrangement as well, but he told me he wanted to get a sound with a small ensemble that would sound like a big band.

Loza: Yeah, you couldn't have had that sound with a whole band, because you still have the bop-type group sound.

Ruiz: I could have got the sound with a big band, but again, it would have sounded like a big band. It's a different thing. But the idea is to make it sound bigger than what it is with the instruments that you have. That's the power of arranging. If you put certain intervals together—even with two horns, if you harmonize two horns in a certain way, you create a bigger sound than if you just did it like in unison or another thing. You have to know when to put the leading tones in, the voice leading and things like that; that comes with experience.

Loza: Now, let me ask you something as a final topic. A lot of people divide the intellect from the intuitive, and I think this is a problem. Music is a form of intellectual communication, so why should it be divided from intuition? What I'm getting at is that if you take a person like Tito Puente, in your estimation, should he be recognized only as this intuitive artist who has these built-in abilities or as an intellectual? In other words, what is his music saying socially, intellectually, philosophically?

Ruiz: To me the end result—now, I can't speak for him or how he feels, but I can say my conception of what's going on—is that the integrity is there, the feeling is there. First of all, the feeling. The feeling of the music that makes the average person who has intellectual capability in different fields—whether it be medicine, whether it be literature, whether it be sports, or whatever—people can feel that music. We've got people coming from all different walks of life that love this record—lawyers, guys on the street—but the feeling first of all. The rest of it is academic—the tools that you need to be able to create, like yourself as a teacher and a writer. You have to know how to write, you have to know where to put your commas. Now you could have all of that, but if you ain't saying nothing, it doesn't mean anything. So what you're saying is your feeling. You're expressing what you're feeling, and then you just use all these literary tools or these grammatical tools to express yourself. But then another guy can come off the street and have a better feeling and have a better message. You can get an old lady, a bag lady, who might have more insight than a guy up on Wall Street.

Loza: She might not be able to write one comma or whatever.

Ruiz: It doesn't make any difference. That's how it works. I do a lot of things in academia too. I do a lot of clinics. What I do is, I find there's a lot of complacency. Not yourself, but there's a lot of great guys who can play, but so many teachers have degrees in classical music, and all of a sudden, this college has to have a jazz program. They're not going to fire the guy.

Loza: Pretty soon they're doing very perverted music because it's being misinterpreted.

Ruiz: Well, you have to be careful with that, because people have spent their life savings sending these kids to school to learn, so what you teach them you should be able to do. There should be some kind of cross-reference. But that all comes out in the wash. In other words, I would never take a teacher who does a blues by Charlie Parker, and I know this guy can't play it, and say it in front of his class, "Man, you've got no business being here. You don't know what you're doing." Because the student automatically will suffer. So what I do is I make the teacher look good in front of the student. All that stuff we'll take back in the back room: "Between you and me, man, listen, I think I wouldn't even do that." Because I don't want to close the door on myself. But I know musicians who do that, who say, "Listen, man, you got no business being here. These kids come out of college, and they can't play a gig in New York City." Even after you do come out of Berklee or wherever, you still have to pay your dues, because there are a lot of fine schools. What I try to do is make sure that I play the song for the kids first. Then they say, "Wow, we never heard that before." I'm talking about Des Moines, Iowa, or Lansing, Michigan. You got little blond-haired girls, nine years old, playing alto saxophone trying to play Charlie Parker. Some of these little girls play better than some of the guys in New York! If they were only able to get the right person. I know a girl called Sue Terry, who is maybe Russian or Jewish or something, but this girl plays her ass off, man. She's fantastic. She's better than some guys.

Loza: It's like the Olympics. All these countries like Mexico and Nicaragua, they could have gymnasts, and they were doing that, but that's not what they do. So that's why the thing to me is not even a reflection of the world society.

Ruiz: Fortunately you do have a lot of guys like yourself who have experience, who have records out, who know what's going on, and that's what saves academia.

Loza: Well, let's hope so.

Ruiz: I know so because I've been around. I get to places that nobody gets to as a performer.

Loza: Well, you're right. Somebody has to make it happen, like bringing Francisco [Aguabella] in to teach at UCLA. He's a faculty member now. We've got Nati Cano teaching mariachi in the department. We've brought out Tito Puente, and we pushed for Kenny Burrell, who's coming out in the fall. He's hired now as a full professor and director of the new jazz studies program. He's bringing in people like Billy Higgins, Oscar Brashear, Harold Land, Garnett Brown.

Ruiz: I've sat on panels with Kenny Burrell, and we had to judge bands at the New England Conservatory, we judged at the Berklee School of Music, and what I never did was give anybody a bad mark, because this relates to people's transcripts. This is kids' futures your dealing with. I only say, "Sounds good but needs more work." Never a negative thing because you have to realize what you're doing. You can't sit up there and say, "I'm so and so and I think——." You have to think of the big picture. This kid's transcript, he's going to try and get a scholarship somewhere [with it]. What you do is going to be taken by the department, by the regents of the college, and use this to determine a person's grade, which might determine their acceptance into an important program.

Loza: I've seen that happen. Some major artists don't know how to teach. They'll do that. They'll say, "Wait a minute, stop and play the right notes." This kid's blowing his ass off; leave him alone, like they left you alone when you were developing.

Ruiz: Because they don't know how to teach.

Loza: One more thing regarding Tito. Have you ever gotten a religious or spiritual impression from the man? What does all this stuff mean spiritually? Metaphysically?

Ruiz: Now you would have to discuss those religious aspects with him, but spiritually to me, it's a good feeling that makes people feel good when we are conveying our frequencies and energies that are unseen, that actually make people forget about their problems and their troubles. Whether it be a physical handicap—like even a person dancing in a wheelchair—people want to get up out of their seats. People who are depressed, they want to hear something good. They go away for that hour that they're listening to the music. They're not listening to any problems. So what do you call that? That's a spiritual healing. When you heal the spirit, that also helps heal the body. I'm sure you've heard of surgeons who say, "I never thought this guy was going to come out of an operation like this. I don't know how he made a recovery like this." So what happened? The spirit takes over. It's something we can't see. We all believe in it in our different ways. But it's all the same thing, and it all comes from one place. It comes from the Creator. So the purpose of us, as musicians, and what Tito is doing, is making people feel good. So if you are on this planet and you're making people feel good, giving them positive energy, that they're actually feeling good, this is better than therapy. These people might spend time on the couch and not get the same feeling with a psychiatrist that they would get from music. People who can't walk that well, they hear the music and all of a sudden get energy. There's a life force that emanates from this music that makes us feel good. That's the idea, the positive thing. This detracts from all the negative frequencies that are around us. So as musicians I feel that we are spiritual healers, and Tito definitely has it. He is probably one of the greatest there ever was at that.

Loza: In other words, like a *santero* or *curandero*.

Ruiz: Yeah, like a shaman or priest or wise man.

Loza: I've always felt as a musician that when I stop playing, I start to get sick, like psychotic or neurotic.

Ruiz: Yes, because you have nothing to do but focus on problems.

Loza: Once you've been at this state, this state that you're talking about, this curing state, this positive energy, and you take yourself out of it, it can be highly damaging. It makes you realize why people have to spend so much negative energy doing negative things, whether its gang-banging or exploiting prostitutes; they're having experiences of it then.

Ruiz: But then again, you get the bad and the good. You get the bitter with the sweet. The thing is to try and get more good than bad because you're always going to run into somebody who is not going to agree with you.

Loza: You've got to deal with it.

Ruiz: But I find that a lot of people who come with negative attitudes and a look in their face—and I can read people because I've been around, professionally for thirty years—you can see it coming. But after we play the music you see a change in these people. All of a sudden they say, "Wow, they're not looking at me now as this Puerto Rican guy" or "this Hispanic person," and the racism and poison has been purged. Now they're saying, "This guy made me feel good. So they're not all bad, are they? After all, maybe I should meet more of these people because I'm feeling better with this guy." It makes people think.

Publicity still. (Photo by Martin Cohen, LP Percussion, 1983.)

Rumba para Monk, a 1989 recording by Jerry González, who performed with Puente during the early eighties and is interviewed in chapter 5. (Courtesy of Sunnyside Communications, Inc.)

Poster announcing a Tito Puente scholarship benefit at Lincoln Center, May 13, 1983.

In concert with UCLATINO, directed by the author, as part of "Noche Mexicana" (UCLA Mexican Arts Series, 1988), which also featured Linda Ronstadt, Poncho Sanchez, Nati Cano, Lalo Guerrero, and Daniel Valdez. (Courtesy of UCLA Mexican Arts Series.)

Puente performing with the UCLA ensemble UCLATINO, directed by the author (at left in trumpet section), 1983. (Photo by Claudia Cuevas.)

Photo in celebration of Puente's star on the Hollywood Walk of Fame. (Photo by Martin Cohen, 1990.)

Publicity still that became the cover image for Puente's 1991 *Master Timbalero*. (Photo by Martin Cohen.)

Poster distributed in New York area announcing the Fourteenth Anniversary Concert of the Tito Puente Scholarship Fund, a tribute to Dizzy Gillespie, Machito, and Mario Bauzá featuring various guest artists at the famed Apollo Theatre in Harlem.

Program cover of the sixteenth annual Tito Puente Scholarship Fund benefit concert, July 27, 1996, celebrating Puente's fifty years in show business and featuring the orchestras of Puente and Johnny Pacheco.

THE FAR SIDE — By GARY LARSON

Aug. 11, 1957: Tito Puente loses the beat

Nov. 3, 1963: Ella Fitzgerald hits a flat note

Sept. 9, 1948: Dizzy Gillespie can't find B♭

July 14, 1974: Oscar Peterson forgets the chords to "Heart and Soul."

Infamous moments in jazz

Puente is advertised along with other jazz greats in a Blue Note Tokyo pamphlet (1996). As of the late nineties, he continued to perform live at the most prestigious clubs throughout the world. (Courtesy of Blue Note Tokyo. Photo transfer by Ko Sasaki.)

Puente is humorized along with other jazz greats on the cover of a greeting card. (The Far Side © 1988 FarWorks, Inc. Used by permission of Universal Press Syndicate. All rights reserved.)

Tito Puente receiving the ASCAP Founders Award in 1994, presented by Sheila E, flanked by ASCAP President Marilyn Bergman and Arturo Sandoval. (*ASCAP Play-back*, Sept. 1994.)

Publicity photo for Tito Puente Jr. and the Latin Rhythm Crew, who recorded a Latin rap album on the EMI Latin label in 1996. (Courtesy of Tito Puente Jr.)

Ray Santos.

Chico Sesma.

Hilton Ruiz.

Poncho Sanchez. (Courtesy
of the Berkeley Agency.)

6

Musical Style and Innovation

I N reflecting on the music of Tito Puente, one must inevitably address the issues of his compositional skill, musical virtuosity, leadership, showmanship, and innovation. With the present chapter I have attempted to deal with all these factors in a brief sketch of and commentary on a diverse selection of his recorded music, representing the more than fifty-year span of his career, from the early years to the present.

Early Repertory

Puente's apprenticeship with the Machito Orchestra during 1940–42 had a profound impact on his early arranging and composing style. His orchestrational approach flowered most, however, in the years following his return from his wartime naval service. First while experimenting extensively with the navy bands and then afterward while studying at Juilliard and learning the Schillinger system with Richard Bender, Puente ventured into musical territory that would eventually become his stylistic trademark. His early recordings, however, steadfastly project the dominant Cuban stylistics of not only Machito and Bauzá but also the earlier Cuban *son* tradition of Arsenio Rodríguez and Beny Moré, among many other essential Cuban stylists.

The compositions "Picadillo," "Abaniquito," and "Esy" typify Puente pieces recorded during the years 1949–51. As historically contextualized in chapter 1, "Picadillo" emerged as a watershed piece for Puente in a number of ways. Composed by Puente when he led his initial orchestra, the Picadilly Boys, in 1948, the tune, which Puente had originally referred to as "un picadillo," or a "mish-mash," was recorded in 1949. The "oriental" flavor with which Puente has often characterized the composition sets itself immediately into motion with an opening brass theme following an eight-bar *tumbao*-patterned solo for bass and piano left hand (see example 1).*

The strictly instrumental (no vocals) arrangement proceeds from the main brass theme into a highly embellished and syncopated piano solo, significantly tapping into the simple yet gripping "orientalism" of the main theme, which is constructed on a combination of a quartal harmonic structure and a somewhat pentatonic melody. The arrangement is an example of musical economy, yet it affords both musician and dancer the opportunity to create and embellish in a most expansive palette of possibilities. Syncopation, harmonic curiosity, and rhythmic consistency and freedom converge in an aural setting that in 1949 emerged as a new sound. Puente inaugurated his innovative principles and style with a highly simple yet interesting piece of music. One of the essentials of this style was his use of the orchestra as a whole, including the brass section, as a percussive device—a trait that would eventually come to distinguish the Puente sound from that of other major Latin music artists.

> I am a rhythmic, syncopated arranger mostly. I am involved with rhythmic forms of a percussive type of arranging where I interject a lot of brass with Latin percussion, because in our music, brass is a very essential instrument due to the fact that many years ago in Cuba some of the *conjuntos,* like in Mexico, were always using trumpets. Then saxes got involved and all that. So my expansion into arranging came when mostly American bands had more extensions into their arrangements, due to the opening of the voicings in the saxophones, which gave it a real fat chord. But the Latin arrangers were not studying enough to be able to do that. We were always with our tonics and triads and sixths, you know. All of a sudden we got hip. We went into major seventh chords; but these types of harmonies don't match your typical Latin music. The only way you can go into an extension of these type of harmonies and keep it basic Latin is if you use the right figuration that goes with the clave, which I was discussing in the percussion class. You've got to have the right bass figuration and the right syncopation of the piano—what we call the *guajeo* in Spanish. It's like a riff. Each riff identifies a different type of music. (Puente 1984)

The following observations of pianist and bandleader Charlie Palmieri expand on Puente's percussive concept:

> I have known Tito Puente since we met at the old musicians union hall almost thirty years ago. He was then the contractor for Fernando Alvarez's Copacabana (nightclub)

---

*Example 1 and subsequent Ascencio Publishing examples in this chapter are arrangements Puente rescored, usually for a larger orchestra, without the original vocal sections.

Picadillo

Edited and engraved by G. Di Lorenzo

Composed and arranged by Tito Puente

Example 1

Piano Solo

Example 1 (cont.)

Samba band, and he gave me the band's piano chart. We worked together as sidemen and as I played with him I heard drumming and timbal playing I had never heard before. His arrangements were ahead of their time. While he was still with the Copa band, Tito organized his group, for which I played piano at the Palladium Ballroom every Sunday afternoon. It was Tito who inspired me to study composition and arranging. Many people still do not know that Tito is a fine pianist and that he was the first to introduce the vibraphone in Latin music (Cugat introduced the marimba). Aside from being a top notch composer and arranger, Tito is most famous for his timbal work. Prior to his drumming popularity, most musicians wanted to be pianists because of Anselmo Sacassás, Gilberto Frank Ayala and Noro Morales. It was Tito who popularized los timbales and inspired hundreds of drummers who followed his steps. (in Salazar 1977c, 26–27)

"Abaniquito," Puente's first major popular hit, was a product of the bandleader's newly formed Tito Puente Orchestra in 1949. Recorded toward the end of that year, the arrangement featured the orchestra's new singer, Cuban *sonero* Vicentico Valdés. Much like "Picadillo," the composition begins with a bass and piano *tumbao* pattern followed by a repeated brass riff, embellished by bongo accents and improvisation, or *repicando*, performed by Manny Oquendo. The vocal structure of the piece is basic: improvised verses (*versos* or *coplas*) answered by a repeated chorus (*coro*). The mostly improvised, playful text is based on the rhetorical motif of the *abaniquito*, a word meaning "little fan." The following is a loose transcription of Vicentico Valdés's improvised *soneos*, or *inspiraciones*, with the repeated chorus incorporating the word *abaniquito*.

Abaniquito	*The Little Fan*
Ocho yo doy por un medio.	Eight I give for a half.
Coro: Abaniquito de a real.	*Chorus:* Little fan for a quarter.
Abanico, abanico, abanico de a real.	Fan, fan, fan for a quarter.
Coro: Abaniquito de a real.	*Chorus:* Little fan for a quarter.
¡Oye, oye, oye ponme a gozar!	Listen, listen, listen, make me enjoy!
Coro: Abaniquito de a real.	*Chorus:* Little fan for a quarter.
Rumbero bueno mira, vamos a rumbear.	Good rumbero look, let's do the rumba.
Coro: Abaniquito de a real.	*Chorus:* Little fan for a quarter.
¡Ocho yo doy por un real!	Eight I give for a quarter!
Coro: Abaniquito de a real.	*Chorus:* Little fan for a quarter.
Mira, mira, no, no.	Look, look, no, no.
Cumbara, cumbara, cumbara ponme a gozar.	*Cumbara, cumbara, cumbara* make me enjoy!

Coro: Abaniquito de a real.	*Chorus:* Little fan for a quarter.
María linda, vamo' a gozar.	Pretty María, let's have fun.
Coro: Abaniquito de a real.	*Chorus:* Little fan for a quarter.
Abanico, abanico, abanico de a real.	Fan, fan, fan for a quarter.
Coro: Abaniquito de a real.	*Chorus:* Little fan for a quarter.
Oye, oye, oye vamo' a rumbear.	Listen, listen, listen, let's do the rumba.
Coro: Abaniquito de a real.	*Chorus:* Little fan for a quarter.
Mira, mira mamá, pa' gozar.	Look, look mama, to have fun.
Coro: Abaniquito de a real.	*Chorus:* Little fan for a quarter.
¡Manteca! Abanico, abanico, abanico, abanico, abanico, mira, pero no, no no no. Cosa buena.	*Manteca!* Fan, fan, fan, fan, fan, look, but no, no no no. Good thing.
Coro: Abaniquito de a real.	*Chorus:* Little fan for a quarter.
Abanico, mira ¡pero pa'gozar!	Fan, look but to have fun!
Coro: Abaniquito de a real.	*Chorus:* Little fan for a quarter.
Oye, mira pa' rumbear.	Listen, look to do the rumba.
Coro: Abaniquito de a real.	*Chorus:* Little fan for a quarter.
Abanico, abaniquito no no [*bis*]	Fan, little fan no no [*twice*]

Of significant interest in the arrangement of "Abaniquito" is a mambo riff following the initial vocal section just cited and based on the Dizzy Gillespie–Chano Pozo melodic riff of "Manteca." It is essential to point out that Puente, at this early date of 1949, was popularizing both on record and especially at the Palladium dance hall the earlier innovative collaborative concepts of Machito, Bauzá, and Gillespie-Pozo in the fusion of Cuban dance music and bop. Puente himself consistently recognized this marriage of musical styles and the importance it played not only in his own stylistic development but also in that of Latin music in general, with specific reference to the mambo.

The mambo differs, let's say from the rumba, in that it concentrates more on the off-beat, the after-beat, like modern jazz—whereas the rumba is mostly *on* the beat. And the mambo has much more syncopation in its melodic form than the rumba. I think any person who digs jazz will dig the mambo. . . . Rhythm is what you dance to, and the mambo is popular because its strong rhythms make for good dance music. What is making it even more successful is the combination of jazz elements with the mambo. Bop, for example, by itself has crazy sounds harmonically, and is not easy to dance to. That's why bop bands are putting in conga drums and adding a mambo flavor to their work. Similarly, in my band, I use certain aspects of jazz. In our arrangements we use some of the modern sounds in the manner of Dizzy Gillespie and Stan Kenton, but we never lose the authenticity of the Latin rhythm. (Puente 1992)

"Esy," another mambo, was recorded by Puente and his orchestra in 1951 and was dedicated to Esy Morales, a Puerto Rican flutist who died in 1950. He was the brother of pianist Noro Morales, with whom he performed in addition to Xavier Cugat. He also led his own band. Like "Picadillo," it is an instrumental, but it differs markedly from the former in its general style, voicing, orchestration, and melodic rhythm. With much more of a jazz influence, the composition is marked by various themes and rhythmic or melodic transitions (see example 2). Harmonically it is deeply textured with a fabric of seventh chords in various inversions, from the initial piano entrance to the trumpet and saxophone figurations that follow respectively at measures 13 and 25. Also of note is the divergent jazz evocation of these two separate horn themes, which are superimposed on the consistent mambo pattern maintained throughout the piece and based on the initial piano entrance, although orchestrated in various combinations both with the rhythm section and brass. In "Esy" Puente thus began to explore even more the integration of Latin and jazz, doing so in an orchestrated version that began to exhibit the development of his own individual mark. The harmonic-melodic complex forged by Puente in the tune again evokes the "orchestral percussion" alluded to earlier and certainly represented a new and innovative turn in the directions that Latin dance music was to take during the early fifties in New York City.

"Mambo Diablo" constitutes another classic recording from Puente's earlier repertory. Significant to this recording was Puente's use of the vibraphone, which he had studied during his Juilliard period. Although other Latin music bandleaders had experimented with the use of marimba, Puente was the first to adopt the vibraphone as a standard option in his orchestra. Once again Puente's innovation bore witness to the impact of jazz, for the instrument had been incorporated in jazz performances some years before, especially by Lionel Hampton and Milt Jackson. The vibraphone eventually came to be a typical instrument in Latin jazz, becoming the featured instrument of ensembles including those of Cal Tjader, Joe Loco, Joe Cuba, and Louie Ramírez, among many others.

Recorded in 1949–51, "Mambo Diablo" is based on a principal motif announced solo by Puente at the outset of the arrangement. Patterned on the syncopated basic theme notated in example 3, the riff does not resolve harmonically or modulate throughout the piece. The brass section punctuates the mambo riff at various points, always reinforcing and accenting the vibraphone as the featured instrument and its line as the "motif" of the composition. Puente improvises fluidly and generously throughout the arrangement, exhibiting the strong integration between mambo and bop that he had already developed. His melodic and rhythmic concepts borrowed directly from both traditions; the blending of these styles, however, was leading to totally new and different forms.

Esy

Dedicated to "Esy" Morales

Edited and engraved by G. Di Lorenzo

Composed and arranged by Tito Puente

Example 2

Example 2 (cont.)

Example 2 (cont.)

Example 2 (cont.)

Example 2 (cont.)

Example 3

Meanwhile, on the dance floor, the paying public adapted to instrumental mambos like "Mambo Diablo" with no apparent conflicts, aesthetic or ideological. In retrospect, the context was radical.

At the same time that he produced these innovative experiments, however, Puente also continued to perform and record typical mambos of the day. Among the scores of recordings he was releasing at the time, his arrangement of E. Duarte Brito's "Dónde estabas tú" shows particularly well how he maintained the traditional and popular Cuban-style mambos. Puente's recording featured Vicentico Valdés on vocals and Al Escobar on piano, the latter playing in a progressive yet typical style of Cuban dance music. One interesting feature of the arrangement is the saxophone riffs that characterized the mambo style of Pérez Prado, who may not have been the most popular Latin bandleader in New York but who had nevertheless influenced not only Tito Puente but also other great bandleaders of the era, from Cuba to the United States, including such notables as Machito, Beny Moré, Miguelito Valdés, and Tito Rodríguez. In addition, the singing style of *sonero* Valdés was another essential ingredient in maintaining the strict Cuban inflections and stylizations important to Puente's artistic philosophy, especially when he was interpreting the more traditional and popular dance repertory; nor did Puente underestimate the significance and meaning of the various lyrics and *inspiraciones* to the dancing and listening public. Although a great many among the Palladium's audiences did not understand the Spanish texts, the majority did, and Puente strove to cater to all his clients.

The RCA Years

In 1955 Puente signed an exclusive contract with RCA Records that extended through 1960. He and his orchestra had already been experiencing notable transitions and changes in terms of style and the market. In spite of Puente's struggle with the company, the RCA years in many ways were conducive not only to his stylistic innovations but also to his desire to reach a larger public. He was now signed to an international record company that was attempting to reach the Latin market, both here and abroad, especially in Latin America. Other artists that RCA was producing, especially at its studios in Mexico City, included Pérez Prado, Luis Alcaraz, and Beny Moré. Puente was now, in a marketing sense, competing on a new level—not a more important level, but a different and in many ways more risky one.

In 1956 Puente recorded the classic *Cuban Carnival* LP, which proceeded to become his first major success with RCA. Just prior to this, in 1955, Puente had recorded his experimental *Puente in Percussion* for Tico Records with percussionists Mongo Santamaría, Willie Bobo, Patato Valdez, Candido Camero, and bassist Bobby Rodríguez, all of whom were still members of his orchestra for *Cuban Carnival*. (As was mentioned in chapter 1, the sequel LP, *Top Percussion,* was recorded for RCA in 1957.) The "orches-trated percussion" concept of Puente's still-evolving style transferred onto *Cuban Carnival,* and the unique and innovative sound of Puente's orchestra became a matter not only of the avant-garde in Latin dance music but also of popular approval. Whether a typical *son*-structured sung mambo or a radical departure in instrumental scoring, all Puente's arrangements and compositions were danceable, and clients continued to attend Puente's performances and to purchase his records.

One of the most distinguishable and innovative cuts on the *Cuban Carnival* album was the opening track, "Elegua Changó." Titled for the names of two of the African and Afro-Cuban Yoruba *orishas* (supernatural patron saints or deities), the piece is an amal-gam of traditional Afro-Cuban drumming and progressive orchestration incorporating multiple effects in texture and phrasing as well as extended harmonic structures and melodic experimentation. Puente had now gone well beyond the normative or typical practices of the day. A blues-toned trumpet solo, making use of growl and plunger tech-niques, largely characterizes the first part of the arrangement. Strategically, he limited the LP to only one such composition, and the public endorsed its inclusion as part of his growing and expanding repertory.

Two pieces on *Cuban Carnival* that eventually became standards in Latin dance music were "Pa' los rumberos" and "Que será mi china." "Pa' los rumberos," which would be recorded by Carlos Santana twenty-five years later, is a driving, dynamic arrangement that also exploited the percussive range of Puente's orchestra. A basic but intensely force-ful chorus theme frames the composition, which is constructed on wide voicings, pierc-ing high-register brass accents, typical saxophone mambo riffs, and extensive conga (Mongo Santamaría) and timbal (Puente) solos and improvisation. Various orchestral and percussive breaks also highlight the classic arrangement. Transcribed in example 4 is the final section of Puente's timbal solo, which culminates the arrangement as the orches-tra blends into the solo, climaxing through a cleverly assembled series of rhythmic and harmonic patterns, notably that of the clave.

Also of interest is the original introduction as compared to the more contemporary one that has become associated with "Pa' los rumberos," which Puente often uses as an introductory number at his performances. After Santana recorded the tune in 1972 (on his *Santana III* LP), Puente decided to incorporate Santana's innovative, rock-flavored introduction and coda, which were based on the riff shown in example 5.

Immediately following "Pa' los rumberos" on the album is the classic and highly loved cha-cha "Que será mi china" (titled "Que será" on the original RCA LP). By the midfifties the Cuban *cha-cha-chá* (or cha-cha) had become the vogue among aficionados of Latin music in the United States and abroad. Although the form was originally stylized largely by Cuban *charanga* ensembles, including those of Enrique Jorrín and Orquesta Aragón, Puente absorbed the traditional flute figurations and unison vocal lines of the style into "Que será mi china," among many other cha-chas that he was orchestrating. Of particu-lar interest in his arrangement of "Que será mi china" is the broken, rhythmic introduc-tion that becomes somewhat of an orchestral motif for the piece, followed immediately by the principal vocal chorus and theme (see example 6).

Pa' Los Rumberos

FINAL TIMBAL SOLO

Example 4

Example 4 (cont.)

Para Los Rumberos

Edited and engraved by G. Di Lorenzo

Composed and arranged by Tito Puente

Example 5

Example 5 (cont.)

Example 5 (cont.)

Que Será Mi China

Example 6

Another track on *Cuban Carnival* that merits attention here is "Cuban Fantasy," which closes the album as the last of eleven pieces. Puente's arrangement of the Ray Bryant composition features his vibraphone on the main head and bridging riffs. A highly jazz-oriented ambience is set in a mambo framework, followed by a tenor saxophone solo with a smooth blues, "cool-jazz" flavor. Puente's "orientalism" again emerges at measure 32 (see example 7), a riff structured on quartal harmonies and a pentatonic melody. Running

Cuban Fantasy

lead sheet

1

Example 7

Example 7 (cont.)

only one minute and fifty-four seconds, the arrangement is a prime example of a romantic, richly assembled and executed economy of sound. Example 7 shows the main theme along with its basic harmonic structure.

In assessing the evolution of Tito Puente's musical style and that of Latin music in general, it is essential to refer to some of Puente's own thoughts, especially those on the issue of rhythmic, percussive concepts as adapted in Latin arranging and figurations and their transformations in jazz settings. This has been a consistent topic of many of my conversations with Puente. The following is a transcript of a lecture he gave at UCLA in 1994:

> Now, I presume you're all arrangers, or you're studying composition and arranging.
> It's very important in Latin arranging to match your figurations. That's why those
> little sticks [claves] are sometimes at the bottom of the score. I'll write the clave beat
> sometimes—

> Every time I write a figuration of some sort as a procedure on the piano, it's a *guajeo*
> [*writes a figure on the board*]:

Guajeo is a version that you can play on the piano. If you're going to be writing a thing like *guaguancó,* you will go like that [plays the piano pattern]. That's the type of figuration you need for that type of music, *guaguancó* music. And also for an up-tempo mambo, but usually for an up-tempo mambo we play it like [*plays the pattern*]—that's the changes you want. They don't sound to me like "Tea for Two" changes. That's what these Puerto Ricans play, "Tea for Two" changes. They can't get into Latin jazz because to get into Latin jazz you've got to get into the real harmonic aspect of the music—a lot of changes. There's a difference between Latin jazz and Latin music. See, a lot of Latin musicians think that they can play Latin jazz, but it's not that easy, because Latin music, once you get away from the harmonic aspect of real typical music, you lose its authenticity and its roots. When you're playing Latin [*demonstrates piano pattern for "Tea for Two" changes*]—that makes it. You just count the two vowels if you want to go through changes. If you keep that figuration, that's what gives you the Latin taste of the music, which makes it different than jazz. Now when you'd be playing Latin jazz, you'd be playing more figuration. . . . That's the difference between Latin and Latin jazz, because I get that question asked by all the Latin musicians when I go to South America . . . some of them are really into the jazz, some are not. But you really have to have a concept of jazz to be able to play Latin jazz.

I was very fortunate that I was born in the neighborhood of Spanish Harlem in New York, and I was brought up with Latino music and jazz music at the same time. So that's why you can combine both musics, because I have the basics of the Latin rhythm and then I studied my years at the conservatory at Juilliard. I studied my harmonics and all that so I could combine most of it with the clave, and that's what made it more interesting music. That's why Latin jazz has become very popular around the whole world, because you take the same jazz melodies that people relate to and then put that Latin influence underneath. That causes excitement to the music, like Dizzy Gillespie did forty, fifty years ago when he had Chano Pozo and he did "Manteca" and "Tin Tin Deo" and "Night in Tunisia" and those kind of real hip tunes. They also had that Latin influence there, and he is one of the masters, one of my mentors between Machito and Mario Bauzá. . . . These people were involved in putting jazz and Latin together. People like Bauzá were responsible for people like us bringing out this kind of music and making it bigger and bigger and worldwide known. And the secret of that is the percussion, naturally, because the Latin percussion underneath these jazz melodies gives more excitement. (Puente 1994)

It was especially during the midfifties that Puente began applying such juxtaposed jazz and Latin techniques in his arrangements and compositions. Two albums in which he specifically sought to combine the elements of Latin and jazz were *Puente Goes Jazz* and *Night Beat,* both surveyed in chapter 1. *Night Beat* featured some especially progressive Puente compositions and arrangements, notably the instrumental "mambo jazz" work entitled "Mambo Beat," featuring solos by Joe Grimm on baritone saxophone, Doc Severinson on trumpet, and Puente on timbales.

Also significantly representing this period was another LP, *Mucho Puente,* which included tracks recorded from 1955 through 1957. The recording represented yet another stylistic and conceptual shift for Puente, who featured a variety of instruments and ensembles with which he was experimenting at the time, notably his vibraphone, Dek-

Tette (a ten-piece ensemble), big band, and ample additions of accompanying woodwinds and strings. The album ranged from classic Latin American compositions adapted to Puente's vibraphone and ensemble, such as "What a Difference a Day Makes" ("Cuando vuelva a tu lado," by María Grever), "Noche de ronda" (Agustín Lara and María Teresa Lara), "Son de la loma" (Miguel Matamoros), and "Almendra" (Abelardo Valdez), to tunes that had emerged here and abroad, including "Lullaby of the Leaves" (Bernice Petkere and Joe Young), "Tea for Two" (Vincent Youmans and Irving Caesar), and "Mack the Knife" (Kurt Weill and Bertolt Brecht), from *The Threepenny Opera,* in which Puente uses an interesting beat on a mambo scheme.

One especially notable stylistic innovation for Latin music at this time was Puente's use of electric guitar, primarily interpreted by Johnny Smith, as well as George Barnes and Al Caiola. Puente makes ample use of his vibraphone, both orchestrally and soloistically, on all but four of the fifteen tracks on the album, all of which he arranged.

One of the most complex and innovative of Puente's arrangements on *Mucho Puente* is that of "Tea for Two," which had become a major hit in popular music of the day. Puente's adaptation of the song, however, is a highly danceable cha-cha in which he maximized the instrumentation of his big band to dynamic effect. The transcription in example 8 shows the basic melodic and harmonic scheme of the opening section and the principal statement of the tune. Following this section are various riff sections featuring different instrumental sections in the orchestra. At one climactic juncture the arrangement transforms into double time and the trumpet section echoes the *guajeo* patterns of the piano, which plays a dynamic role throughout the arrangement.

Dance Mania

Recorded in New York City in November and December 1957 and released in 1958, *Dance Mania* was considered by many critics to be Puente's career watershed. By the time the LP was recorded, Puente was already established as a bold arranger and an innovative composer in the musical world. With the release of this recording, however, he also established something of a precedent for Latin music, for his eclectic, experimental approach became even more popular with the public. The record's innovative mosaic of sound was characterized by a diversity of new arrangements and musicians as well as a highly integrated mix of musical ideas and styles. One of the major differences in Puente's band and sound by this time was *sonero* Santitos Colón, who had joined the orchestra in 1956, although *Dance Mania* was his first recording with the ensemble. Unlike the majority of Puente's previous vocalists, Colón was not Cuban and did not adhere to what some might refer to as a strict or typical Cuban style of singing in terms of both tonal inflection and the execution of improvised *inspiraciones*. His new, distinctive style was especially marked by a high vocal register and a less strict, sometimes nonrhyming improvisation in which he did not implement some of the more traditional *copla* poetic forms, which Cuban *soneros* had tended to retain in both innovative and traditional streams. Of spe-

Tea for Two

condensed score

Example 8

Example 8 (cont.)

Example 8 (cont.)

cial attention on *Dance Mania* was Colón's exquisite rendition of the bolero "Estoy siempre junto a tí," composed by Pepe Delgado.

"El cayuco," the initial track of the LP's eleven arrangements, became an immediate hit with the dancing and listening public. Opening with a syncopated interplay of riffs and breaks among the saxophone and brass sections, the piece is structured on a *son montuno* rhythmic base but displays a cha-cha orientation in its arrangement and vocal motif, both textually and stylistically. A *coro*, notated in example 9, follows the instrumental introduction, followed by brief *soneos* by Colón.

Coro

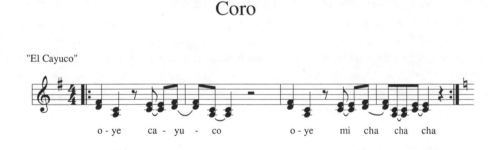

Example 9

One of the interesting aspects of "El cayuco," as with some other arrangements on the LP, is the lack of any instrumental solos. Brass and woodwind riffs, interplay, and breaks highlight the piece in a manner that lends itself to a typical yet modern interpretation for the period. Puente continued to make a practice of catering to the evolving yet traditional eclecticism of his Palladium dance public. Thus, the album ranges from arrangements like "El cayuco," based on a vocal and ensemble emphasis, to pieces exhibiting complete instrumental arrangements, to ones featuring extended, innovative, and virtuosic improvised solos among both the horns and percussion. The second track of the LP, "Complicación" (composed by Francisco Aguabella), although a typical popular dance *guaguancó,* follows a formula similar to that of "El cayuco."

A highly interesting arrangement for the period follows, that of "3-D Mambo," a "mambo jazz instrumental" composed and arranged by Ray Santos, who performed as alto saxophonist at different points in the Puente orchestra, although not on *Dance Mania.* Literally a hybrid of a mambo underpinning supporting a swing overlay of ensemble orchestration, the composition is largely structured on a principal theme built on a mambo riff introduced in the brass and diversely recycled in the saxophone section. A short two minutes and twenty-three seconds long, the piece served as a dance segue to which the public became highly attracted. The piece symbolized the interaction of Latin and swing dance aficionados and lent to the growing relationship of these two publics meeting on dance floors at clubs such as the Palladium, as well as in record shops and jazz clubs.

Also included on the album was another of Puente's major compositions, "Hong Kong Mambo" (example 10). By this time Puente's use of the "oriental" sound had become part of his stylistic persona, and he continued to exploit the concept in creative fashion. Based on a basic mambo riff with a heavy jazz feel and inflection, the piece opens with Puente stating the unitary theme on marimba (using it for the first time in place of the vibraphone), again evoking the emerging Latin jazz sound of the period as personified through other vibraphonists, such as Cal Tjader.

But Puente was also able to exploit the wider dimensions of his large orchestra, which differed from the small groups of Tjader and other artists experimenting with the Latin jazz formula. Again, Puente was defying the promotional odds of both dance halls and Latin jazz circles when arrangements such as "Hong Kong Mambo" became standards for both contexts. And through it all, people kept dancing.

Yet another arrangement on the album that would become a long-lasting standard in the Latin dance repertory was "Mambo gozón." A high-energy composition by Puente, the piece opens with one of his stylistic orchestral break introductions, followed by a solo piano *guajeo.* At the seventh measure (letter A in example 11) the saxophones, voiced in fifths, enter in the form of the *guajeo,* counterpointed eight measures after by the brass section of trumpets and trombones.

The main *coro* enters immediately after this instrumental introduction. Upon the opening *coros* of "A gozar este rico mambo, a gozar" ("to enjoy this rich mambo, to enjoy"), Santitos Colón immediately begins his *inspiraciones* (see example 12).

The *coro* section is followed by an orchestrated interlude (or bridge) and then repeated. A shortened version ("a gozar") is repeated three times, accented by bridging breaks and followed each time by an orchestrated build constructed of double eighth-note patterns, culminating each time with a percussion solo. The last appearance of this section ends the arrangement as shown in example 13.

As with many of Puente's mambos, "Mambo gozón" is representative of the typical progression of the mambo by the midfifties among Latin dance bands, especially those

Hong Kong Mambo (excerpt)

Tito Puente - marimba

Example 10

Mambo Gozon

Edited and engraved by G. Di Lorenzo

Composed and arranged by Tito Puente

Example 11

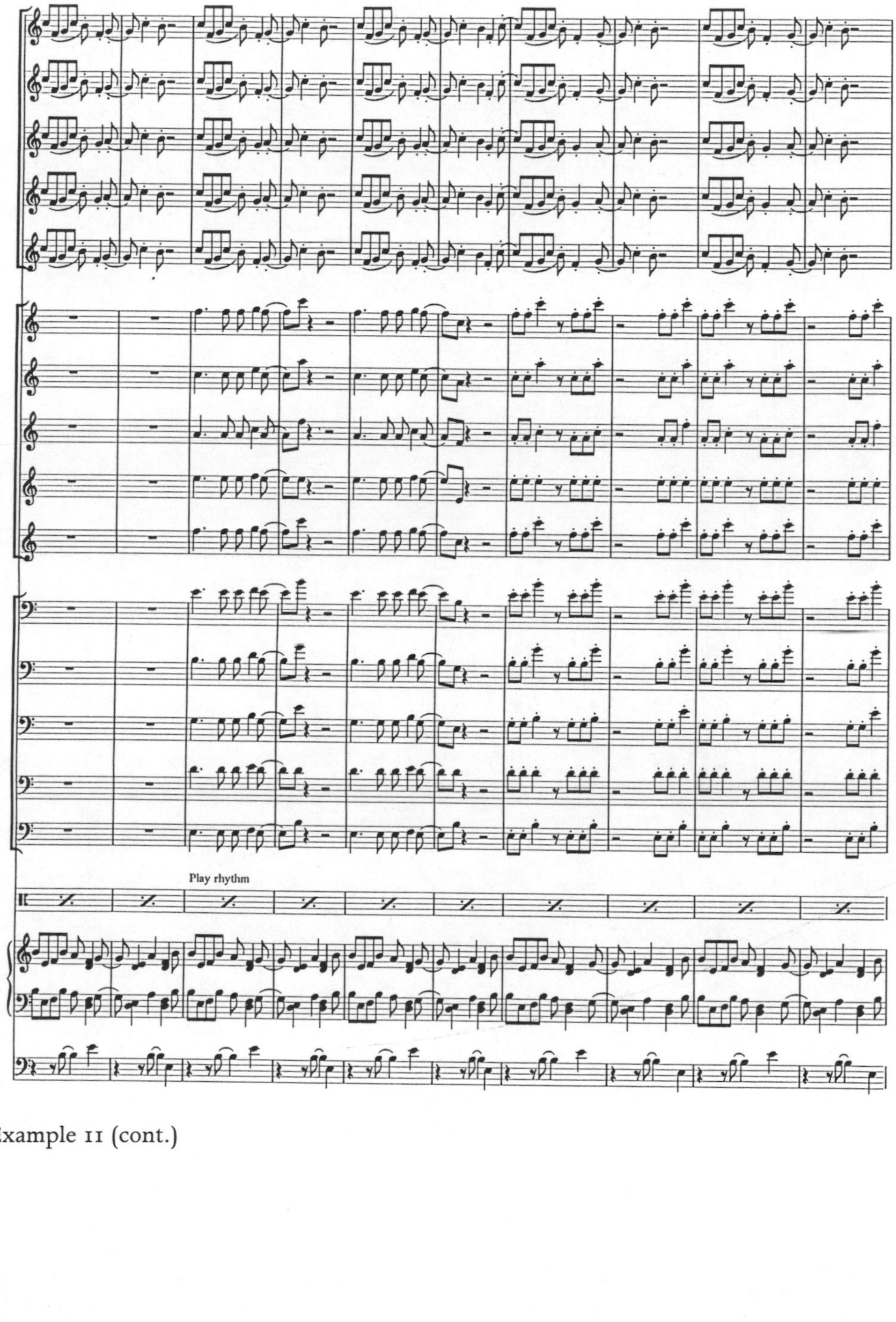

Example 11 (cont.)

Example 11 (cont.)

"Mambo Gozon"

- zar es - te ri - co mam - bo   a go - zar   a go-

Example 12

Example 13

Example 13 (cont.)

of New York City. With respect to certain of the genre's practices, however, Puente's mambos pushed the envelope with their harmonies, instrumentation, and consistently changing employment of his "orchestral percussion" and resultant stylistic character.

The mambo had originally been a "riff" section of the more formalized Cuban *son* structure and was previously used by Cachao and Orestes López in Cuba. Many traditional *guarachas,* for example, continued to be constructed with a complete verse section, a *coro* and *inspiración* section, and a separate "mambo" section, which also became part of the classic Cuban *danzón.* In the hands of the modern mambo practitioners of the fifties such as Puente, Machito, Rodríguez, and Prado, the mambo had become a basic formula structured mainly on instrumental riffs and embellished with various *coro* sections. Notable changes in tempo or specific rhythmic patterns were not the rule in the mambo during the period immediately before and after Puente's *Dance Mania,* which in many senses epitomized and culminated the mambo style of the late forties through the fifties.

Into the Sixties

In 1960, in his presidential inaugural address, John F. Kennedy proclaimed the "New Frontier" as a metaphor for the future of the nation and the world. The following decade would see radical social change and shifts in culture. Tito Puente was no exception to the spreading philosophical, technological, and social transformations that came to be symbolized by the sixties.

In 1960, for example, Puente immersed himself in a project of musical innovation and complexity. In his own words, it had for years been his "contention that jazz and Latin could be combined into a powerful force in music where listeners and dancers could enjoy these great rhythms together" (Morrow and Puente 1993). Puente proceeded to team up with Buddy Morrow, a bandleader and trombonist, in a project culminating in *Revolving Bandstand,* a series of recording sessions where both Puente and Morrow simultaneously performed arrangements shifting, or "revolving," from one orchestra to the other. Morrow made the following comments on the challenging nature of the project:

> When we talked about making this album, the first thing that came to mind was— will it work? Just imagine, *two full orchestras,* in other words two completely different rhythm sections and brass sections not to mention the saxes, individual leaders, different arrangers. The recording was a huge task if only because of the "time-lag"— the split second difference from the execution of a note by one musician to the ears of another as much as twenty or thirty feet away; yet they must perform as one or the whole effect and excitement is lost. Certainly a challenge in every respect. (Morrow and Puente 1993)

The double arrangements of an assortment of standards were scored independently by Puente and George Williams. Each arrangement, none of which incorporated vocals, literally shifted from one band to another, changing in rhythmic and harmonic style from jazz swing to Latin rhythms, including mambo, cha-cha, and bolero. The transitions between these sections usually occurred at strategic points—for example, the change from principal theme to bridge. A well-developed logic and structure emerged to a strong and uniquely molded synchronous and contrasting effect.

One example of the contrasting arrangements is Puente's treatment of the jazz classic "Autumn Leaves." Introducing the tune with vibraphone on a soft ballad-paced, bolero rhythm, Puente scored an interesting orchestral accompaniment using brass and woodwinds. The bridge section of the main theme changes to a cha-cha rhythm with increasingly accented, syncopated brass riffs, returning to the bolero rhythm on the final melodic phrase. The arrangement then shifts to Morrow's orchestra, rhythmically transforming to a swing beat, with the trombone and saxophone section scored in an interesting collage of the initial theme, which is then restated by the full orchestra, especially incorporating the trumpet section on the melody with trombone counterthemes. Returning to the principal harmonic section, Puente enters on an improvised vibraphone solo, followed by Morrow's statement of the bridge melody on trombone. A short bongo solo (José Mangual Sr.) at the final measures of the bridge leads back to Puente's orchestra and the bolero rhythm in an interplay of the main theme, played first by Puente on vibraphone with Morrow's trombone in counterpoint and then by Morrow with Puente's embellishments. An innovative coda of descending chords featuring Puente's vibraphone closes the arrangement with a cadenza by Puente and a final tag of three full orchestra chords.

A contrasting track on the *Revolving Bandstand* LP is George Williams's arrangement of "Harlem Nocturne," a highly popular instrumental hit of the period composed by Earle Hagen and recorded by numerous artists. Beginning with a medium-paced swing tempo, the arrangement is introduced by the piano and electric guitar vamp interplay shown in example 14.

A dark jazz mood set, Morrow's full orchestra begins the principal theme in harmonized orchestration with some saxophone and guitar counterphrasing, the guitar exploiting the opening piano vamp figure throughout the harmonic progression of the melody. The main theme then shifts to Puente's orchestra on a cha-cha rhythm, beginning with unison tenor saxophones on the first section of the head, followed by the fully harmonized saxophone section. Although not double time, the cha-cha feel gives the arrange-

Example 14

ment a doubling sense at this point because of the abrupt rhythmic change, though the piece nevertheless continues to flow smoothly. Harmon-muted trumpets provide an interesting staccato, yet mellow, backdrop of counterparts, accenting the syncopated cha-cha beats of the Latin rhythm section.

At the bridge the arrangement returns to Morrow's orchestra in swing, with the full brass and woodwind sections harmonizing the melody. The descending figure of the closing of the bridge section is scored for Morrow's trombone. The bridge melody is now repeated in full as it revolves to Puente's orchestra, again in cha-cha with muted, staccato trumpets delivering the melody in a Latin syncopation. Flute and saxophones end the section on the descending pattern, which segues the piece back to Morrow's orchestra and the main melodic theme, this time stated by guitar (Al Casamenti) in a swing mode. Muted trumpets and the trombone section generate interesting supporting figures, and the baritone saxophone echoes the initial piano vamp, closing the section. The main theme is repeated by Puente's ensemble, again in cha-cha, with the guitar now playing the melody up an octave. The second phrase of the theme is taken over by Morrow's band in swing, flowing gracefully into a coda section marked by the initial piano and guitar vamp, with flute and saxophones restating the principal melodic motif of the tune.

The *Revolving Bandstand* LP displayed the experimentation that Puente had exhibited since his earlier bands, but his ideas were expanding even more by the sixties, and his growing international stature and the artistic respect that he enjoyed within the music industry made recording easier. Although *Revolving Bandstand* did not use the more traditional dance framework that Puente had to this point consistently provided for his audience, the public reacted positively, and so did musicians. Latin jazz was invigorated because of the recording, although it was not released until 1963; nevertheless, Puente's newer experimentation with the jazz mix began directly to affect younger musicians, many of whom would be spearheading the new salsa movement by the late sixties and early seventies. One such musician was Ray Barretto, who played congas in Puente's orchestra in 1960 and recorded on the *Revolving Bandstand* sessions.

Puente continued his prolific recording output through the sixties. His progressive yet traditional concepts were especially marked during this period by a number of dynamic vocalists who not only flavored his arrangements but influenced his composing and arranging techniques and still-evolving style. In 1961 he used the highly respected Cuban vocalist Rolando La Serie on his LP *Pachanga in New York*. In 1962 Puente recorded the LP *Y parece bobo* (on Al Santiago's Alegre label), which featured Chivirico Dávila, a Puerto Rican *sonero* who sang in the typical Cuban tradition while adding an individual, at times humorous, touch and spirit. Dávila's *inspiraciones* echoed much of the earlier art of Cuban *soneros* Beny Moré and Vicentico Valdés. It was also during this period that Puente recorded *The Exciting Tito Puente in Hollywood* (later reissued as *Tito Puente Now*). The recording featured Cuban flutist Rolando Lozano, who had located to Los Angeles during the midfifties.

In 1965 Puente recorded *Tito Puente Swings La Lupe*. Featuring the highly talented Cuban *sonera* La Lupe, the LP typified the many recordings that would follow where

Puente collaborated with female vocalists, notably La Lupe (Lupe Yoli) and Celia Cruz. One such effort, *The King and I/El rey y yo* (1967), is a vivid example of Puente's traditional yet progressive movement at the time. Pieces on the recording, all vocal arrangements, ranged from typical Cuban *guaracha, guajira, son montuno,* and cha-cha to a Mexican-composed bolero, a Puerto Rican *plena,* and the Beatles' ballad "Yesterday." Of special interest for its arrangement and vocal quality is the bolero "Ruega por nosotros," featuring La Lupe's passionate vocals and Puente on vibraphone. Composed by Alberto Cervántes and Rubén Fuentes, the piece was originally scored for mariachi. Fuentes is considered by many to be the most influential stylist and composer-arranger in the Mexican mariachi style through the last fifty years; he directed Linda Ronstadt's landmark *Canciones de mi padre* LP. Also of interest is that Puente recorded the dynamic and exciting "La salve plena," a traditional-style *plena* based on a Puerto Rican folk and dance genre and infrequently recorded by the Latin dance orchestras of New York's Palladium era. Also included on the LP are three pieces composed by La Lupe, "Cumba, Cumba," "Oriente," and "Mi gente." "Oriente" received major radio airplay and become a hit within the Latin music industry. Climaxing the LP is La Lupe's rendition of the religiously themed "Rezo a Yemayá," incorporating the Yoruba-derived Lucumí dialect, *batá* drums, and another innovative orchestral arrangement by Puente. Prior to *The King and I,* in 1966, Puente recorded the first of his albums with another female vocalist, Celia Cruz. Originally from Havana, Cruz was beginning a historic association with Puente that has lasted into the late nineties. She has performed and recorded extensively as a solo artist and is acclaimed as the most influential vocalist of contemporary Latin music.

The LP with Cruz was titled *Cuba y Puerto Rico son . . .* ("Cuba and Puerto Rico are . . .") and represents yet another innovative mixture of tracks, each based on distinctive rhythms from Cuba, Puerto Rico, the Dominican Republic, and Colombia. As with the music he directed for La Lupe, Puente penned arrangements specifically designed for Celia Cruz and tended to use compositions of others. The LP included the following pieces and their appropriate rhythmic/dance structures:

1. La guarachera: Cuban *guaracha*
2. Mi desesperación: "rock"
3. La plena bomba me llama: Puerto Rican *plena* and *bomba*
4. Desencanto: Cuban *bolero-chá* (combination of bolero and cha-cha)
5. Cumbiando: Colombian *cumbia*
6. Tinicué: Cuban *afro* (based on Afro-Cuban religious chants and rhythms)
7. No hay amigos: Cuban *guaguancó*
8. Me acuerdo de tí: Cuban bolero
9. No juegue con el diablo: *ritmo vereguá*
10. Herencia gitana: *bolero zambra*
11. La rueda: Cuban rumba
12. Salve pa' tí: Dominican merengue

Of the diverse, dynamic arrangements on the LP, one that bears attention as a "trade-mark" Celia Cruz interpretation is "La guarachera," a power-driven composition based on the traditional Cuban *guaracha* musical form and composed in a contemporary style by *sonero* Chivirico Dávila. The initial verses of the opening piece begin as follows:

La guarachera	*La guarachera*
Abran paso que aquí traigo yo	Make way, here I bring
en mi voz un saludo cordial.	in my voice a cordial greeting.
Guarachera me llama la gente.	*Guarachera,* the people call me.
Yo con Tito Puente voy a guarachar.	I with Tito Puente am going to dance *guaracha.*
Vengan todos a oirme cantar,	Come everybody to hear me sing,
con mi coro que viene allá atrás.	with my chorus coming behind me.
Yo sí soy guarachera conciente	Yes, I'm a conscientious *guarachera*
y este rico ambiente	and this delightful ambience
me pone a inspirar.	makes me improvise.
Coro: Guarachera, bonco.	*Chorus:* Guarachera, bonco.
Inspiración: Bonco, bonco, bonco rumba buena.	*Improvisation:* Bonco, bonco, bonco good rumba.
Coro. Guarachera, bonco.	*Chorus:* Guarachera, bonco.
Inspiración: ¡Me llaman la guarachera!	*Improvisation:* They call me the *guarachera*!
Coro: Guarachera, bonco.	*Chorus:* Guarachera, bonco.
Inspiración: Boncooo, boncooo, boncooo, boncooo.	*Improvisation:* Boncooo, boncooo, boncooo, boncooo.
Coro: Guarachera, bonco.	*Chorus:* Guarachera, bonco.
Inspiración: Bonco, bonco, bonco que la rumba.	*Improvisation:* Bonco, bonco, bonco, what a rumba.
¡Vaya a guarachar!	Go do the *guaracha*!
Coro: Guarachera, bonco.	*Chorus:* Guarachera, bonco.
Oye, Tito Puente,	Listen, Tito Puente,
guarachea conmigo.	do the *guaracha* with me.
¿A ver si es verdad chico?	Let's see if it's true, man.
Coro: Guarachera, bonco.	*Chorus:* Guarachera, bonco.

The typical Cuban *guaracha* form includes a main verse, often sung in satiric or humorous *coplas* (rhymed poetic couplets in four-line stanzas), and frequently employs a multichord harmonic scheme through the melody of the verse. In his arrangement of "La guarachera" Puente inserts a "mambo" section with brass riffs that bridge to a *coro* section, including ad-libs by Cruz and an extended timbal solo that begins with a creative, humorous vocal-timbal interplay between Cruz and Puente. The *típico* Cuban feel is one of high intensity and progressive authenticity, in Puente's arrangement and Cruz's vocals.

Among all the vocalists in the field of Latin music, male or female, Celia Cruz has emerged as the leading exponent of the art form, as Puente has of his—thus the very popular and accepted analogy of Tito as "the king" (from the instrumental-orchestral perspective) and Celia as "the queen" (from the vocal perspective). Although she was preceded by others, Celia Cruz became the figure most associated with and responsible for the changing role of women in her art. For his part, Puente must be given credit for incorporating numerous other women vocalists in his performances and on his recordings, including La Lupe, Abbe Lane, La Lloroncita, Sophy Hernández, Noraida, Millie P., Yolanda Duke, and La India.

With the advent of the seventies Puente's music continued to change, to adapt to new concepts, and to maintain the essential ingredients and integrity of Latin music. One LP that forcefully exhibits these qualities of time and culture is the 1973 release *Tito Puente and His Concert Orchestra*. Versatility, diversity, contrasting colors, rhythmic vitality, and expressive precision earmark this important album and set of compositions.

On the LP Puente performs on timbales, *kintos* (small timbales), vibraphone, marimba, melodica, electric piano, timpani, tambourine, miscellaneous percussion, and "rock drums." Invited as a special guest on the album is pianist Charlie Palmieri (piano, organ, and melodica), who plays on all tracks. The rise of jazz influence, endemic to other musical styles from the late sixties through the midseventies, is reflected in many of the arrangements on the recording. At the same time, however, the integrity of traditional *típico* Cuban rhythms and articulate arrangements epitomize the album.

One such cut is "El rey del timbal" (originally released in 1952), which became the major hit associated with the LP. Composed and arranged by Puente, "El rey" lives up to his name by demonstrating virtuoso musicianship on the timbales, around which the arrangement is built. After a sixteen-bar percussion introduction, the full orchestra enters on the main theme (see example 15). Immediately following the eight-bar theme and a rapid timbal break is the *coro* and main verse, the latter sung by Frankie Figueroa:

El rey del timbal	*The King of the Timbal*
El rey del timbal soy yo. La ley, soy yo. (*bis*)	The king of the timbal, I am. The law, I am. (*twice*)
Repicando por aquí, y tumbando por acá. El rey, soy yo. El rey del timbal soy yo. La ley, soy yo.	Beating over here, and knocking over there. The king, I am. The king of the timbal, I am. The law, I am.
Coro: Soy el rey del timbal.	*Chorus:* I'm the king of the timbal.
Inspiración: Repicando por aquí, y tumbando por acá mamá.	*Improvisation:* Beating over here, and knocking over there, mama.

Coro: Soy el rey del timbal.	*Chorus:* I'm the king of the timbal.
Inspiración: Tito, el rey del timbal.	*Improvisation:* Tito, the king of the timbal.
Que yo te voy a cantar Mangual.	That I'm going to sing to you, Mangual.*
Coro: Soy el rey del timbal.	*Chorus:* I'm the king of the timbal.
Inspiración: El rey, el rey de los cueros.	*Improvisation:* The king, the king of the skins.
El rey del timbal.	The king of the timbal.
Coro: Soy el rey del timbal.	*Chorus:* I'm the king of the timbal.
¡Arranca Tito!	Take it away, Tito!

Climaxing the second portion of the arrangement is Puente's timbal solo, which to many became another benchmark for mastery of the instrument and the hallmark of the composition. Example 16 is a transcription of the solo, which Puente recorded on two separate tracks dubbed together.

Also readapted on the LP from his earlier repertory is Puente's "Mambo Diablo" in a totally renovated arrangement. Incorporating much of the contemporary, progressive jazz practices of the period, Puente utilizes extended chordal structures throughout the arrangement, especially in the addition of an extensive introduction, where he employs a variety of orchestral textures, syncopated counterthemes, and a wide range. As on his original version of "Mambo Diablo," Puente states the head of the instrumental tune on vibraphone. Highlighted on the newer recording are highly jazz-influenced improvised solos by Puente on vibraphone and Don Palmer on soprano saxophone.

Another notable track on *Tito Puente and His Concert Orchestra* is the richly textured and arranged *son montuno* "Ah! Ah!" with a freshly executed *coro* section of Frankie Figueroa, Vitín Avilés, Adalberto Santiago, and Yayo El Indio. Puente's arrangement of the title track for the film *Last Tango in Paris* is also included, making use of electric guitar (with wah-wah, reverb, and distortion effects), melodica, and other instrumentation added to his orchestra of five trumpets, five saxophones, two trombones, bongo, congas, drums, bass, and keyboards. Added instrumentation is also incorporated by Puente in his arrangement of Spanish composer Manuel de Falla's *Ritual Fire Dance*, including organ, electric piano, melodica, bass saxophone, timpani, flute, and piccolo, among other instruments. Featured on this extensive, innovative, and experimental arrangement are solos on piano (Palmieri), alto saxophone, and trumpet. (Of interest throughout the recording is the baritone saxophone performance by René McLean, son of noted jazz alto saxophonist and composer Jackie McLean.) Also distinguishing the complex sequence of orchestral colors and counterpoint are dynamic experimental solos by Puente on electric piano and Palmieri on organ.

---

* This refers to the percussionist José Mangual.

El Rey Del Timbal

Edited and engraved by G. Di Lorenzo

Composed and arranged by Tito Puente

Example 15

Example 15 (cont.)

El Rey del Timbal

TIMBAL SOLO

Example 16

Example 16 (cont.)

Example 16 (cont.)

Example 16 (cont.)

The year this LP was released, 1973, represented much in the areas of artistic experimentation and cultural change, and again, Puente adapted to the contexts of the time. The sepia photo of Puente on the album's cover shows a gracefully aging *timbalero* with an "afro" hair style and a three-piece, double-breasted, wide-lapeled pin-striped suit. Puente's youthfulness was not simply a look; in the minds of many, he was performing at a more intense and higher level of virtuosity than ever in his career. Carlos Santana, an icon of the rock movement from San Francisco, had already recorded two of Puente's older compositions, "Oye como va" and "Pa' los rumberos," both of which had already become major international hits. Puente was not only in the limelight of two generations of music; he had become a legend.

Throughout the midseventies, another factor that profoundly affected Puente's role as a master musician was that of a growing and expanding pan-Latino identity in the United States. Young Puerto Ricans, Chicanos, Cubans, Dominicans, Central Americans, and other Latin Americans who were living in the country began to unite in a political, social, and cultural momentum that constantly sought symbols, leaders, and common expression in the arts. The salsa movement was in full drive, and younger musicians and artists, as had Carlos Santana, looked to Puente for inspiration and leadership. His musical concepts were now the models for younger bandleaders, composers, and arrangers based in New York, such as Willie Colón, Larry Harlow, Sonny Bravo, Johnny Rodríguez,

Dave Valentín, Jerry González, and Hilton Ruiz, among scores of others. In addition to Santana's band, other West Coast groups that implemented his musical style included Malo (led by Jorge Santana, who was eventually featured on a recording of the Fania All-Stars), Azteca (which included Pete and Coke Escovedo), El Chicano, Tierra, and Cold Blood. Abroad, salsa bands and artists were emulating Puente's legacy, including Oscar D'León in Venezuela, Lobo y Melón in Mexico, and a Panamanian named Rubén Blades.

For Puente, something else occurred that represented change on a musical level. With his 1973 LP Puente had named his ensemble a "concert" orchestra. Although the majority of the arrangements were danceable, a good part of the album was conceptualized for the concert hall, signified by Puente's cutting-edge renditions of his own "Mambo Diablo" and Falla's *Ritual Fire Dance*. Puente's musical goals had expanded in terms of what he was now attempting to do with his music and where and how he went about doing it. And as always through the course of history, mass musical movement could not be separated from the industrial-ideological complex.

The Legend Continues

In 1977 the release of Puente's LP *The Legend* exemplified the musical and social place that the Latin music industry was according Puente, in many ways a crowning of his prolific influence on an art form that was now popular not only in the pan-Latino movement but also—as always—within international sectors that straddled the categories of musical styles, age, ethnicity, and class, among other cultural classifications. The album was nominated for a Grammy Award.

Significantly the title track of the LP was composed by the young Rubén Blades, who by this period had come to New York from Panama and was doing much work for the Fania record label. Blades had studied law in Panama and had developed a unique and exciting blend of musical style and political ideology through both his compositions and his exceptional talent as a *sonero*. In 1980 Blades and Willie Colón would collaborate as coleaders on the Fania LP *Siembra,* which became the best-selling LP in the history of salsa up to that point.

In writing "La leyenda," Blades was composing an homage to Puente's inevitable characterization as a legend. Blades's lyrics also represented the overwhelming sentiments of the new generation of *salseros* emulating Puente, the bandleader who toward the end of the arrangement is described in a *coro* as "el rey del timbal." The musical arrangement by Louie Ramírez is highly reflective of the emerging salsa styles of the period, for it includes smooth, interlocking orchestral textures; a wide range of dynamics; and notably, a progressive harmonic scheme incorporating extended chordal structure and close harmonic voicing. These harmonic qualities are especially evident in the piano *guajeos,* "comping," and embellishments. One significant contrast to the new, contemporary salsa of the younger bandleaders of the period was the size of the orchestra. Puente was still maintaining full brass and woodwind sections (the latter progressively exploited in Ramírez's arrangement by means of highly percussive and melodic dynamics and variations), in addition to a full rhythm section of piano, bass, congas, bongos, and timbales. Also included is Puente's work on vibraphone, electric piano, synthesizer, and timbalitos, the smaller, high-pitched timbales on which Puente performs an extensive solo at the end of the arrangement. All lead vocals on the album are by Santos Colón, who had by this time been working with Puente for twenty years. Singing *coro* were Adalberto Santiago, Tito Allen, and Puente.

All but two of the arrangements on *The Legend* were done by Puente, and all include vocals except for a Puente composition that many critics have cited as the most noteworthy, innovative, and in a musical sense, controversial of the LP. As Max Salazar pointed out in chapter 3, some liked it and some did not, largely because the innovative work was included in an album that, although arranged in a modern vein, was still traditional Cuban dance music. Puente titled the instrumental "Fiesta a la King"; in it he experimented with new ideas involving the use of a creative, multisectioned, principal melodic theme constructed on jazz-style voicings and melodic phrasing. Rhythmically the piece adheres to traditional Cuban structures, especially that of the reverse clave of *son montuno*. John Coltrane had left his indelible mark on jazz, Latin, and popular music, and the tenor solo encompassing the first *montuno* section of the arrangement shows his influence, a predominant stylistic practice that had climaxed by the midseventies. Following the tenor solo, Puente improvises a solo on the vibraphone, swinging fluidly and gracefully webbing a sound matrix in which percussive, melodic, and harmonic elements interact colorfully.

The LP also addresses a rich side of the romantic as expressed through the bolero, "Qué falta tú me haces," by Bobby Capó, which Santos Colón interprets in his rich and distinctive vocal style. Another innovative and imaginative piece on the LP is Puente's "Bombata," a juxtaposition of Puerto Rican and Cuban musical idioms making use of the Afro-Cuban religious *batá* drums adapted to the Afro–Puerto Rican *bomba* rhythm and song form. In the seventies a large contingent of Latinos and people of other backgrounds in the United States became greatly interested in the folkloric, religious origins of Afro-Cuban music and its relationship to the development of salsa. Again, as he has throughout his career, Puente continued to conceptualize and personify the juncture of the musical and the social.

The garnering of Puente's first Grammy Award in 1978 supports this social and musical equation. With the salsa movement in full steam, the icons of Latin music were finally beginning to be recognized in the "mainstream" U.S. music industry. But Puente's Grammy for *Homenaje a Beny* signified much more than mere industrial or ideological success for the Latin market and Latin culture. With this LP Puente was paying tribute to Beny Moré, a seminal Cuban artist whose music had led to the evolution of a salsa as pure as that of Machito and Puente. In effect, Puente risked alienating segments of the industry on the one hand because a "tribute" album could seem nationalistic and on the other hand because the non–Latin American public and market scarcely knew who Moré was.

But the "Latino renaissance" and the "salsa explosion" of the late seventies proved to be buttresses, not deterrents, for Puente and his consistently innovative energy. The Moré LP became popular among various sectors of the market. The older Palladium veterans gravitated toward the nostalgia of Moré's repertory on the LP and the consistent dance character of all the arrangements. The younger audience had by this time reaffirmed Latin dance, which was also being fueled by the late seventies "disco craze," which had borrowed considerably from Latin dance styles such as the mambo and cha-cha.

The *Homenaje a Beny* album, produced by Louie Ramírez, includes ten tracks, mostly tunes originally composed or recorded by Moré and rearranged in a more contemporary format. Original Moré compositions include "Qué bueno baila usted" (*son montuno*), "Bonito y sabroso" (mambo), "Dolor y perdón" (bolero), "Se me cayó el tabaco" (*son montuno*), and "Santa Isabel de las lajas" (*son montuno*). *Coros* on the album are sung by Tito Allen, Rubén Blades, Adalberto Santiago, and Puente. Puente's outstanding and powerful arrangement of "Qué bueno baila usted," one of Moré's most popular tunes, emerged as one of the hits of the LP to receive major radio airplay (illustrating the significance of this composition is the fact that a Cuban documentary highlighting the life and music of Moré was titled after the song). Comparing Puente's 1978 arrangement with Moré's original recording popular during the early fifties reveals a progression of musical ideas and stylistic evolution based on the traditional Cuban *son,* whose style Moré greatly influenced in the form's earlier stages. Puente was "modernizing" a sound through new arrangements, but neither the rhythmic patterns of the Cuban *son* nor the integrity of the choreography was compromised. Puente's arrangement of "Qué bueno baila usted" employs five different *soneros* and clearly punctuated, syncopated brass and woodwind figures constructed on widely voiced chordal combinations. Harmonically Puente did not use as experimental an approach as he had in the seventies repertory previously analyzed here—that of the *Concert Orchestra* and *The Legend* LPs. Improvising *inspiraciones* dedicated to the memory of Moré on the arrangement are Celia Cruz, Adalberto Santiago, Ismael Quintana, Junior González, and Héctor Casanova.

Celia Cruz's powerful interpretation of Moré's hit "Yiri Yiri Bon" (composed by Silvestre Méndez) and a duet featuring Cruz and Cheo Feliciano are finely executed recordings and arrangements by Puente and Marty Sheller, respectively. Another cut on the album that merits significant attention is Moré's "Bonito y sabroso," vocally interpreted by Néstor Sánchez and arranged by Eddie Martínez. The classic melody of the main verse is sung faithfully to Moré's original version, but Martínez's arrangement displays the stylistic changes that had occurred in Latin music orchestration and performance practice in the thirty years since Moré's initial creative activity and popularity, especially with respect to the metamorphosis that had taken place in New York City and its various influences of jazz and a pan-Latino, multicultural ambience. Example 17 includes transcriptions of the introduction and principal verse section of both versions of "Bonito y sabroso," the first from Moré's original recording and the second from Puente's tribute album to the Cuban innovator. One can easily observe the contrasting orchestral parts accompanying the original, unaltered vocal verse.

Bonito y Sabroso

Beny Moré version

Example 17

Example 17 (cont.)

Example 17 (cont.)

Bonito y Sabroso

Puente version

Example 17 (cont.)

me u-ven las cin-tur-as y los hom- bros i-gua-li-to que las   cu - ba - nas

Con   el sen-ti - do del rit - mo   pa -   ra bai-lar y go - zar

has - ta pa - re - ce es - toy en la Ha - ba - na   cuan - do bai - lan - do veo una mex-i-ca-

Example 17 (cont.)

Example 17 (cont.)

Throughout his arrangement Martínez incorporates various bridge sections with uniquely exciting contrapuntal orchestrations modulating through various tonal centers and comprising extended harmonizations and range. The original verse (at points in unison or harmonized by the *coro* section), *coro,* and Néstor Sánchez's *inspiraciones* on the recording are structured as follows:

Bonito y sabroso

Pero qué bonito y sabroso
bailan el mambo las mexicanas.
Mueven la cintura y
los hombros
igualito que las cubanas. [*bis*]

Con el sentido del ritmo
para bailar y gozar.
Que hasta parece que estoy en
   La Habana,
cuando bailando veo
a una mexicana.
No hay que olvidar que México y
   La Habana,

Pretty and Tasty

Oh, but how pretty and tasty
Mexican women dance the mambo.
They move their waists
and their shoulders
the same way as Cuban women. [*twice*]

With the sense of the rhythm
to dance and have a good time.
It even seems that I'm in Havana,
when dancing, I see
a Mexican woman.
Don't forget that Mexico and Havana
are two cities that are like sisters.
To laugh and sing.

son dos ciudades que son como
   hermanas.
Para reír y cantar.

Pero qué bonito y sabroso
bailan el mambo las mexicanas.
Mueven la cintura y
los hombros
igualito que las cubanas. [bis]

Oh, but how pretty and tasty
Mexican women dance the mambo.
They move their waists
and their shoulders
the same way as Cuban women. [twice]

Coro: Mueven la cintura y
los hombros.

Chorus: They move their waists and
their shoulders.

Inspiración: Lo bailan en México, en
   La Habana.
Mueven la cintura y
los hombros.

Improvisation: They dance it in
   Mexico, in Havana.
They move their waists and
their shoulders.

Coro: Mueven la cintura y
los hombros.

Chorus: They move their waists and
their shoulders.

Inspiración: Cuando lo bailas conmigo
me tiras unos pasos,
mamita, que me asombro.

Improvisation: When you dance it with me
you throw me some steps,
little mama, that amazes me.

Coro: Mueven la cintura y
los hombros.

Chorus: They move their waists and
their shoulders.

Inspiración: Ven y baila como yo.
En la posición que tú te pongas
yo me pongo.

Improvisation: Come and dance like me.
In the position you place yourself,
I put myself.

Coro: Mueven la cintura y
los hombros.

Chorus: They move their waists and
their shoulders.

Inspiración: Tan linda que yo no me
   puedo contener.
Bailando con Isabel yo me asombro.

Improvisation: So pretty that I can't
   control myself.
Dancing with Isabel, I amaze myself.

Coro: Mueven la cintura y
los hombros.

Chorus: They move their waists and
their shoulders.

Inspiración: Beny Moré esto es para tí,
aunque sé muy bien que muchos
no te alcanzan ni
los hombros.

Improvisation: Beny Moré, this is for you,
although I know very well that
many don't even reach
your shoulders.

Coro: Mueven la cintura y
los hombros.

Chorus: They move their waists and
their shoulders.

Inspiración: Vengan a bailarlo conmigo.
Este ritmo no se llama sorongo.

Improvisation: Come dance with me.
This rhythm isn't called "sorongo."

Coro: Mueven la cintura y los hombros.	*Chorus:* They move their waists and their shoulders.
Inspiración: Báilalo tú aquí. Trae a tu hermana, dilo, que me pongo.	*Improvisation:* Dance it here. Bring your sister, say it, so I'll be ready.
Coro: Mueven la cintura y los hombros.	*Chorus:* They move their waists and their shoulders.
Inspiración: ¡Como dijo Beny! Muchacha mira, como yo gozo en La Habana.	*Improvisation:* Like Beny said! Girl, look, how I have a good time in Havana.

In 1979 and 1985 Puente recorded volumes 2 and 3 of *Homenaje a Beny,* again featuring various vocalists interpreting new arrangements of Moré's repertory. Throughout this period, as throughout his career, Puente continued to use different vocalists in performance and on his recordings. In addition to many of his previous vocalists, the following *soneros* appeared on his recordings from 1979 through the eighties: Frankie Figueroa, Héctor Lavoe, Ismael Miranda, Pete "Conde" Rodríguez, and Camilo Azuquita, among others.

In 1980 one of these singers, Frankie Figueroa, recorded on an important album by the Puente orchestra, *Dancemania 80's* (Tico), titled after the prolific and highly successful *Dance Mania* RCA LP of 1958, which had been followed by a sequel album in 1963, *More Dancemania* (RCA). Figueroa was an articulate, strong-voiced, dynamic *sonero* who often performed in concert using the motions of a boxer for his rhythmic accents and showmanship. He worked extensively with Puente's orchestra.

The *Dancemania 80's* album was another sign of the consistent quantity and quality of Puente's production and his adaptation to new audiences. Six of the nine tracks were his own compositions, and he penned all the arrangements. The opening track, a *guaguancó* titled "La generación del 80" ("The Generation of the Eighties"), composed by Puente and introduced and embellished by another of his exciting, powerful brass and woodwind orchestrations, referred in its verse to the newer, contemporary dancing public for whom Puente was now performing. Concluding the arrangement is another of Puente's classic timbal solos, another tour de force—this one being played by a man fifty-seven years of age literally beginning another stage in his unprecedented career.

La generación del 80	*The Generation of the Eighties*
Generación del ochenta, bailen mi guaguancó. Generación del ochenta, bailen mi guaguancó. Cuando yo me criaba en el barrio de verdad los muchachos me decían que yo no estaba en na'.	Generation of the eighties, dance my *guaguancó.* Generation of the eighties, dance my *guaguancó.* When I was growing up in the real barrio the kids told me that I was nothing.

Guaguancó, vengan todos
a bailar.

Coro: Generación del ochenta,
bailen mi guaguancó.
Generación del ochenta,
bailen mi guaguancó.

Cuando yo me criaba
en el barrio de verdad
los muchachos me decían
que yo no estaba en na'.
Guaguancó, vengan todos
a bailar.

Coro: Generación del ochenta,
bailen mi guaguancó.
Generación del ochenta,
bailen mi guaguancó.

Inspiración: Esto mamita
se ha puesto bueno,
con Tito y su tambor.

Coro: Generación del ochenta,
bailen mi guaguancó.
Generación del ochenta,
bailen mi guaguancó.

Inspiración: Tito Puente
el rey de los cueros.
Caballero,
hay que quitarse el sombrero.

Coro: Generación del ochenta,
bailen mi guaguancó.
Generación del ochenta,
bailen mi guaguancó.

Inspiración: Lo goza, lo goza to'
el mundo entero.
Oye mira, soy sonero.

Coro: Generación del ochenta,
bailen mi guaguancó.
Generación del ochenta,
bailen mi guaguancó.

Inspiración: Nadie comprende
lo que gozo yo
cuando Tito Puente toca los cueros.

Guaguancó, come everyone
and dance.

Chorus: Generation of the eighties,
dance my *guaguancó.*
Generation of the eighties,
dance my *guaguancó.*

When I was growing up
in the real barrio
the kids told me
that I was nothing.
Guaguancó, come everyone
and dance.

Chorus: Generation of the eighties,
dance my *guaguancó.*
Generation of the eighties,
dance my *guaguancó.*

Improvisation: This thing, little mama
has gotten good,
with Tito and his drum.

Chorus: Generation of the eighties,
dance my *guaguancó.*
Generation of the eighties,
dance my *guaguancó.*

Improvisation: Tito Puente
the king of the skins.
Sir,
you have to take your hat off to him.

Chorus: Generation of the eighties,
dance my *guaguancó.*
Generation of the eighties,
dance my *guaguancó.*

Improvisation: They savor it,
the whole world savors it.
Listen, look, I am a *sonero.*

Chorus: Generation of the eighties,
dance my *guaguancó.*
Generation of the eighties,
dance my *guaguancó.*

Improvisation: No one understands
what I enjoy
when Tito Puente plays the skins.

Coro: Generación del ochenta,	*Chorus:* Generation of the eighties,
bailen mi guaguancó.	dance my *guaguancó.*
Generación del ochenta,	Generation of the eighties,
bailen mi guaguancó.	dance my *guaguancó.*
Inspiración: No es tercero	*Improvisation:* He isn't in third place
ni segundo	nor in second
¡Tito Puente siempre será el primero!	Tito Puente always will be the first!
Coro: Repica el timbal.	*Chorus:* Beat the timbal.

A variety of Latin rhythms in a modern mode characterizes the balance of the album. Two cha-chas on the LP are of contrasting interest and innovative style and craftsmanship. "Digan que sí," composed by Puente, utilizes a rich, mellow orchestration textured by harmonized flutes, synthesizer, trombone pedal point, and a muted trumpet section. The timbre of this blended sound deviates from the *típico* Cuban base while simultaneously adhering to the traditional Cuban cha-cha style in terms of rhythmic structure, danceability, and a close re-creation of the classic Cuban *charanga* sound, especially in the use of unison vocals, synthesizer (replacing violins), and flute figurations. Notable in the midinstrumental section are clever handclaps and fluidly moving, interlocking orchestral parts. Culminating this progressive cha-cha arrangement is a "recalled" concluding section similar to many of Puente's classic codas of his earlier orchestrations. The other cha-cha on the LP, Puente's arrangement of "El que sabe sabe," composed by Ernesto Duarte, represents another innovative interpretation of the cha-cha genre. Using a combination of *charanga*-style vocals, closely voiced orchestrations, and a smooth jazz phrasing in the brass and woodwind interludes, in addition to strategically placed saxophone mambo riffs and building brass break sections, Puente threads a neat fabric of coherent and well-paced effect. Another unique facet of the composition is the cleverness of the text:

El que sabe sabe	*He Who Knows Knows*
Oyeme bien para que comprendas.	Hear me well, so you understand.
Oyeme bien para que comprendas.	Hear me well, so you understand.
No te pongas a escuchar	Don't go listening
esos cantos de sirenas	to those siren songs
ni trates de averiguar	or try to understand
como está la vida ajena.	how the others live.
Coro: Oyeme bien para que	*Chorus:* Hear me well, so you
comprendas. [*bis*]	understand. [*twice*]
No por mucho	Not because one rises so
madrugar	early in the morning
se amanece más temprano.	does the dawn break earlier.
Acuérdate del refrán	Remember the refrain
y legisla bien mi hermano.	and legislate well, my brother.

| *Coro:* Oyeme bien para que comprendas. *[bis]* | *Chorus:* Hear me well, so you understand. *[twice]* |

El que sabe, sabe
y él que no
¡que aprenda!

He that knows, knows
and he that doesn't
should learn!

Coro: Oyeme bien para que comprendas. *[bis]*

Chorus: Hear me well, so you understand. *[twice]*

El que sabe, sabe
y el que no
¡que aprenda!

He that knows, knows
and he that doesn't
should learn!

In the second section of the arrangement, Puente introduces and alternates the *coro* section, which becomes the highlighting feature of the piece, with orchestrations again exerting smoothly textured, closely harmonized jazz phrasing adapted to the cha-cha syncopations (see example 18).

Another innovative, progressive Puente composition on the LP is "Ye-Ye," an up-tempo instrumental mambo characterized by intensely tight, syncopated horns and a fast, driven rhythm section featuring intricate timbal work. Vocal effects are used minimally yet effectively, dressing the complex orchestration with "Ye-Ye" on the vocal motif. Orchestrated pyramids among the brass and woodwinds build to different sections of the arrangements in dynamic fashion, bridging the various melodic and rhythmic motifs through extended, progressive harmonic structures.

Topical elements particularly highlight two of Puente's other compositions on *Dancemania 80's.* "En el barrio" is a more traditionally arranged *guaguancó* with a verse reflecting on the positive side of life in the Latin quarters of the city. Again, Puente juxtaposes themes expressing Latinos' current social sentiments of identity, which had heightened by the late seventies and the early eighties. Latin pride and identity were reaffirmed by themes such as the barrio and other cultural realities of Latinos in the United States. Such themes were highly popular and commonly adopted by many salsa artists of the day, especially the younger, politically and socially conscious bandleaders and *conjuntos,* such as Héctor Lavoe, Conjunto Libre, Rubén Blades, Willie Colón, Sonora Ponceña, and El Gran Combo. Also of topical interest, in a more humorous and satirical setting, is the text of Puente's "Le robaron los timbales" depicting the theft of his timbales while on tour, forcing Puente instead to play the timbalitos.

On the same LP Puente resurrects and recycles, through a new arrangement, a bolero that he had composed and recorded earlier in his career, "Sin amor." The verse reflects the romantic creativity and spirit that Puente continued to maintain as part of his repertory, which consistently combined tradition and innovation. He is featured on vibraphone throughout the arrangement, which also features the sensuous voice of Frankie Figueroa.

El Que Sabe Sabe

condensed score

Example 18

Sin amor	*Without Love*
Dios mío,	My God,
¿por qué no encuentro en esta vida	why don't I find in this life
tan siquiera un amor	at least one love
que me haga feliz?	that would make me happy?
Dime,	Tell me,
yo no puedo seguir	I can't go on
sin tener un amor	without having a love
para mí, para mí.	for me, for me.
A veces en mi soledad	Sometimes in my loneliness
yo me pongo a pensar	I begin to think
que la vida sin amor	that life without love
es una llama	is a flame
que se extingue sola.	that extinguishes itself.
Por eso,	For that reason,
Dios mío, yo te pido ahora	my God, I ask you now
que me des un amor	that you give me a love
que me haga feliz eternamente.	that would make me happy forever,
Yo no puedo	I cannot
más estar	be any longer,
sin un amor.	without a love.
A veces en mi soledad	Sometimes in my loneliness
yo me pongo a pensar	I begin to think
que la vida sin amor	that life without love
es una llama	is a flame
que se extingue sola.	that extinguishes itself.
Por eso,	For that reason,
Dios mío, yo te pido ahora	my God, I ask you now
que me des un amor	that you give me a love
que me haga feliz eternamente.	that would make me happy forever.
No, no puedo más estar	No, I cannot be any longer,
sin un amor.	without a love.

Latin Jazz and Beyond

Around 1978–79 something unique and different began to happen for Tito Puente and the music for which he had become known: the music was about to expand. As noted in chapter 1, during this time Puente went on tour with Martin Cohen's LP Jazz Ensemble, which soon evolved into the Tito Puente Latin Jazz Ensemble (also known as Tito Puente and His Latin Ensemble). What resulted from this excursion has led to twelve Latin jazz albums by Puente on the Concord label since 1983, in addition to four others on Tropijazz (RMM). With the notable exception of his 100th LP, *The Mambo King,* plus a few other albums within this period, the majority of Puente's last twenty-plus albums have been dedicated to the Latin jazz idiom. This observation, however, bears some clarification.

First, some of these albums labeled as Latin jazz include many compositions and arrangements that verge more on Latin dance music or salsa. Moreover, like the majority of Latin-based music, most of Puente's Latin jazz is *danceable,* for it is based on the precisely executed, traditional forms and rhythms of Cuban *son,* cha-cha, and mambo, among many others. This has been a sensitive issue for Puente:

> I remember I went to the recording company and I went to the president and I told him I was gonna record "Lush Life." You're gonna record Duke Ellington's "Lush Life"? So I told him, "No, it's not Duke Ellington's; it's Billy Strayhorn's work 'Lush Life.'" "You're gonna record that?" "Yeah, this Puerto Rican boy's gonna record 'Lush Life,' baby." And I did it. They can't believe a Latin artist could dig into that kind of music without really going into the thing. "Donna Lee" by Charlie Parker, or Miles Davis, or Monk things, or Coltrane things: "Giant Steps." How do you even win a Grammy Award? I was just telling Prof. Loza, one year I did a live album in San Francisco and I was up for a Grammy Award and they took me off of the nomination. So I asked the president—who's still there, who is a musician, Greene—I asked him, "What is wrong?" I love to talk to musicians, 'cause that way when they ask me a question, I think they know what the hell they're talking about. I love to ask them if they know what I'm talking about. Now this is the president of NARAS, still today there. So I asked, "So what's wrong with that album? I want you to tell me why I can't be nominated for that album I did in San Francisco." He couldn't give me an answer. I said, "Well I'm gonna give you a week, because if not, I'm gonna call a press conference and I'm gonna put NARAS down." So he finally got back to me. Now I was on top; really, I had a lot of people on top of him. I wanted to find out *why.* Was it political things, or why don't they give Grammys to people that deserve the Grammy? So he told me that I didn't have any Spanish titles on my tune. See, I had John Coltrane's "Giant Steps." I don't even remember how to say "Giant Steps" in Spanish. "Paso mi Step," something like that. "Gigante de Paso!" I didn't use no trap drummer. My bass player was going "dun-dun-dun-dun" [*simulates the syncopated bass* tumbao]. We were playing Latin music to John Coltrane's "Giant Steps." This is our Latin jazz interpretation. (Puente 1994)

Puente, in addition to many other Latin music artists (notably Eddie Palmieri) and the Latin Categories Screening Committee of NARAS, lobbied extensively for a Latin jazz category, which was finally added (although in the jazz field) for the 1993 Grammy Awards. Nevertheless, before the creation of the category, three of Puente's twelve Concord recordings garnered Grammy Awards, including his first on the label, *On Broadway.*

Two essentials particularly earmarked Puente's venture into his next musical era, the eighties, during which time the majority of his recordings and concert dates would be in the Latin jazz format. One element was his innovative approach to developing a new repertory, notably, his adaptation of jazz or popular standards or traditional tunes to Latin rhythms and forms. The other essential was his instrumentation, through which he again demonstrated his remarkably innovative approach and imagination.

A prime example of this admixture of concept and stylistic development is the title track to the *On Broadway* LP (1983), Puente's first recording released by his Latin Ensemble. The arrangement for "On Broadway," a major R&B doo-wop hit originally recorded by the Drifters (and composed by Cynthia Weil, Barry Mann, Jerry Leiber, and Mike Stoller), had recently been rerecorded by guitarist and singer George Benson and again became a radio hit. Puente recycled and adapted the tune, constructing its melodic and harmonic scheme over a cha-cha rhythm and featuring Edgardo Miranda's electric guitar on the main theme. The jazz-R&B-Latin blend becomes clearly apparent in this arrangement, as Pablo Guzmán notes in his liner notes describing the album's music. Guzmán recognizes Puente's eight band members as highly talented and diverse individuals "who, like Tito, have one foot in the Latin swing that is salsa and another in the world of Afro-American improvisation that is jazz. The result is a rich and potent blend" (Guzmán 1983).

Following a guitar solo and return to the main theme of "On Broadway," the arrangement shifts to a *guajira* feel, continuing to feature Miranda, but now on the Puerto Rican acoustic *cuatro,* a five double-stringed guitar-type instrument similar in sound to the Cuban *tres,* which was one of the original instruments with which the traditional Cuban *son* was developed. A double-time section follows, featuring dynamic flute work by Mario Rivera, finally referring to the opening cha-cha rhythm and texture with the main theme again played by Miranda, although this time on *cuatro* instead of electric guitar.

Especially evoking a more *típico* Latin vein on the album is Puente's offering on vibraphone of "María Cervantes," composed by Puerto Rican pianist Noro Morales, to whose memory the arrangement is dedicated. Also reminiscent of an earlier era in Puente's career is "Jo-Je-Ti," named for and featuring bongo player Johnny Rodríguez, conga drummer Jerry González, and Puente on timbales and similar in concept to "Ti-Mon-Bo" on Puente's 1957 *Top Percussion* LP, which featured Puente, Mongo Santamaría, and Willie Bobo.

Another two exceptional arrangements on the *On Broadway* LP are Puente's "T.P.'s especial" and "First Light," a composition by jazz trumpeter Freddie Hubbard, who originally recorded the tune on his *First Light* album. Puente's "T.P.'s especial" is an interesting adaptation of a bop-inspired head superimposed on a *son montuno* rhythmic base and features Alfredo De La Fé on violin exhibiting much of the *charanga* idiom with which he was familiar. Also featured are solos by Mario Rivera on tenor saxophone and Jorge Dalto on piano, the latter in a section toned down in dynamics and without bell patterns, a typical practice in Latin arrangements.

Words such as *dark, sweet,* and *progressive* can certainly be used to describe the sections of Puente's Latin Ensemble on Hubbard's "First Light," which already exhibited a strong Latin influence. Placed onto a typical cha-cha rhythm, the piece features Mario Rivera on soprano saxophone, Jerry González on flugelhorn, and Jorge Dalto on electric piano, all three displaying modern, progressive ideas on their respective solos and other embellishments throughout the arrangement. Especially interesting are Alfredo De La Fé's use of syncopated pizzicato effects (at times in conjunction with the piano *guajeo*), in addition to Dalto's rich harmonic enhancements and strategic atonal comping and other effects. Puente executes some precise, rich fills on timbales toward the end of the arrangement, climaxing its coda in excellent, dynamic form.

The *musical* blend of Puente's Latin Ensemble also involves the blending of diverse young virtuoso artists, a blend that has characterized all Puente's music and ensembles since his earliest performances and recordings (and helps to explicate Puente's consistent problem with the idea that "crossover" is a recent phenomenon). His ensemble of 1983, however, represented a newer and somewhat different blend—one of a completely new generation and new breed of young Latin musicians. Apart from trumpeter and trombonist Jimmy Frisaura, a New York Italian American who by this time had been performing with Puente for close to forty years, and New York–bred Puerto Rican bassist Bobby Rodríguez, by then with Puente for almost thirty years, the ensemble comprised a mix of young musicians reflecting the pan-Latino movement and artistic momentum of the period. Perhaps most notable among such individuals was *conguero* and trumpeter Jerry González, to whom Puente consistently referred as the young "New Rican" of the band, a name referring to the baby-boom-era youth of Puerto Rican heritage born in New York City. At thirty-four years of age, González was more than young enough to be Puente's son (Puente was at this time sixty years old). González was also somewhat of a colorful figure and involved in much of the musical experimentation of the seventies, particularly with regard to a group he had led, the Grupo Folklórico Experimental. Based in New York City, the ensemble experimented with jazz, Afro-Cuban, and Afro–Puerto Rican genres, performed often at the New Rican Village, and recorded a number of LPs. González had also been extensively involved with Conjunto Libre, a salsa group that had been experimenting with the intersections of jazz and Latin music. In addition to his virtuosic, progressive trumpet style, comparable to major stylists of the period such as Freddie Hubbard and Woody Shaw, González was a highly talented conga drummer with a unique, innovative flair and at times unorthodox, yet tradition-based, technique. Instead of playing the usual two or three conga drums of different pitches, he commonly played four or five, creating a new richly textured layer of sound.

The other members of the ensemble also displayed diverse pan-Latino identities. Violinist Alfredo De La Fé was Cuban and brought an experimental ambience to the group via his progressive *charanga* violin approach. The Cuban *charanga* ensemble and style at this time had experienced a revival in new formats, especially in New York City and Cuba. Pianist Jorge Dalto was originally from Argentina and likewise represented the young progressive wave of Latin and jazz musicians of the period. He had formerly performed and recorded with George Benson and was also recording his own LPs as a leader. New York Puerto Rican bongo player Johnny Rodríguez had been instrumental in the formation of one of New York's most innovative salsa groups, Típica '73. Mario Rivera, originally from the Dominican Republic, was a prolific master of the woodwinds and experimented extensively on flute and soprano and tenor saxophones. Puerto Ricans Ray González (trumpet) and Edgardo Miranda (guitar, *cuatro*) were prolific musicians who not only enhanced Puente's ensemble but attested even further to Puente's utilization and recognition of the emerging new breed of Latin jazz musicians.

Leaving the ensemble after *On Broadway* was Alfredo De La Fé, who eventually continued his performance and recording career in Colombia. Also leaving was Jerry González, who returned to work with his Fort Apache Band, with which he subsequently recorded a number of albums and which he still led as of 1999. He was replaced by New York–based *conguero* José Madera. González, nevertheless, must be given credit for leaving his imprint on Puente's newest venture.

Many critics consider *El rey* (1984), Puente's second album on Concord, to be one of Puente's definitive recordings, along with *Dance Mania*. One of only four live-concert albums Puente ever released, *El rey* was recorded at the Great American Music Hall in San Francisco in May 1984. In the liner notes to the LP, Hugh Wyatt assesses the significance of the live date, claiming that "*El Rey*'s style of music should always be *live* since the music is always fiery and highly combustible. I like it also because of the call and response between his superb lot of musicians and the audience, both of whom seemed to have given hugely of themselves" (Wyatt 1984). Many musicians see the album as presenting a solid, highly inclusive repertory of jazz and Latin, where Puente experiments with both the juxtaposition and the intersection of jazz and Latin structures—rhythmically, harmonically, melodically, and in terms of form, arrangements, and instrumentation.

Quite appropriately, the recording opens with the tune that was by this time a worldwide classic, "Oye como va," being performed in the same city in which Santana had made it part of rock lore over a dozen years before. From a musical point of comparison, it is interesting to note the metamorphosis of the piece from Puente's original 1963 recording through Santana's 1970 hit to the live 1984 interpretation on *El rey*.

"Oye como va" is a cha-cha bearing a strong resemblance to Cachao's "Chanchullo," which was arranged and recorded by Puente and his orchestra in 1959 on his *Mucho Cha-Cha* LP, featuring both Johnny Pacheco on flute and percussion and Ray Barretto on congas. Puente's "Oye como va," which unlike Cachao's tune incorporates a *coro* section, utilizes devices similar to those in "Chanchullo," such as ample *charanga*-style flute embellishments and improvisation, related brass riffs, and markedly similar breaks at the ends of the principal phrases, all on a syncopated piano cha-cha riff that has come to personify the Puente composition (see example 19).

An interesting facet of the rhythmic and harmonic articulation is the harmonic effect created by the repetitive A-minor seventh chord with a suspended fourth resolv-

Example 19

ing to a D⁷ (in the left hand only), which is quite different from the piano *guajeos* more commonly used for the cha-cha pattern (although the Cachao/Puente pattern can also be called traditional). Whereas "Oye como va" is similar in this aspect to "Chanchullo," Puente negotiates a much different bass *tumbao*. Although identical in rhythmic formation, Puente's bass line differs melodically, in essence resolving (along with the left-hand piano part) the harmonic suspension of the piano pattern (the right-hand D played throughout the two-measure pattern) by implying a i⁷sus.–IV⁷ progression (see example 20). In sum, it lends well to a unique, leading effect.

Example 20

Although "Oye como va" is similar to "Chanchullo," it cannot be called the same tune. Also of interest is the fact that Puente, as did Santana on his Latin rock experiment, used organ in place of piano on his original 1963 version, although not the same Hammond B-3 setup used by Santana's organist, Gregg Rolie. Santana replaced the flute and horn riffs with his guitar to great effect. Otherwise, however, Santana's arrangement is basically a duplicate (minus some extra *coro* and horn sections in Puente's arrangement) with a different instrumental texture and a fused rhythmic base of rock-R&B and cha-cha.

On the *El rey* LP pianist Jorge Dalto opens "Oye como va" and is followed by fast-paced flute embellishments by Mario Rivera, who solos extensively throughout the arrangement, and Bobby Rodríguez's improvised electric bass figures. A horn-section break cues the percussion, the horns proceeding to duplicate in harmony the piano pattern. The trademark break of this tune (see example 21, which shows the piano part) cues the *coro* section and the following solo on bass, in addition to closing the arrangement.

Another two Tito Puente classics are recorded on *El rey:* "Ran Kan Kan" and "El rey del timbal." Whereas Puente's original 1949 recording of "Ran Kan Kan" featured vocalist Vitín Avilés with orchestra, the more up-tempo 1984 live recording serves primarily as a vehicle to showcase Puente's still intricate, vibrant, and creative timbal dexterity. "El rey del timbal" is performed without vocals, unlike the original 1973 version with Puente's Concert Orchestra, and is also executed at a much faster tempo. As on the origi-

Example 21

nal, since the piece is essentially a showcase of his percussive ability, Puente improvises extensively, at one point performing a solo cadenza on a set of four timbales. Throughout the album the percussion section of Francisco Aguabella (conga), Johnny Rodríguez (bongos, congas), and José Madera (congas, timbales) provides a consistently strong and exciting support and rhythmic framework on which Puente builds a diversity of sound. Also especially significant for the recording is the participation of the veteran Cuban musician Francisco Aguabella, who had performed with, recorded with, and composed for Puente, especially during the fifties and thereafter.

El rey also features Puente on vibraphone, both on "Autumn Leaves," where he adapts the introduction and coda from his original arrangement on the *Revolving Bandstand* LP (recorded in 1960), and on a medley incorporating the jazz classic "Stella by Starlight" and "Delirio," a classic bolero composed by César Portillo de la Luz.

Finally, perhaps the most innovative tracks on *El rey* are two John Coltrane compositions, "Giant Steps" and "Equinox," which are innovative in several respects. Few established Latin artists, especially those of Puente's generation, had begun to experiment with the fusion of the progressive, postbop jazz of artists such as Coltrane, Miles Davis, and Freddie Hubbard. The two Coltrane pieces Puente included on the album were experiments that not only proved successful but facilitated the continuing evolution of Latin music. Rhythmically and texturally, the musical base of these fusions was still the traditional forms of cha-cha, mambo, *son montuno, guaguancó,* bolero, and other Afro-Cuban genres of music and dance. And clave persisted as the timekeeper of Puente's newest experiments.

Puente's arrangement of "Giant Steps" vividly and creatively attests to the previous remarks. Puente adapts Coltrane's intricately designed tune to a highly up-tempo pace, constructing it on a rhythmic framework based on a 3-2 clave. Following a percussion introduction and the statement of the head by the ensemble is Mario Rivera's punctuating and passionate tenor sax solo navigating the tune's constant modulations. Capping Rivera's improvisation is a horn interlude of rapidly fired sixteenth-note phrases bridging to Jorge Dalto's rich piano solo, also played over Coltrane's complex and rapid series of chord changes that defines the composition. Horn riffs enter after Dalto's solo, accenting a timbal exposition by Puente that powerfully climaxes the arrangement. Puente again demonstrates his imaginative, vibrantly energetic virtuosity on four timbales, creating a mosaic of melody, rhythm, and harmony.

On Coltrane's "Equinox" Puente converts the four-beat meter to an Afro-Cuban 6/8 *compás* and clave rhythm, using the following basic *cáscara** pattern:

---

* *Cáscara* is the term used in Afro-Cuban styles for various rhythmic patterns usually played with sticks on the sides of the metal timbal shells. In the rumba and other folkloric traditions this practice varies, and sticks usually strike the wood part of a drum or other instrument. Literally *cáscara* (Sp.) can be translated as "bark," as that of a tree.

The horns enter in a flow of free improvisation, leading to the melodic head, phrased by Rivera's soprano saxophone and González's flugelhorn, echoed in imitative counterriffs by Jimmy Frisaura's valve trombone. Rivera and González both solo, Rivera echoing the Coltrane legacy and González sounding a smooth, Hubbard-inspired, yet individual improvisation. Dalto's piano solo that follows incorporates sensuous elements of blues, richly clustered tertian and quartal harmony, and complex counterrhythms. Puente's intense timbal work serves again as a climactic build to close the arrangement.

Yet another piece that bears mention on this milestone album is "Linda chicana," a Mark Levine cha-cha orchestrated in a fluid, interactive texture that creatively exploits the horn section of Mario Rivera on flute, Jimmy Frisaura on trombone, and Ray González on trumpet.

With the sad and unfortunate death in 1984 of Jorge Dalto, who had battled cancer and to whom Puente often referred as "my man on the piano," the piano position in Puente's Latin Ensemble was filled by Sonny Bravo. The veteran yet young pianist had performed extensively in the Latin music and jazz circuit, notably with Johnny Rodríguez in the innovative and dynamic Típica '73 ensemble.* Like Dalto, Bravo brought arranging skills in addition to his performance ability. The rest of the ensemble that had recorded *El rey* remained intact (with the exception of Francisco Aguabella, whose participation on the *El rey* live recording was actually more of a guest appearance). As of this point Puente's Latin Ensemble was characterized by people who formed the nucleus of the band, notably Bravo, Jimmy Frisaura, Johnny Rodríguez, Bobby Rodríguez, José Madera, and Mario Rivera.

Puente continued to release recordings with his Latin Ensemble by putting out his third Concord album in 1985, *Mambo Diablo,* with special guest George Shearing. This time Puente received his third Grammy Award. Pianist Shearing, a veteran and revered jazz artist, recorded one track on the album, his own classic composition "Lullaby of Birdland," using a *son montuno* structure based on a 2-3 clave figure. Puente rearranged not only the title track of *Mambo Diablo* but also another of his older classics, "Que será mi china," here retitled simply "China." Both arrangements feature Puente on vibraphone and Mario Rivera on flute. Billy Strayhorn's "Lush Life" is treated to an innovative and fluid arrangement by Puente and Bravo, structured at first on a bolero rhythm and transforming into a cha-cha. The arrangement features Puente on vibraphone and Mario Rivera on tenor saxophone. Possibly the most innovative arrangement on the album is that of Paul Desmond's jazz classic "Take Five" (originally recorded by the Dave Brubeck Quartet), arranged here by Puente, who transforms the tune's 5/4 meter into a four meter in cut time, at points (i.e., the bridge) adapted to a *guaracha* dance feel with the piano pattern on the main theme structured as shown in example 22.

Featured on the arrangement of "Take Five" are Mario Rivera on tenor saxophone, Ray González on flugelhorn, and Puente on timbales. Puente's arrangement of the head

---

* Rodríguez's father (percussionist Johnny "La Vaca" Rodríguez), a Puerto Rican, and Bravo's father (bassist Elio Osacar), a Cuban, were highly significant musicians of the Afro-Cuban styles.

Take Five

PIANO INTRODUCTION

Example 22

is a creatively designed counterpoint of the three horns of Rivera, González, and Jimmy Frisaura, doubling on trumpet. The final recapitulation of the main theme uses close-voiced and fluid horn-section lines, leading to the close of the tune.

Other arrangers sharing tasks on the album include conga drummer José Madera ("Lullaby of Birdland" and "Pick Yourself Up"), Marty Sheller ("Eastern Joy Dance"), and Sonny Bravo ("No pienses así").

Puente's next album was *Sensación,* which used the same personnel and was recorded in December 1985 (again in San Francisco) and released in 1986. The ensemble did a new version of Puente's 1978 "Fiesta a la King," and the title track, Omar Hernández's "Que sensación," is arranged by Sonny Bravo in a vocally charged salsa format that converts into an up-tempo *bomba* section. "Guajira for Cal" is a Puente composition dedicated to Cal Tjader, who had died in May 1983. Puente plays vibraphone on the arrangement, along with jazz vibraphonist Terry Gibbs, who appears as a guest artist and also performs as a soloist on Puente's *son montuno* arrangement of Duke Jordan's "Jordu." Additional guest artists on the recording include John Santos on bongos on the classic César Portillo de la Luz bolero "Contigo en la distancia." Santos also sings *coro* on "Qué sensación," along with Sonny Bravo, Juan Ceballos, and Mario Rivera. Puente also did the arrangements of three classic, historic standards composed by jazz artists Thelonious Monk ("'Round Midnight"), Clare Fischer ("Morning"), and Chick Corea ("Spain").

Noting the dexterity and musical virtuosity that Puente was still demonstrating at the age of sixty-three, Enrique Fernández made the following clever and meaningful metaphoric comments on his liner notes to the *Sensación* LP.

If anything beats hearing Tito on record—and his productions have copped Grammy after Grammy—it's seeing him on stage. There's no performer in pop, rock or R&B that can outpower Tito on stage. Even when he's just rat-tat-tatting the beat, his energy surge ignites the drums. And when he solos, his compactness explodes until what you see is an octopus that somehow got caught in a tropical storm with a drumstick clutched in each tentacle. Two arms up in the air, in Tito's trademark "shoot-the-cuff," at least two arms on each drum, and a couple more working the cowbell and cymbal. *Octopuente.* (Fernández 1986)

Puente's next album on Concord, *Un poco loco* (1987), represented yet another prolific mix of jazz and Latin and featured both Puente's Latin Ensemble and his orchestra. The title track is the classic Bud Powell composition "Un poco loco," a challenging, intricate bop tune interpreted by Puente's Latin Ensemble on a mambo-influenced arrangement based on a 3-2 clave rhythmic structure. Also of note on the album are two Puente pieces: "Chang," which bears a structure similar to, although more developed than, that of his early "Picadillo," and "Machito Forever," composed for Puente's early mentor and dedicated to his memory. "Chang" opens with a gong strike, followed by the *son montuno* pattern uniquely accented by marimba, piano, and bass and the principal riff voiced for Mario Rivera's overdubbed soprano saxophone and melodica. Jimmy Frisaura and new ensemble member Piro Rodríguez enter later on trumpets with interesting countermelodies, riffs, and texturally effective chordal pyramids. A Spanish, flamenco ambience among the horns complements Puente's solo marimba work. In sum, the arrangement is a dynamic, contemporary interpretation of Puente's original "Picadillo."

Puente's arrangement of "Machito Forever" is for his full orchestra, brought into the studio to record two tracks, the other being Ellington's "Prelude to a Kiss." The harmonically progressive instrumental introduction to "Machito Forever" utilizes a variety of voicings and textural combinations evident in the opening measures (see example 23).

Especially notable on the *Un poco loco* album are three blues- or funk-based tunes superimposed on Latin rhythms: Moe Koffman's "Swinging Shepherd Blues (Goes Latin)," Benny Golson's "Killer Joe," and Chucho Valdés's "Tritón." The closing selection on the album is Puente's "Alluya," a percussion and vocal arrangement based on the chants and rhythms of Afro-Cuban religious music. Guest musicians performing on various sections of the album include Pete Escovedo (congas) and Rebeca Mauleón (synthesizer) on "Prelude to a Kiss," as well as Juan Ceballos and John Santos joining Puente on the *coros* to his salsa-oriented "El timbalón."

On his next three Concord releases Puente continued to expand and enhance his arrangements with extra musicians on specific pieces. In 1988 he recorded *Salsa Meets Jazz,* featuring Phil Woods, one of the world's leading jazz alto saxophonists. Tracks on the album ranged from Freddie Greene's "Corner Pocket" to Neal Hefti's "Repetition," and from Puente's "Guajira Soul" to Dizzy Gillespie's "Con alma." In July–August 1989 Puente recorded his 1990 release, the highly acclaimed album *Goza mi timbal,* for which he won a fourth Grammy Award. The album included arrangements by Puente, Brian Murphy (in collaboration with Puente), and Marty Sheller, and adaptations by Sonny

Machito Forever

Edited and engraved by G. Di Lorenzo

Composed and arranged by Tito Puente

Example 23

Example 23 (cont.)

Example 23 (cont.)

Trumpets 1 & 5

Example 23 (cont.)

Example 23 (cont.)

Example 23 (cont.)

Example 23 (cont.)

Bravo and José Madera. Of particular interest on this collection are several classic and complex jazz tunes, including two by Sonny Rollins, "Airegin" (an often recorded piece whose title Rollins created by spelling *Nigeria* backward) and "Pent-Up House," Miles Davis's "All Blues," and Thelonious Monk's "Straight, No Chaser," the latter a refreshingly innovative and involved arrangement by Murphy and Puente. Also of interest on the album are Bravo's adaptation of Chucho Valdés's "Cha Cha Chá" and Madera's adaptation of Puente's "Ode to Cachao." With "Ode to Cachao" Puente had composed a tribute to the great Cuban bassist by combining elements in a cha-cha highly reminiscent of both his own "Oye como va" and Cachao's "Chanchullo." Featured on the piece is bassist Bobby Rodríguez. Puente also wrote a new arrangement of his classic "Picadillo" for the album, renaming it here as "Picadillo a lo Puente." Also noteworthy are some of the comments made by Hugh Wyatt in the liner notes to the album concerning Puente's hybrid of Latin jazz in addition to Puente's close friendship with his fellow musician Jimmy Frisaura:

> Mergers are the staple of Wall Street and provide the drive behind the stock market, but they rarely work in music. Just picture a wild discordant crew of traders on the floor of the Exchange and you have an idea of the hodgepodge of sounds this blending of music usually brings. A smooth amalgam of notes may be what the mergers want—but it's often not what they get.
>
> In the 1960s and 1970s, Miles Davis, Weather Report, John McLaughlin, the Heath Bros., and a few other bands melded jazz and rock idioms to the satisfaction of the masses and put fusion on the pop music map.
>
> But it must be noted that the resultant music was viewed as suspect by the jazz cognoscenti. They argued that they didn't care if some of the top innovators in jazz were leading the fusion movement. They still saw it as an excessive watering-down of one of the most important forms in modern music—jazz.
>
> But, in the midst of this cacophony of bickering, Tito Puente, the genius, was involved in a merger and acquisition that would make the traders on Wall Street stand up and take note. He was not only mixing a number of different Latin modes, which later would earn him the title of "El Rey" (The King of Salsa). Tito, who dislikes the name "salsa," was busy creating a marriage between jazz and Latin.
>
> Nowhere is his union more soothingly evident than on this recording, his 99th in a career that has spanned more than four decades. El Rey's fusion would not deal with both diverse modes in a perfunctory manner. It would take on the most complex elements and musicians in jazz—from the far-out dissonance of Thelonious Monk to the unprecedented thematic development of Sonny Rollins . . .
>
> Although jazz and Latin might seem to be at the opposite ends of the musical spectrum, they are not. Jazz musicians, especially Duke Ellington and Dizzy Gillespie, used Latin rhythms and other elements in the 1930s and 1940s to provide a boost and an exotic flavor to their music. Though brilliant, the music is nonetheless intellectual and often pontifical.
>
> One final note. Tito has dedicated this outing to his "main man," Jimmy Frisaura, who suffered a heart attack. What is both touching and intriguing at the same time

is the fact that Tito originally canceled the recording session because of Jimmy. But Tito said he had a dream on Saturday, the day after he had canceled the recording.

On Sunday, he scheduled a rehearsal, and by Monday his entire band was actually recording. Two days later, in what is perhaps one of the fastest recording sessions in the history of electronics, Tito and his band completed this remarkable recording. The music sounds as if it took them six months to record, for the simple reason that this may be the most dynamic recording El Rey has ever made.

Wall Street would be envious. (Wyatt 1989)

Out of This World, Puente's eighth consecutive Concord release and *officially* the ninety-ninth of his career, was recorded in December 1990. It was released in 1991, soon after he had received his star on the Hollywood Walk of Fame. On the album he uses an eleven-piece ensemble, expanding his Latin Ensemble with the addition of José "Papo" Rodríguez (a regular member of Poncho Sanchez's ensemble) on bongos and *chékere,* Charles Sepúlveda on trumpet, Michael Turre on baritone saxophone and flute, and Papo Vásquez on trombone.

For his 100th album, recorded and released in 1991 and titled *The Mambo King* in the light of his recent work on the film *Mambo Kings,* Puente made a decision that was of great importance to him, that of recording the album with his large dance orchestra, with which he still performed, although on a more limited basis than before his Concord years. Also of significance was that the album would be released through the RMM record label, which had just been incorporated by Puente's longtime business agent, Ralph Mercado. The album received distribution through Sony, the world's largest record company.

As reviewed in chapter 1, *The Mambo King* featured numerous vocalists who had worked with Puente throughout his career. The arrangements are in an updated, contemporary style and feature Puente on timbales, vibraphone, and synthesizer (for string sounds). The list of musicians in the orchestra is impressive: Sergio George, Sonny Bravo, and Paquito Pastor (piano); Johnny Torres, Bobby Rodríguez, and Rubén Rodríguez (bass); Johnny Rodríguez and Papo Pepín (congas); Marc Quiñones (timbales); Ray Colón and José Madera (bongos); David "Piro" Rodríguez, Charlie Sepúlveda, Ite Jerez, Bomberito Zarzuela, Brian Lynch, Barry Danelian, John Walsh, and Chocolate Armenteros (trumpet); Papo Vásquez, Luis López, Conrad Herwig, Lewis Kahn, and Víctor Vásquez (trombone); Bobby Porcelli, Mitch Frohman, Mario Rivera, Steve Sax, Pablo Calagero, Rolando Briceño, Pete Yellin, and Bob Francheschini (saxes); Johnny Pacheco (percussion); and Ray Sepúlveda, Néstor Sánchez, Sergio George, and Johnny Rivera (*coros*).

Much of the album is highly reminiscent of Puente's earlier dance hall era, especially his days at the Palladium and especially on the tracks featuring *soneros* Celia Cruz, Ismael Miranda, Santos Colón, and Oscar D'León. On the *guaracha* "Celia y Tito," composed by Johnny Pacheco and arranged by José Madera, Celia Cruz sings the following verse and ad-libs dedicated to Puente. As she did on frequent occasions with Puente through many years, Cruz trades improvised vocal motifs with Puente's timbales in the *montuno* section of the arrangement.

Celia y Tito

¡Vaya, azúcar pa' Tito Puente!
Yo he tenido la dicha de cantar
con tenores, baladistas
y sopranos.
Y he compartido con los mejores salseros
a los que quiero como si fueran mis
    hermanos.

Ahora estoy invitada a compartir
con un grupo de salseros
sin igual.
La invitación viene de un
gran amigo.
Es Tito Puente mi hermano,
El rey del timbal.

Cuando llegué de Cuba
Tito me puso a gozar
y ahora, es el número cien
es que yo quiero
con mi voz reciprocar
y ahora, es el número cien
es que yo quiero
con mi voz reciprocar.

¡Y dice!
Esta guarachera ahora le viene a cantar
por que el número cien de Tito
sí lo quiero vacilar.

Coro: Oye Celia
pon a Tito a gozar.

Inspiración: Eee. Yo sé que cuando yo
    empiece
él va querer repicar.
Pero yo no lo dejaré, ¡caramba!
porque me quiero inspirar.

Coro: Oye Celia
pon a Tito a gozar.

Inspiración: A Tito Puente señores
siempre le agradeceré
él fue quien me acompañó
cuando de Cuba llegué.

Celia and Tito

All right, sweetness for Tito Puente!
I've had the pleasure to sing
with tenors, balladeers,
and sopranos.
And I've shared with the best salseros,
whom I love like my own brothers.

Now I am invited to share
with a group of salseros
without equal.
The invitation comes from a
great friend.
He's Tito Puente, my brother,
the king of the timbal.

When I arrived from Cuba
Tito gave me joy
and now, it's number 100
it's what I want to give back
with my voice
and now, it's number 100
it's what I want to give back
with my voice.

And it goes!
Now this *guarachera* comes to sing
because with Tito's number 100
I really want to have fun.

Chorus: Listen, Celia,
Give Tito joy.

Improvisation: Eee. I know that when I
    start
he's going to want to chime in.
But I won't let him, *caramba*!
because I want to express myself.

Chorus: Listen, Celia,
Give Tito joy.

Improvisation: To Tito Puente, sirs,
I will always be thankful;
he's the one who accompanied me
when I got here from Cuba.

Coro: Oye Celia
pon a Tito a gozar.

Inspiración: Esa amistad que tenemos
es casi como de hermanos
y si sigue este timbeque
durará por muchos años.

Coro: Oye Celia
pon a Tito a gozar.

Inspiración: Que sí lo pongo a gozar,
que sí lo pongo a tocar
porque a Tito Puente le llaman, señores,
el rey del timbal.

Vaya, Tito Puente, demuéstrale al mundo
que de verda' tú eres,
el rey del timbal.
Vaya, Tito Puente, bótate ahora
el ráfago que yo te pago.
Ahora Tito!

Coro: ¡Repica tu timbal!

Inspiración· Mira que llegaste al cien

Coro: ¡Repica tu timbal!

Inspiración: en tu carrera triunfal.

Coro: ¡Repica tu timbal!

Inspiración: Sigue ahí que tú vas bien

Coro: ¡Repica tu timbal!

Inspiración: Te respetamos por tu
talento

Coro: ¡Repica tu timbal!

Inspiración: Cuando te inspiras
así lo siento.

Coro: ¡Repica tu timbal!

Inspiración: Eee, repica, repica, repica,
repica, repica
¡Tito ahí te dejo eso!

Coro: ¡Repica tu timbal!

Chorus: Listen, Celia,
Give Tito joy.

Improvisation: That friendship we have
is almost like that of brothers
and if this playing continues
it will last for many years.

Chorus: Listen, Celia,
Give Tito joy.

Improvisation: Yes, I make him have fun,
yes, I make him play,
because they call Tito Puente, sirs,
the king of the timbal.

All right, Tito Puente, show the world
that you really are
the king of the timbal.
All right, Tito Puente, let it go now
the blast that I pay you for.
Now, Tito!

Chorus: Beat your timbal!

Improvisation: Look, you made it to 100

Chorus: Beat your timbal!

Improvisation: in your triumphant career.

Chorus: Beat your timbal!

Improvisation: Keep on, you're doing
well.

Chorus: Beat your timbal!

Improvisation: We respect you for your
talent.

Chorus: Beat your timbal!

Improvisation: When you express yourself,
that's how I feel it.

Chorus: Beat your timbal!

Improvisation: Eee, beat it, beat it, beat it,
beat it, beat it
Tito I leave it to you!

Chorus: Beat your timbal!

After *The Mambo King* Puente seemed ready to begin another series of 100 albums. In the subsequent seven years he released an additional eleven (not including numerous reissues and recompilations). Eight of these have alternated between the two major labels for which he was recording, Concord and RMM/Tropijazz, the latter distributed by Sony Records. In his various recording projects of this period, Puente used a variety of ensembles in addition to his regular Latin Ensemble and his large orchestra, notably his Golden Latin Jazz All Stars.

The Concord studio dates recorded during this time included four albums: *Mambo of the Times* (1992), *Royal T* (1993), *Master Timbalero* (1994), and *Special Delivery* (1996), featuring Maynard Ferguson. On the well-sculpted, eclectic *Mambo of the Times,* Puente again used an expanded ensemble of eleven musicians (besides himself), a combination that enabled him to generate either his small group sound or one closer to his large orchestra. The diverse mix of a traditional concert sound and innovative ideas makes the album one of his most creative endeavors. The various tracks include jazz classics arranged by Puente and Brian Murphy, such as Billy Strayhorn's ballad "Passion Flower," here made into a bolero rhythm, and "Things to Come," by Gil Fuller and Dizzy Gillespie. The latter arrangement features both trumpeters, Charlie Sepúlveda and Piro Rodríguez, as soloists; Sepúlveda's improvisation is impressive homage to Gillespie's trumpet style and technique. Mario Rivera solos on both tenor and baritone saxophones. "Japan Mambo," composed and arranged by Puente, was inspired by his 1958 "Hong Kong Mambo" from the *Dance Mania* album, although in an indirect sense only. Familiar are the mambo rhythm section riff and the melodic use of marimba. "Baqueteo" is a traditional instrumental *guaracha* arranged by José Madera and making use of Brian Murphy's synthesizer work emulating the sound of the traditional Cuban *tres* guitar-like instrument. "Mambo King" is a contemporary Puente composition characterized by a progressive structure and arrangement over a traditional mambo and rhythm. Nick Jiménez's "Mambo of the Times," as its title implies, is a new and innovative mambo version using jazz-phrased lyrics in English. Arranged by Oscar Hernández, the voices of Tito Allen and Alexandra Taveres are set in an interesting and dynamic harmonic scheme. Perhaps one of the most innovative arrangements is Puente and Murphy's version of Fats Waller's "Jitterbug Waltz," converted from its original waltz structure into a 4/4 meter and utilizing typical Latin rhythms and an interesting, syncopated interpretation of the head on vibraphone. The balance of the album includes Marty Sheller's arrangement of "If You Could See Me Now" (Tadd Dameron and Carl Sigman), Murphy and Puente's arrangement of "The Best Is Yet to Come" (Cy Coleman and Carolyn Leigh), and Gil López's arrangement of his own "El titón."

In 1992 the new Tropijazz label, an affiliation of RMM and Sony, released the first of two albums featuring Tito Puente's Golden Latin Jazz All Stars. The all-star group for the first album, recorded live at the Village Gate in New York and assembled by Puente and the musical producer of the album, Jack Hooke, featured (in addition to Puente) the following virtuoso masters of Latin jazz: Mongo Santamaría (congas), Paquito D'Rivera (alto saxophone), Dave Valentín (flute), Claudio Roditi (trumpet), Hilton Ruiz (piano),

Giovanni Hidalgo (congas), Ignacio Berroa (drum set), Andy González (bass), and Mario Rivera (tenor saxophone). The ensemble interprets Puente's "Oye como va" in addition to "New Arrival," composed and arranged by Ruiz, and Miles Davis's "Milestones," arranged by Brazilian trumpeter Roditi. The second Latin Golden All Star album (1994) headlined by Puente was recorded in the studio and titled *In Session*. Distinguishing the album is the guest appearance by legendary jazz musician James Moody, who arranged, sang, and played tenor saxophone on his own classic composition "Moody's Mood for Love," which also features Puente on vibraphone. The musicians on *In Session* were the same as those on the first Golden All Stars recording, with the exception of Paquito D'Rivera and the replacement of Claudio Roditi by Charlie Sepúlveda. In another excerpt from one of his UCLA lectures, Puente made the following comments with regard to his Golden Latin All Stars:

> Now I'm involved mostly with a Latin jazz ensemble. . . . Because of economics, the situation of carrying a big band around the world becomes nearly an impossibility. I think I'm the only guy that has three bands now. I have the Latin Jazz All Stars, the Golden Men of Latin Jazz, and a big band, so I may be crazy. I don't even know how we can manage two bands. But the thing is, we try to get the minimum amount of men to get the big-band sound. That's where I'm at now. You tell that to somebody on the street and they don't know what you're talking about. Booking agents will send you to some job around the world; they don't know what kind of music you play, what kind of people you're catering to, or what kind of dancing. All kinds of different bilingual problems we have because, naturally, Latin jazz is mostly instrumental, but when you play with a big band you have vocalists in there, so that's what they call salsa music.
>
> [With the] Golden Men we have a guest artist, Arturo Sandoval, trumpet player; Paquito D'Rivera, great alto; Claudio Roditi, beautiful trumpet player, Brazilian; Mario Rivera plays great tenor, flute, and soprano saxophone; on flute we have the great Dave Valentín, great flute player; on piano we have this kid named Hilton Ruiz, beautiful piano, great Latin jazz piano. These are not typical Latin musicians; they play good jazz. On bass we have Andy González, one of our top Latin jazz bass players; on drums we have a fellow Cuban guy, Ignacio Berroa is his name, and he used to play with Dizzy Gillespie's band, very good drummer; and then on conga we have Mongo Santamaría, our master *conguero;* and then we have this kid Giovanni Hidalgo, great conga, plays four congas the fastest, real, real fast. On this [the second] album my guest artist is James Moody. On this album James Moody sings "There I go, there I go," the old tune "Moody's Mood for Love." Before we went to Europe on the last trip, I lined them all up; I said, "All you guys are stars. I don't want nobody asking me for an advance. I don't want nobody asking me what time you start work. I don't want nobody asking me what you're playing or what you're gonna wear. I am an invited guest artist." And they all laughed. "I'm not the leader; I'm an invited guest artist. They just put my name to that, but that's not even my band. The only reason they put my name to that is because all you guys put together, you ain't got the name I got, see? That's why you guys are here." So we did all of Europe—great. Wonderful work. One was the session album, the other one we did live at the Village Gate in New York. So the only way I read my name in there was me—T.P., Turnpike, I don't know. (Puente 1994)

Puente's Concord releases of 1993 and 1994 continued to reflect his reference to both bop and traditional Latin rhythms framed in continually changing colors. On *Royal T* Puente's Latin Ensemble interprets Charlie Parker's "Donna Lee" (arranged by Michael Turre), Horace Silver's "Tokyo Blues" and "Virgo" (both arranged by Sonny Bravo), and Charles Mingus's "Moanin'" (arranged by trombonist Sam Burtis, who also performs on the record). Newcomers to Puente's ensemble on this recording include Bobby Porcelli on alto and baritone saxophone, Arturo Velasco on trombone (previously of Poncho Sanchez's Latin jazz ensemble), and Tony Luján on trumpet. Puente's *Master Timbalero* (1994) includes arrangements of jazz classics "Bloomdido" (Charlie Parker); "Nostalgia in Times Square" (Charles Mingus), over dubbed with a live track of Times Square's urban noise; and "Enchantment" (Horace Silver), in addition to a highly interesting arrangement by Paquito Pastor of the traditional Japanese melody "Sakura." Puente's "Azu Ki Ki," adapted by José Madera, was dedicated to the memory of music producer Bill Graham and featured Puente's progressive arranging skills and piano work by Sonny Bravo.

Puente proceeded to record another eclectic album, *Tito's Idea* (1995), on the Tropijazz label. The album featured Hilton Ruiz's arrangement of and exceptional performance on the title track, a cocomposition by Puente and Ruiz, in addition to a guest appearance by Steve Turre, who plays trombone and conch shells on Puente's composition "Asia Mood," on which Puente performs richly on marimba. In 1996 Puente recorded another Tropijazz project of special note and attention, *Jazzin'*, on which he collaborated with the young New York Puerto Rican hip-hop vocalist India in addition to featuring as special guest the Count Basie Orchestra, directed by trombonist Grover Mitchell. Because of the significance of the album, Alfredo Cruz's complete liner notes merit a reading as part of this musical-cultural analysis.

> It has been my good fortune over the past fifteen years or so, to have been acquainted with Tito Puente. A true musical master of our time, "El Rey" is one of the few remaining pioneers of our music. When I heard that he was planning to do a recording with India and the Count Basie Orchestra, I got really excited.
>
> Just as Duke Ellington, Count Basie, Machito, Stan Kenton, Xavier Cugat, Pérez Prado and others have personalized and defined the big band setting, through the decades Puente also has repeatedly proven his prowess and facility with this style of music. Having been raised in Spanish Harlem during the innovative heyday of Latin music, Tito was exposed early on to the evolving sounds of Jazz and Be-Bop. The influence of that era has given Puente a creative edge and musical diversity that has come to define his expressive musical personality.
>
> This new recording of Tito's featuring the vocals of young singing sensation, India, and the world renowned Count Basie Orchestra (CBO) is another testament to the on-going legacy of the marriage between Latin music and Jazz. The link between these styles has been a lifelong mate of Tito Puente's and he commented to me that this project is the realization of a dream.
>
> In featuring a big band guest artist, Puente wouldn't consider limiting the project to a single prestigious name. "Why not bring the whole band in as my guests instead

of just one guy?" thought Tito. Always the innovator, he thought featuring an entire big band as the guest artist(s) would make this recording a first in the Latin field.

Marking the continuation of a musical tradition for Puente, we are treated here to the big band sound of CBO, Tito's distinctive beat and the soaring vocals of an internationally recognized Nuyorican songstress. It is quite refreshing to hear the raw, gutsy and urgent vocals of India on this recording.

Blasting out of the Bronx in 1992, India has established her solo career as an undisputed and international rising star. Her CD, "Dicen Que Soy," went triple platinum and she's received prestigious awards throughout Latin America. India's success and popularity in the Latin music world comes after an already well established run in the urban "hip hop" music field.

India is part of a renaissance among young Latino performers who, after experiencing promising and successful careers in various segments of the non-Latino music scene, have "rediscovered" their Latin music traditions. These performers guarantee the continuation of our valuable traditions and at the same time, they attract a whole new crop of fans and consumers to Latin music.

For this recording Tito directs India through her first full fledged Jazz experience. Tito said, "She's one of the best vocalists we have in the Latin field . . . in both languages!" "Her funky urban feel and bilingual capacity categorize India's unique style." With El Maestro's musical guidance on this record, India eases from Latin-with-Jazz to Jazz-with-Latin, on both a combination of known standards and some new compositions as well.

Tito Puente's energy has inspired and sparked musicians, dancers and listeners alike around the globe for many years. I am positive that after you listen to this recording you will agree that he shows no sign of slowing down. Long live the King! (Cruz 1996)

The title track and opener on this album is Hilton Ruiz's arrangement of his own composition "Jazzin'." An intricate, bop-flavored head comprises two distinct melodies of challenging, "zigzag" intervallic shape, performed eloquently in unison by Puente on vibraphone, India on scat-style vocal, and Ruiz on piano (see example 24). At the age of seventy-three Puente punches out the complex head with clear phrasing, equaled by India, two generations his junior.

"Jazzin'" and another three tracks on the album are performed by Puente's "Latin Ensemble," which in addition to the previously cited musicians now included Mitch Frohman (baritone saxophone), Ray Vega (trumpet), Ite Jerez (trumpet), John Benítez (bass), Horacio "El Negro" Hernández (drum set), and Luisito Quintero (percussion).

The Count Basie Orchestra accompanies Puente on four arrangements on the album: "Take It or Lose It," composed and arranged by Puente (performing timbales); "Crazy He Calls Me," composed by Bob Russell and Carl Sigman and arranged by Puente and featuring a section of Afro-Cuban religion–based *batá* drums and chants performed by Milton Cardona; and "What a Difference a Day Makes" ("Cuando vuelva a tu lado"), composed by María Grever (English lyrics by Stanley Adams) and arranged by Marty Sheller.

Jazzin'

Example 24

Example 24 (cont.)

The Identification of Style

The musical style of Tito Puente and its various innovative shifts, contours, and qualities are reflected in the musico-social analyses I have offered in this chapter. But I have only "chipped the iceberg." Puente's repertory of about 500 compositions and 116 albums could occupy volumes of analysis and reevaluation. Puente has played a number of roles, including that of musician, composer, orchestrator, and philosopher. At times his role has been camouflaged by such multiplicities, but we must face one matter of fact. Whether it is heard in a timbal solo, an improvisation on marimba, or an orchestration, Puente's sound is unmistakable to any ear that has learned it, and this is perhaps the essential quality of all major stylists and innovators through the ages. Like Beethoven and Ellington, Puente has simply balanced the equation.

Tito Puente and His Orchestra's third album, originally released in 1956 on RCA. The LP featured Latin percussionists Mongo Santamaría, Willie Bobo, Carlos "Patato" Valdez, and Candido Camero; it proved to be a major breakthrough for Puente in his early career. (Courtesy of the RCA Records Label, a unit of BMG Entertainment.)

Including tracks recorded from 1955–57, *Mucho Puente* comprised an eclectic selection of contemporary Latin American and North American classics, for example, "What a Difference a Day Makes," "Noche de ronda," "Son de la loma," "Tea for Two," "Almendra," and "Mack the Knife." (Courtesy of the RCA Records Label, a unit of BMG Entertainment.)

Reissue cover for Puente's *Dance Mania* album, released in 1958. (Courtesy of the RCA Records Label, a unit of BMG Entertainment.)

Cover of a combination reissue of two of Puente's highly acclaimed albums, *Top Percussion* and *Dance Mania*. (Courtesy of Bear Family Records.)

The King and I—El rey y yo featured Puente's orchestra and Cuban *sonera* La Lupe, who recorded with Puente on various occasions during the sixties in addition to performing with him. The LP is characterized by an eclectic set of compositions and arrangements. (Courtesy of Tico Records.)

Among Puente's numerous recordings with Celia Cruz was the highly acclaimed *Cuba y Puerto Rico son* . released in 1966 on the Tico label. (Courtesy of Tico Records.)

Reflective of the dynamics and experimentation of the early seventies was the LP *Tito Puente and His Concert Orchestra,* a highly diverse and significant album and set of compositions. Charlie Palmieri performed on various keyboards, and the LP premiered "El rey del timbal," which would rapidly become another of Puente's classics. (Courtesy of Tico Records.)

Puente's first Grammy Award nomination was made for his 1977 LP *The Legend.* The album represented a keen transition in Puente's career and included his innovative new sound of "Fiesta a la King" in addition to the title track "La Leyenda," which was composed by Rubén Blades as a dedication to Puente. (Courtesy of Tico Records.)

Puente received his first Grammy Award for his LP *Homenaje a Beny* [*Moré*], released in 1978 and featuring *soneros* Celia Cruz, Cheo Feliciano, Santos Colón, Ismael Quintana, and Adalberto Santiago. The album was produced by Louie Ramírez. (Courtesy of Tico Records.)

Puente continued to demonstrate his composing and arranging skills with the 1980 album *Dancemania 80's,* featuring *sonero* Frankie Figueroa. Puente at this time was maintaining both his smaller Latin Ensemble and the large dance orchestra featured on this album. (Courtesy of Tico Records.)

Puente's first album on the Concord Picante label earned him his second Grammy Award in 1983. Puente would continue the Latin Ensemble format with Concord into the late nineties with international acclaim. (© 1983 Concord Records, Inc.)

Puente's landmark *El rey* album, his second for the Concord label, released in 1984. (© 1984 Concord Records, Inc. Photo by David Fischer.)

Mambo Diablo, Puente's 1985 album, which received a Grammy Award in the "Latin Tropical category"; it was Puente's third Grammy Award and his second on the Concord label. Special guest on the album was jazz legend pianist George Shearing, recording his own composition "Lullaby of Birdland" with Puente's Latin Ensemble. (© 1985 Concord Records, Inc. Photo by Bob Shamis.)

Named for the title track composed by jazz great Bud Powell, *Un poco loco* (1987) featured Puente's Latin Ensemble and Orchestra. Included on the album was Puente's composition in tribute to Machito, "Machito Forever." (© 1987 Concord Records, Inc. Photo by David Fischer.)

Puente was awarded his fourth Grammy Award for *Goza mi timbal* (1990). (© 1990 Concord Records, Inc. Photo by David Fischer.)

Tito Puente's 100th album, *The Mambo King,* released in 1991 and featuring many of the artists with whom Puente had worked; it was produced by Johnny Pacheco. (Courtesy of RMM Records.)

Bill Cosby wrote the liner notes for Puente's *Mambo of the Times,* released in 1992. Puente and Cosby developed a close friendship through the years and collaborated on a number of television and musical projects. (© Concord Records, Inc. Photo by David Fischer.)

Puente's third ensemble, his Golden Latin Jazz All Stars, recorded its first album in 1992–93 live at the Village Gate in New York City. The recording featured a number of the finest Latin jazz artists in the world. (Courtesy of RMM Records [Tropijazz].)

In 1994, and at the age of seventy-one, Puente had become even more acclaimed as "the master" or "el maestro." He continued to record with great pace and energy, and his music remained as explosive as ever. In *Master Timbalero* he performed on timbales, timbalito, vibes, marimba, and other percussion. Max Salazar wrote the historically rich notes for the album. (© 1994 Concord Records, Inc. Photo by Martin Cohen.)

Jazzin' (1996) signified both the new and the old, featuring vocalist India in addition to the Count Basie Orchestra. The title track was composed by pianist Hilton Ruiz; the album also included standards such as "Love for Sale," "Wave," "Going Out of My Head," and "What a Difference a Day Makes" (Cuando vuelva a tu lado)." (Courtesy of RMM Records [Tropijazz].)

7

Identity, Nationalism, and the Aesthetics of Latin Music

I N the realm of Latin American music and Latin American culture in general, the issues of nationalism and identity have been common analytical and figurative concepts. From the "nationalistic" use of folk and indigenous materials in the music of composers Heitor Villa-Lobos and Carlos Chávez to the use of song as political metaphor and protest, identity has been a dominant issue in Latin American culture and, I might add, world culture through the centuries.

The present momentum in the formulation of "salsa" musical and dance expression has been largely associated with a variety of identities. These have included associations based on a number of cultural constructs, such as religion, ethnicity, politics, change, innovation, and the artistic virtuosity of the venerated master musician, dancer, or performer—the high priest of a religion of art.

The diversity of such underlying constructs extends beyond the major historical artistic basis of contemporary Latin music, that of the Afro-Cuban musical tradition. Although still firmly based on the foundation of Afro-Cuban forms, the expressive framework of Latin musicians has evolved stylistically and varied extensively in terms of context, theme, and nationalist or ethnic sentiment. The music has also become quite universal, with salsa groups such as Orquesta de la Luz from Japan becoming Grammy Award nominees. Nonetheless, even among Latino artists, who constitute the majority of the contemporary Latin music enclave, the many innovators and stylists have come not only from New York and the northeast United States, representative of their local Cuban, Puerto Rican, or Dominican population, but also from other sectors of the United States (especially California and Florida) and, perhaps more significant in terms of historical precedent, from various sectors of Latin America. Many Afro-Cuban forms evolved in other parts of Latin America—for example, Cuban Pérez Prado's orchestra in Mexico—in a sphere of social and national context separate from that of the New York Palladium and its New York ambience. Artists such as Oscar D'León from Venezuela, Rubén Blades from Panama, Lobo y Melón from Mexico, and a large number of *conjunto* groups from Puerto Rico—for example, Cortijo, Ismael Rivera, Sonora Ponceña, and El Gran Combo—have emerged as messengers of salsa and Latin music no less important than the New York artists. Additionally, the social messages of the style have addressed this ever-growing geographical terrain. Although significantly more directed toward a "pop" market, salsa may now have a broader appeal across the Latino world than ever before, especially given the inter-American popularity of "salsa" artists such as Marc Anthony, José Alberto, Lalo Rodríguez, Luis Enríque, Tito Nieves, Grupo Niche, Joe Arroyo, Gloria Estefan, and Juan Luis Guerra (whose style is actually based on the Dominican merengue and *bachata* dance forms), among many others, all representing various Latin American countries or U.S. Latino sectors (the evolution of salsa as a pan-Latino development and symbol has been significantly examined by Frances Aparicio [1998]).

In the light of these observations concerning the evolving identities, markets, and aesthetics of Latin music, I feel compelled to raise in this study an issue that has become a focal point for some contemporary scholars: the "Cubanization" of Puerto Rican culture and musical expression, particularly in New York City. In his article "Puerto Rican Music and Cultural Identity: Creative Appropriation of Cuban Sources from Danza to Salsa," Peter Manuel confronts the "issue of cultural identity" that "has been particularly controversial and active among Puerto Ricans" (1994, 249). Manuel notes that "Puerto Rican nationalist intellectuals as well as popular opinion have long embraced salsa—for example, as opposed to rock—as a characteristically (albeit not exclusively) local music." Manuel's aim in the article is not to question the "validity of the virtually unanimous Puerto Rican conception of salsa and *danza* as local in character" but "to explore the process by which Puerto Ricans have appropriated and resignified Cuban musical forms as symbols of their own cultural identity." He does note, however, a "potential contradiction" concerning historical "fact" and the origins of the music: "A significant qualification and potential contradiction lies at the heart of the allegedly indigenous character of salsa and its island antecedents, for in stylistic terms, most of the predominant Puerto Rican musics, from the nineteenth-century *danza* to contemporary salsa, have been originally derived from abroad—particularly from Cuba" (249).

In my estimation, such analytical viewpoints are problematic. For one thing, many Puerto Ricans might question the point of concentrating on the idea that "most of the predominant Puerto Rican musics . . . have been originally derived from abroad." With their modest population (compared to larger "nation-states") of a little over six million in both Puerto Rico and the United States,* why should people of Puerto Rican heritage be expected to restrict themselves to "island" culture and identity?

Moreover, the issue of Cuban musical culture itself can be seen as a similar contradiction. The forms that have historically constituted Cuban national styles have in fact migrated, diffused, and adapted from a number of geographic and national origins, including Nigeria, Ghana, and the Ivory Coast, among numerous other West and Central African locations (as well as Spain and other European contexts). In the literature Afro-Cuban *batá* drums are not often considered a nationalistic contradiction, when in fact they derived directly from the Nigerian *bàtá* drums of the Yoruba culture and their associated religious context; nor are they, through time, referred to as specifically "Nigerian" drums. The diffusion of musical expression and religious ideology has not represented a contradiction in Cuba concerning the emergent nationalist character of Afro-Cuban music as "Cuban"; rather, it has produced a quite flexible, although conflictual and diverse, convergence of philosophies.

Another point of discussion can be centered on the issue that a place such as multicultural Nigeria and its Yoruba migratory cultural history can be tied to numerous past intercultural connections and national identities in various sectors within the north and west of Africa. "Borrowed" and shared cultural forms have consistently signified the emergence of nationalist, "indigenous" symbols. In the *nueva canción* movement of Latin America, Andean forms became one of the most vivid features of the musical style and certainly elicited a nationalist association that strongly reinforced the verbal content of the song, yet the singers of the movement were largely not Aymara- or Quechua-speaking peoples. In southeastern Mexico the *son jarocho* developed as a cultural convergence, within a specific time frame, of indigenous, African, and European interests. But the *son jarocho* did ultimately become *identified* as Mexican, and it has recently become associated with numerous Chicano artists in the United States, for example, Los Lobos, Fermín Herrera, and Francisco González (see Loza 1992, 1993).

Puerto Rico and Cuba, as Manuel does note, have been linked historically and culturally for centuries, even before Spanish colonization. Furthermore, Latin America must be considered a cultural entity much like that of other continental areas, for example, the United States, Europe, and East Asia, where intercultural expression ultimately signifies various national identities and "characters." The regional variants of various Latin American countries or even regions of these countries frequently take on the character of Latin America as a larger "nation" similar to the United States and its regional state or geographical variants and thus identities. Since before and after the Civil War, the issue of North and South in the United States has represented not convergence of nationalist identities and styles but rather their divergence.

---

* The Puerto Rican population in the United States is reported as 2,727,754 in the U.S. Census of 1990. The population of Puerto Rico is reported as 3,522,037 in the *World Almanac and Book of Facts* (1995), 670.

The Multicultural Matrix of Latin Music

Since the early experiments and innovations of Cuban musicians Arsenio Rodríguez, Machito, and Mario Bauzá during the thirties, Latin music in the United States has developed as a reflection of its intercultural matrix. The exposure to and experience with jazz that Bauzá adapted in his early arrangements with the Machito Orchestra became both the musical and cultural framework on which Latin dance orchestras, Latin jazz, and salsa would emerge. Puerto Ricans, Cubans, and other Latinos began to interact with African American and white jazz musicians more than ever before in either the United States or Latin America. The other apex of this convergence was the multicultural complex and the human, industrial environment of New York City. The audiences that began to form in the Palladium and other dance halls were, like those of jazz, highly integrated, notwithstanding the elements of discrimination and segregation that still existed in a large part of the society.

Thus, Machito and Bauzá did not simply continue to stylize or develop a Cuban music. Yes, their musical concepts did "Cubanize" jazz; but jazz also "jazzified" their music in both its dance hall and concert contexts. Puerto Rican Juan Tizol's work with Duke Ellington, the Machito Orchestra, bebop, Charlie Parker, Dizzy Gillespie, and Chano Pozo (referred to Gillespie by Bauzá) all represented not only a growing and multicultural matrix but a changing matrix of style, expression, and thought with various ideological sources and factors.

This multicultural and often "transethnic" ambit that characterized the Latin music movement of the fifties, of course, has not remained a strong social reality, especially since the "salsa explosion" of the seventies, when the music became heavily identified and socialized as a pan-Latino expression and movement not separated from the current political environment of the period. Following the civil unrest and civil rights movement of the sixties, Latinos throughout the United States pursued causes similar to those that had been initiated by African Americans.

Thus, it was especially during the sixties and thereafter that the numerous Latino and African American musical genres converged in diverse forms throughout the United States. The boogaloo style was one of the earlier syntheses of Latin music and R&B, epitomized through New York artists such as Joe Cuba, Joe Bataan, and Willie Colón. In California such intercultural compatibility or "resolution" (as opposed to "intercultural conflict") took form through the artistry of Carlos Santana, Azteca, and Malo in San Francisco and Thee Midniters, Lil' Ray Jiménez, El Chicano, and Tierra in Los Angeles.

Such intercultural compatibility among Latinos and African Americans has been noted and rationalized by artists and critics citing a number of theories. Crediting Machito as the cultural mediator who "stood at the juncture of Caribbean and Afro-American musical traditions," Juan Flores provides some significant analytical insight concerning the interaction of Puerto Ricans and African Americans in musical and aesthetic choices, tracing the contemporary hip-hop of both communities to the fifties and sixties.

These years saw the dawning of the second-generation Black and Puerto Rican communities in New York; it was the time when the first offspring of both migrations, many of them born and raised in New York, were settling into their new situation. They comprised, and still today comprise, the two largest nonwhite groups in the city. They came from southern, largely rural backgrounds; they lived in the same or bordering neighborhoods, attended the same schools, and together occupy the most deprived and vulnerable place in the economic and cultural hierarchy; they are the reserve of the reserve. Small wonder, then, that young Blacks and Puerto Ricans started liking the same kinds of music, doing the same dances, playing the same games, and dressing and talking alike. Their common experience of racist exclusion and social distance from their white-ethnic peers drew them even closer. In groping for a new idiom, young Blacks and Puerto Ricans discarded rural trappings and nostalgic "down home" references, but retained the African rhythmic base and improvisational, participatory qualities of their inherited cultures. In so doing, Black and Caribbean peoples came to recognize the complementarity of what seemed to be diverse origins. (1988, 34)

Flores's analysis lends itself to further expansion. The intercultural compatibility of African Americans, Cubans, Puerto Ricans, and other Latinos was forged through social and cultural relationships, traditions, and aesthetic forces. Marginal societies became sensitized to what Flores refers to as complementarity. Instead of instantiating the separatist predictions and fears of many contemporary social and political critics, individually identified cultural communities synthesized the art and ideologies on various levels and in various sectors. Multiculturalism tended to unify and in the process provided much fodder for creativity—but such is the historical pattern of art and many marginal communities throughout the world.

The Case of Tito Puente

Earlier I alluded to the multicultural ambit of the Palladium era represented by artists such as the orchestras of Machito, Tito Puente, and Tito Rodríguez, among many others. In addition to benefiting from the interaction of Latinos and African Americans, however, Latin dance music in New York City, especially during the fifties, attracted large audiences from the "white" public, including dancers and aficionados from Italian, Jewish, Irish, Polish, German, English, and other European heritages. As Max Salazar mentioned earlier in chapter 3, the social context of the Palladium era integrated the races. With more specific reference to Tito Puente, Salazar eloquently expressed the same point of analysis in the program notes that he wrote for the "Discovery Day Concert" honoring Puente at Lincoln Center's Avery Fischer Hall in 1977: "For the last twenty-five years, Tito Puente has accomplished more with his music in improving race relations than any scientific study. Since 1949 he has thrilled Anglos with mambos, cha chas, Latin jazz, pachangas, bossa-nova, and guaguancós. To the non-Latins the Spanish lyrics seemed unimportant. Puente's music made the point. The almost one-thousand tunes in his repertoire firmly established 'TP' as Latin music's most productive and progressive leader" (Salazar 1977c).

Attesting to the context of this multicultural ambit are the reflections of songwriter Mort Shuman, who credited much of his creative development to Latin music in New York. "The Puerto Rican influence was very strong in New York. You had terrific bands like Tito Puente, Tito Rodríguez, and [Cuban] Machito. There was a great ballroom, the Palladium at 53rd and Broadway, and every Wednesday night was mambo night. You'd get two or three bands on the same bill. The place was jam packed with people who worked in factories. Cleaning ladies. It was a great melting pot and the catalytic agent was Latin music. I was there every night it was open" (in Escott 1988).

Perhaps one of the most significant aspects of Puente is that he became enmeshed with various generations—the adults, the children, and the babies of the forties through the nineties. Race and intercultural relations have taken different courses during these years, but Puente has attempted to adapt to each era. It can be said that he has taken more of the multicultural versus nationalistic course, consistently emphasizing the international popularity and charisma of his music and himself. At the same time, however, he has often been active in the artistic and political solidarity of the Latino community in the United States. On some particular political fronts, however, he has expressed no interest; for example, he has not performed in or visited Cuba since before the 1959 revolution.

In assessing Puente's relationship to and perception of these issues of identity, nationalism, and the multicultural ambit, some of the artist's own statements shed light on his philosophy. In 1981 Puente expressed the following thoughts:

> It's very difficult to put a big Latin band on the Johnny Carson Show. He doesn't need me. He has a big band of his own there. I can't go on by myself. Buddy Rich goes out there. He does it by himself, but that's jazz; they can go in. Count Basie—I've seen him play by himself [on the show], but you'll never see a Latin artist go by himself. You can't, because they can't play our music, they can't interpret it. They're great musicians, naturally, but you can't play a *guaguancó* on Johnny Carson because the people that he caters to don't know what *guaguancó* or a typical Latin tune is, so you have to go with a semicommercial thing. Maybe an "Oye como va" they might understand, or a "Tico Tico," a Brazilian thing, or "Chin Chin Chi"—Cugat type music, and that's not my music, really, so it's a challenging thing. You're in between, and then you don't know what to do. . . . So we're Latins and yet we're not. We still got to play commercial music for the masses [and shows such as] Johnny Carson. Then our Latin people put us down for playing that type of music, so we're in the middle of both sequences. And when you cater to masses you never know which way you're heading. You could become lucky or not. You have to know what direction you're going, and it's very difficult.
>
> But I have always had a big, large English-speaking audience, and I always, as we say in Spanish, "Plantao bandera"—wherever I go I represent more or less, the Puerto Rican people. . . . Wherever I go, [wherever] I travel, they ask me, "What are you?" I say "I'm Puerto Rican." Bam, bam, bam, I talk. But I am international, too. I play

for all kinds of people, and they dance to my music and I have all kinds of a following; so I don't want to tag myself . . . but when they ask me who I am, I represent Puerto Rico. In festivals . . . like in Venezuela, "La Festival de la Canción," I represent Puerto Rico. . . . The State Department has never sent me to South America and . . . embassies representing the United States. But yet they send Woody Herman playing for the Latin embassies down there, and I wrote six of the arrangements, and I recorded an album with Woody Herman. They sent Dizzy Gillespie also . . . and Herbie Mann; the *State Department* for the *Latins* down there. They haven't sent one Latin band down there . . .

I've been in Mexico with my orchestra, played right there, and I've gone to see the State Department concert to see Sarah Vaughn singing there! In Mexico. And everybody's Mexican, Spanish. And she was jazz, beautiful, and she gives me recognition 'cause she's my friend, but yet this is the Latin State Department Centuries Band. There hasn't been no Latin band that's been able to do that yet. The American bands are doing that. So we have all these problems, really, and there's a lot to talk about there. And our representation is not being done the right way. So therefore, to play in the White House like I've done [shows that] there are new doors that are opening up. I think it's going to be easing up in the decade. It'll take another decade to do it. I hope I'm around to finish it up, but I'm starting it and I have a feeling it's going to be there. It's going to make it. (Puente 1981)

Certainly Puente's words must be considered somewhat prophetic. Since these words, recorded in 1981, Tito Puente has continued to perform for every U.S. president and to receive major national and international honors and recognition. During the same 1981 interview Puente also commented considerably on the state of the Latin music industry as a business.

We have a major problem [in] that we don't have *Latin* executives in our business—people that are well studied. In other words, you'll always find the owners of Latin companies are other races than Latin. The people that are making money in Latin music are not Latin people. They're other people, other nationalities. The people involved in television—we don't have no big Latin producer or big Latin director. We don't have great Latin arrangers. I mean we have a few South American arrangers, but in this country we don't have the Quincy Jones or people of that category—or Henry Mancini. Sure we have Lalo Schifrin, but he came through Dizzy Gillespie and had a connection in Argentina. He's out there.

What we need is executive-type people in our public relations, executives in our recording companies, executives in magazines, and exposure to the media, radio, and airplays. We need executives, *Latin* executives, that know of our music and culture, that could be able to go out and present something. I'm on the board of governors for the Grammy Awards, and why do they have me there? They have me there because I represent the Latin category, let's say, and they could send me to Nashville, Tennessee, where I'll meet people there, where[as] if they send another Latin person down there to talk or categorize our music. . . . They'll listen to me because I'm Tito Puente. I'm a known bandleader, an artist. But if you send somebody else that maybe knows more about how to present their music, they won't accept them at this point.

So therefore, that's why we need our young people to go to school, continue their education, don't quit school, don't be disappointed. Don't feel bad, disillusioned, 'cause I know times are bad and the music business is a very rough business. I'm asked by some people, "Would you do it again if you had to?" Yes, I would do it again because God put me into this world to do this and this is what I have to do, and he made me creative. I don't come from a musical family, so any talents I have I would say he gave them to me mostly. It was his wish, and I thank him for it very much. There may be a lot of young people here of our people that are very talented also, but it has to be developed. They have to go to school, learn how to use the tools, the books, and go to the conservatories and learn how to play the instruments. And then when you get out there, because everybody graduates at the same time, and everybody has the same books . . . doctors, dentists, everybody has the same education. Then they spread out, they go into their own field and they develop a following and a business or their professions. Same thing in the music field. Then you develop, you become creative, you become arrangers, you become executives. You go into marketing or whatever. The music business is a very, very, very big multimillion dollar business. You go into recordings and you go into media and you go into video, because you'll be coming up in our future videotaping and videorecording, digital recording. And producers, we need good Latin people that can evolve into producing good digital records, good videotapes, putting shows together, and choreographers. This goes for dancers, too. Ballets, singers, opera singers, all involved with music.

So our young people should study, and in the future you'll always find that all of a sudden the recognition is there. Like a José Ferrer—he's there, a Puerto Rican. He's one of our top great artists. How many José Ferrers do we have? We have a lot of young people coming up, but it takes time. A lot of people, like Miriam Colón, will develop . . .

We have a lot of Hispanic people in this country, and all we need is the people and the forefront. What they're doing in the political scene—a lot of Hispanics—there's congressmen all over the country. They're all over in California, in Sacramento. We have a lot of Mexican people out there that are into big politics, recognition. We had one person that was running for mayor in New York not many years ago, so we have a lot of big, big people in that field. So why not in the music field? And the big thing— so that we can put our music to be recognized throughout the world. That's what my object is—to get recognition for our Latin American music throughout the whole world, where throughout, when people talk about one kind of music in Europe, they can compare it with Latin music. When they talk about it in Japan, Latin music is right at their level. Whatever kind of music they discuss, Latin music could be at their level. And to get that we need the education and the experience and the creativeness of our young people coming up today to do their will in this decade now. If not, we're going to lose everything we have. (Puente 1981)

Since these 1981 transcripts, many of Puente's concerns have resolved themselves in creative, productive fashion; others have remained problematic. One of the issues Puente raised was that of the lack of Latino record executives. In 1981 Jerry Masucci, an Italian American, had achieved a high level of success in recording and marketing the Latin music style salsa under his Fania label. Martin Cohen not only was the chief executive of Latin Percussion, Inc., but also initiated and managed Puente's Latin Jazz Ensemble, which eventually became the bandleader's principal and highly successful musical project through the eighties and nineties. Puente's recording outlet for this Latin jazz period was Concord Records, owned by Carl Jefferson.

By the nineties, however, Puente was recording on two other labels as well, RMM and Tropijazz, both owned and managed by Ralph Mercado, Puente's longtime business manager, and distributed through Sony Records (formerly Columbia Records), one of the leading international record companies, with corporate ownership based in Japan. The emergence of Mercado's record companies by the midnineties represented a new and significant shift in the Latin music industry, especially that associated with salsa and Latin jazz artists. By this period Sergio George, who had been the predominant arranger and producer for many of Mercado's productions (including work on Puente's 100th album), had also initiated a production and recording company, thus also emerging as a competitive actor in the newly changing market. Simultaneously, the Latin divisions of Sony and EMI Records continued to expand internationally, primarily in the area of "pop," which by this time was incorporating major influence from the new "*salsa erótica*" artists such as Luis Enríque, Eddie Santiago, Tito Nieves, and La India.

As commercialization of Latin music spread, the music was adapted and changed markedly. Another issue emerged, one echoed in Puente's 1981 transcript: many of the Latin music aficionados complained of what they perceived as major artistic compromise and a decaying musical quality. Puente's response to the situation of change has been outspoken yet moderate. He actually promoted and produced one of the younger artists, Millie P., who for some years performed with his ensembles during the late eighties. He has also been critical of much of the new salsa, however, noting its lack of spontaneity, improvisation, dynamics, and traditional structure. At the same time, Puente has seemed to appreciate and applaud the growing emergence of Latin executives and producers, for he has worked with many of them, in the production of both recordings and performances.

Puente's emphasis on the importance of formal education is readily apparent in the 1981 interview with Patricia Wilson Cryer. It was actually during this same period that I met and started working on projects with Puente. At the time, I was a doctoral student in music at UCLA, and I always felt that Tito paid particular attention and respect to that aspect of my work. It is certainly one of his more passionate premises, and the primary one on which he envisions the destiny of Latin culture within United States society.

From this vantage point, it might also be significant to cite Puente's apparent interest in the pan-Latino movement, which has occurred on a diverse spectrum, especially since the end of the sixties. With his references to the growing solidarity of Latino politicians, artists, and other professionals throughout the United States, Puente has emerged as one of the leading advocates for Latino unity in the country. Although not as lyrically direct as artists such as Rubén Blades, Puente has managed to focus on political issues at various critical points and places. His role in educational projects is possibly his principal activism in this area, for example, his scholarship foundation, his honorary doctorates, and his continual seminars and workshops at various schools and universities throughout the world.

Certainly one of Puente's priorities, as elicited in the 1981 transcript, is that of the recognition and development of Latin music as a major world art form. By taking Latin music into countries previously unexposed to the art, Puente has facilitated its world transmission. As a performer of Latin music (as conceived in this book), he has traveled to more parts of the world than any other artist to date and has become an international institution. The goals he expressed in 1981 have been achieved to a greater extent than even he might have imagined.

It is also significant to reflect on Puente's comments concerning the lack of Latins in the media, especially television. This is an area that has remained extremely problematic. A national study published in 1996 revealed that whereas 3 percent of personalities appearing on television during the fifties were of Latino heritage, the figure had decreased to 1 percent by the midnineties (Center for Media and Public Affairs 1996, 6). These statistics became a highly controversial and disturbing issue to the Latino community in the United States, estimated to constitute about 11 percent of the national population (Ybarra-Frausto and Gutiérrez 1997). As of 1996 the issue continued to foment much controversy and political action in the arts industry in general. *People Weekly's* cover story for its March 18, 1996, issue was the controversy over the fact that only one African American had been nominated for the 1995 Academy Awards (out of the 166 major categories). *People* referred to the situation as a "Hollywood Blackout" and a "national disgrace." The Reverend Jesse Jackson proceeded to mobilize minority groups nationally in protest of the state of the film industry, especially citing the lack of African Americans and other minorities in executive positions. The *Los Angeles Times* published the following excerpt as part of its front-page story the day following the internationally televised Academy Awards show staged at the Music Center of Los Angeles County: "The protests were being billed as a launching pad in a campaign spearheaded by Jackson and his Rainbow Coalition to fight what he called 'race exclusion and cultural violence' within the motion picture industry. He said Hollywood continues to resist employing people of color in influential decision-making positions and that it hides behind the terms of 'creativity and artistic license' to resist diversity" (*Los Angeles Times,* Mar. 26, 1996, p. 21).

One vivid example of some of the Motion Picture Academy's inflexibility was expressed by Frank Berry, author of the *People Weekly* article, citing the elimination of a Los Lobos film-track song as a nominee for an Oscar:

> The absence of adequate Hispanic representation probably accounted for its most notorious recent blooper. What happened was that "Canción del Mariachi," Los Lobos's guitar-driven ballad in last year's *Desperado,* was nearly declared ineligible for consideration as Best Original Song because its Spanish lyrics were deemed "not intelligible" by the Academy's music branch. (The Academy later blamed a "clerical mistake" for the ruling.) Frank Lieberman, the Academy's spokesman, says that data on its racial demographics "is not information that we keep," but that there is "no voting [by] color in the Academy." (Berry 1996, 51)

Much of this reflects the critical perspective of Tito Puente in his previously cited thoughts on the music industry and the difficulty Latin musicians have experienced in their attempts to "mainstream" and market their product. Mirroring Puente's stance on the problem of the Grammy Awards was a recent statement made by Latin artist Willie Colón via e-mail:

> Winning the Grammy has nothing to do with talent. . . . It doesn't even have anything to do with sales or airplay. It's about money and name recognition. It's about record companies buying hundreds of general memberships and voting in a block for a slate of their artists. . . . There are artists out there who have made their fame and fortune as minor league pop stars and have found the secret of getting a guaranteed Grammy for their mantle. Record a "Tropical" album! That way they can use their pop name recognition on the General voting members of the Academy and "steal" a Grammy. . . . Today, all "Latino Musics," from Julio Iglesias to Milton Nascimento to Lil Joe to Tito Puente to Gloria Estefan, must compete for three (3) slots. Gospel music has eight (8). I [have] continued to press for more categories or a separate Latino Grammy to which a NARAS (National Academy of Recording Arts and Sciences) official snorted before the membership one night, "Everyone in Latin America is in bed with somebody. We need to know where everybody is when the lights are out." Hello! Is this the old pot calling the kettle black? . . . I . . . was subsequently voted out of my seat on the Board [of Governors of the New York chapter of NARAS]. I was one of the very few people who was not being paid to sit on that board. The others worked for different companies and trade associations and would come to the meetings on company time. These are the people who make the decisions.
>
> I really can't be happy for Linda Ronstadt, Gloria Estefan, David Byrne, or Paul Simon when they are nominated in our category because it almost always means that some artist like myself, the Gran Combo or Celia Cruz, who has lived for this music, will be overlooked and possibly miss a once in a lifetime opportunity because of someone's little musical excursion. . . . It's too late for many to get their due but the word has to be spread so that it will be more difficult and eventually impossible for NARAS to continue this arrogant fraud. We deserve better. ("The Grammy Deception," by William Anthony Colón, sent Feb. 29, 1996, via e-mail)

The issue of the arts industry and its integration with Latin culture in the United States is one that merits much more discussion, analysis, and critical assessment. As George Lipsitz has eloquently noted, we learn both of place and of displacement through music, in effect constituting a "poetics of place" (Lipsitz 1994, 4). The views of Tito Puente among many other artists of various cultural perspectives attest to the issue as a pervasive one in contemporary society, especially in the light of the aesthetic, cultural questions that I have raised in this chapter.*

There are, of course, contrasting perspectives on the issue. Some will point to the fact that artists such as Estefan have included leading Latin music artists such as Tito

---

*In a separate study (Loza 1998) I pursue the dynamic of Latin music's popularity and adaptation in Asia and Europe, where it enjoys a far more prolific level of engagement than has been developed by non-Latino U.S. musicians and industry. Why is this so? Is there a possible hypothesis that could be linked to linguistic aesthetics, abilities, or intercultural conflict and prejudices?

Puente, Cachao, and numerous others on her Grammy-winning tropical albums, in effect promoting and giving deserved recognition to these great artists. Likewise, Ronstadt made use of leading Latin musicians and arranger Ray Santos on her Grammy Award–winning album *Frenesí*. In addition to finally adding a Latin jazz category to the Grammy Awards in 1996, NARAS has also initiated a major plan for a specific Latin American Grammy Awards. Colón's arguments, however, represent the sentiments of many Latin music artists, producers, critics, and aficionados.

The multicultural challenges posited by the constant globally diversifying music industry and market demand serious critical assessment of the needs of individual "cultures" versus the frequently (and now predominantly) larger society. Jacques Maquet (1979) has suggested that culture is based on society, although one can argue the opposite. But Maquet observes a basic flaw in much contemporary thought and analysis: the "multicultural interpretation" is often focused on the issues of diversity and difference rather than on the condition of human interaction, for example, the music industry or society. Maquet makes no claims as to the egalitarianism of society; he speaks only to its inevitable, manipulative, and expanding dominance in the world at large.

The Aesthetic Locus of Latin Music

In his treatment of art from an anthropological perspective, Maquet defines an "aesthetic locus" as follows: "It does not seem that a society maintains an equally intense aesthetic interest in all the things made within its borders. There are certain privileged fields where awareness and performance are higher, where expectations and efforts converge. The class or classes of objects that are localized in these areas of heightened aesthetic consciousness constitute the aesthetic locus of a culture" (Maquet 1979, 30).

It is through conceptual frameworks such as those of Maquet that we can attempt to understand, perhaps on a more meaningful basis, the art and aesthetic locus of Tito Puente and his place in Latin music and its world community. From his earliest days as a professional artist, Puente has created and worked within a matrix of constant dialectics: the tension between his own work and style and the external forces at work—namely, the public and the music industry. Puente manipulated this dialectic in a number of ways. One can also interpret the other side of this equation, one in which the public and the industry manipulated him.

But Puente's manipulative verve has driven the equation. Although he consistently detected the wants and needs of the public and the techniques and strategies of the industry, Puente was able to integrate the elements of another of Maquet's constructs, that of a societal, productive, and ideational triadic. From the societal ambits of the Palladium and the international effects of his music to the productive contradiction of recording industry issues such as the Grammy Awards and the lack of Latino representation, to the ideational incorporation of Afro-Cuban religious themes and music on albums such as *Cuban Carnival* and *Top Percussion,* Puente has manipulated this interactive matrix in a most creative way.

Another mode of thought conducive to such analysis is that of Johannes Wilbert, who suggests that life as expressed through culture can be examined on three specific levels, the cosmic, the cultural, and the telluric. Through the physical, material form of *cultural expression,* the concepts of *cosmic form* (those of spiritual or religious philosophy) and *telluric form* (which encompasses the environment, flora, seasons, and lifecycle) converge into a fuller concept of meaning, purpose, and the interrelationships of so-called life categories, including expression, culture, and the cosmos.

As with Maquet's triadic, Wilbert's three-part model can illuminate the interactive case of Tito Puente, who has negotiated Wilbert's three levels through his cultural production. Predominantly working within the urban, industrial context, his telluric and in part cultural environment, Puente has utilized the physical cultural forms of music, dance, and lyrics to negotiate a matrix of goals, including aesthetic fulfillment, financial sustenance, economic production, spiritual motivation, and social and moral standards, among other possible conceptualizations.

A number of scholars, such as Duane Champagne (1989) and Maria Williams (1996), have been critical of a dominant trend in the social sciences and humanities to "compartmentalize" the factors and functions of a culture. To Champagne, Williams, and others, culture and its collective expression is composed of interactive, inseparable meanings and functions where the spirit is not separated from the body or the universe. I might also allude to the tendency by many in the so-called positivist or materialist schools of thought to separate the intellectual from the intuitive. Puente's art has personified the union of these various areas of meaning, action, and purpose. His musical manifestations cannot be compartmentalized socially, ideologically, or productively, although I do not negate the usefulness of various approaches to *assess* his work on such bases of analysis. But we cannot permit the analysis to become the meaning. As Albert Murray eloquently assessed in *The Hero and the Blues,* it is the "artist, not the social or political engineer or even the philosopher, who first comes to realize when the time is out of joint. It is he who determines the extent and gravity of the current human predicament, who in effect discovers and describes the hidden element of destruction, sounds the alarm, and even . . . designates the targets" (Murray 1973, 11).

In the final analysis, the aesthetic locus of Tito Puente is large—indeed, worldwide—and it is an integrated, interactive matrix of ideation, society, and production. It is a cross-section of the cosmic, the cultural, and the telluric. Crossing cultures through the other categories of these conceptual frameworks, Puente was able to *access* not only a universal "language" but a universal art and ideology and a universal soul.

And the soul thus leads us back to the union of the intuitive and the intellectual, conducive to Benedeto Croce's idea of the "supremely real" domain of the metaphysical. In addition to Croce, numerous twentieth-century philosophers and artists, including José Vasconcelos, Teilhard de Chardin, Deepak Chopra, John Coltrane, and Carlos Santana, have ultimately detected the connection between art, the universe, and a unity of all life in a metaphysical, mystical body. The interactive, organic cells of Puente's music reflect and express this higher unified form.

The Reclamation of Culture

In previous studies I have applied the concept of aesthetic and cultural "reclamation" through a conceptual, cyclical model revolving as an interacting wheel of tradition, reinterpretation, and innovation (Loza 1992, 1993, 1994a). The innovation of Tito Puente and his music can certainly be understood as a product of his involvement with tradition and his reinterpretation of it. But innovation is not necessarily the result of any artist's reinterpretations of tradition. Whereas Puente experimented extensively while still being able to feed a traditional appetite, others maintained unchanging recipes. The notable aspect of Puente has been his ability to maintain the integration of the cycle of tradition, reinterpretation, and innovation.

As a specific example of this process, we may first look at Puente's use of Cuban musical forms. As critiqued previously in this chapter, Manuel's conceptualization of much Puerto Rican music (in New York and Puerto Rico) as representing a "creative appropriation" of Cuban music partly implies that nationalist motives inspired Puerto Rican musical identity.

Tito Puente's early years of enculturation in Spanish Harlem were contoured less by an exclusive Puerto Rican identity than by a bilingual, multicultural ambit and his exposure to many cultural concepts and values. Although Puente, in a number of his statements documented in this book, has expressed his interest in asserting his Puerto Rican heritage, he has simultaneously personified through his musical expression and enterprise the issues of a pan-Latino and international aesthetic. He did not co-opt Cuban music because of a nationalist motive or because of its religious correspondences, such as *santería*. Puente has openly and consistently stated throughout his career that he "plays Cuban music," and he has grappled with the evolved term *salsa* as well as with concepts such as "crossover," for he has realized the historical inevitability of such fusion and cultural interchange. In addition to working with Cuban and Puerto Rican musical forms, Puente has gravitated strongly toward jazz, European classical music, and Mexican and South American forms, among many others. Furthermore, supporting my previous reference to the African origins of Cuban music, Puente has consistently referred to "Mother Africa" as the primary source of his music, a perspective that far outdistances provincial nationalist theories. Puente might well agree with an interesting comment made by a Cuban composer who has resided in the United States since the late fifties, Aurelio de la Vega.

> For me, true musical nationalism is the one of Vivaldi, of Beethoven, of Debussy, of Crumb, for example—composers who, without citing folklore melodies or waving flags, have attracted the attention, the admiration and the respect of the world for the countries (shall I better say "human communities") where their powerful art developed . . . all of them created incredibly personal masterpieces, which, although expanding beyond national frontiers, expressed ideas and sounds with their own vocabularies, delivering their works without preconceived ideas about political, or geographical boundaries. (in Erin 1984, 3)

There is another dimension to Puente's aesthetic and cultural reclamation, that of his constantly evolving musical style that rotates on the cyclical conceptual wheel of tradition, reinterpretation, and innovation. Puente has made a practice of recycling past concepts and restylizing them, revitalizing them, and giving them new meaning while reaffirming their original meanings. A list of examples would include his treatment of tradition through musical arrangements such as "Picadillo," his original "mish-mash" composition recorded in 1949, which he later reinterpreted in more modern compositions or arrangements, notably on the LP *Un poco loco* (1987), where he disguises the tune, retitled "Chang," in a progressive, innovative mode. On his Grammy Award–winning *Goza mi timbal,* Puente directly reinterpreted his classic arrangement, renaming it "Picadillo a lo Puente."

But Puente's reinterpretation of his own and others' music was not simply a career afterthought during the eighties and nineties. It was in the fifties that Puente first experimented with traditional Afro-Cuban drumming as the exclusive content of his early LPs *Puente in Percussion* (1956) and *Top Percussion* (1958). Other examples of converging religious and popular tradition include arrangements or compositions such as "Elegua Changó" on his *Cuban Carnival* LP of 1956, a remarkably innovative experiment that nonetheless achieved success on the dance floor. It was on his highly acclaimed *Dance Mania* album that Puente first adapted the marimba, an African-derived instrument with origins in Central America and southern Mexico, where he acquired the one he brought back to New York. On this album, as on his "Hong Kong Mambo," he reinterpreted the role of the marimba using a theme that he associated with the Far East (he would reinterpret this basic theme on a 1992 composition entitled "Japan Mambo"). From his early days to his recent ones, Puente's multicultural experiments continued to invigorate and renovate the energy and imagination of dancers, musicians, and record executives.

On his important LP *Tito Puente and His Concert Orchestra* (1973), Puente reaffirms the role of his rumba-driven timbal virtuosity while juxtaposing it with an assortment of orchestration concepts and instrumental experimentation. The album *The Legend* (1977) literally paid homage to the tradition and innovations of Puente through Rubén Blades's text and music. Another vehicle on that album that attests to Puente's consistent innovation was his "Fiesta a la King," a composition that surprised many traditionalists of Latin music yet reinvigorated many others.

Puente's reinterpretations of classic pieces from jazz to Latin and their combinations constitute another notable product of his innovative, interpretive arrangement skills and conceptualization. His composition "Machito Forever," dedicated to his mentor, represents Puente's utilization of traditional Latin musical frameworks constructed with numerous new and progressive harmonic, melodic, and rhythmic experimentation. Such experiments, although new and different, emulated the experimental spirit of Machito as much as they did the use of traditional Latin rhythms and structure. In his contemporary tribute "Ode to Cachao," Puente invokes the traditional *charanga* texture and cha-cha format with musical echoes of both Cachao's "Chanchullo" and his own "Oye como va," two compositions related historically and musically. Again, the arrangement is traditional yet modern—or what some may today refer to as postmodern, for it incorporates not only a mosaic of the past and the present but also, more important, the mutual contradictions and relationships of both. In Puente's rerenderings of his classics "Oye como va" and "Pa' los rumberos," he incorporates readaptations of Santana's experiments with the compositions. On one of his most recent albums, *Jazzin'*, Puente, with vocalist La India, reinterprets classic Latin American and jazz standards including María Grever's "Cuando vuelva a tu lado" ("What a Difference a Day Makes"), Antonio Carlos Jobim's "Wave," and Cole Porter's "Love for Sale." On another scale of innovation have been Puente's consistently creative adaptations of the giants of the jazz repertory, including the music of Fats Waller, Charlie Parker, Dizzy Gillespie, Thelonious Monk, Miles Davis, and John Coltrane. Metamorphosing, for example, Coltrane's "Equinox" into an Afro-Cuban 6/8 interpretation or his "Giant Steps" into an accelerated clave pace signifies Puente's unprecedented approach and ability to innovate on the innovative.

The list of examples could go on and on. Throughout his over fifty years in music, Tito Puente has constantly allowed his passion for innovation and tradition to meld an art form that continues to change while retaining its integrity as an intercultural vehicle for human expression. Puente has discovered a multitude of modes for his reinterpretations of an art form and its many meanings—meanings that have also remained the same.

The Limits of the Word

Throughout this chapter it has been my aim to address the issues of identity, nationalism, and aesthetics and their relevance to the art of Tito Puente. Such analysis, based on historical data and creative artifact, can claim to arrive at only a fraction of understanding and must be understood as only selected criteria of judgment; even this judgment may result in a multiplicity of meanings. In the final analysis, words will not begin to suffice for the infinity of realities, physical and metaphysical, that can be arbitrarily attributed to human expression—in this case, the art of music and the question of its meaning. In this both Maestro Puente and I, after substantial discussion, are in agreement. Words have their limits. However, we do not negate the challenge of these words as part of our art and the learning of it. We offer the following words of Michel Foucault, from his *Archaeology of Knowledge,* who has, we believe, made a valuable point.

> This rarity of statements, the incomplete, fragmented form of the enunciative field, the fact that few things, in all, can be said, explain that statements are not, like the air we breathe, an infinite transparency; but things that are transmitted and preserved, that have value, and which one tries to appropriate; that are repeated, reproduced, and transformed; to which pre-established networks are adapted, and to which a status is given in the institution; things that are duplicated not only by copy or translation, but by exegesis, commentary, and the internal proliferation of meaning. Because statements are rare, they are collected in unifying totalities, and the meanings to be found in them are multiplied. (Foucault 1993, 119–20)

8
The King and I

Tito Puente and His Universal Society

In assessing the lifework of Tito Puente, it seems most useful to me to view the effects of one of his typical performances as an analogy for his effects on the world. In May 1996, after Tito had read a preliminary draft of this book, we met to discuss some of his ideas for the project and problems associated with it. He invited me to attend his concert that same week at the House of Blues in Hollywood. It was a Cinco de Mayo event, and the club was jampacked. The analogy lies in the context and experience of the performance. Puente led his fifteen-piece band in musical compositions dating from his earliest days to the present, including arrangements such as "Pa' los rumberos" (with which he opened); "Cayuco," from his *Dance Mania* era; Miles Davis's "All Blues"; "Nica's Tempo" (featuring alto saxophonist Bobby Porcelli), from the recent *Tito's Idea* album (during the performance of which he commented on the Grammy problem); his staple crowd pleaser "Oye como va"; the Gipsy Kings' "Bamboleo"; and Selena's pre- and post-mortem hit "Amor prohibido" (the latter two featuring vocalist Yolanda Duke). The opening show had featured Francisco Aguabella's drum ensemble performing rumbas and Afro-Cuban religious music.

But this amalgam of Latin American popular culture interpreted by means of rumba, mambo, cha-cha, *guaracha,* and bolero surpassed any specific ambit of ethnicity, economic class, gender, age, religion, sexuality, fashion, physical typology, or sociopolitical ideology. The room, holding over a thousand people, included women, men, Latinos, African Americans, white Americans, Asians, Africans, Europeans, Arabs, Catholics, Jews, Protestants, Muslims, Buddhists, singles, married couples, unmarried couples, single and coupled gays and lesbians, people aged twenty-one to seventy-five, dancers, listeners, musicians, janitors, lawyers, reporters, maids, doctors, bartenders, and bouncers. As he has done at many performances like this one, Puente commented on how the whole atmosphere reminded him of his early days in New York's Palladium.

In *City of God* St. Augustine formulated a concept relevant to the image that I have presented here. Augustine analogizes good and evil with two cities: one of spirits devoted to divine truth and goodness—the city of God—and one of evil men and angels who spurn God, an earthly, materialist city of lesser values. In discussing this notion, Vernon Bourke has pointed to our world, where "all human history and culture may be viewed as the interplay of the competing values of these two loves and of these two cities" (Bourke 1958, 10).

In today's growing debate on the goal of "world culture" and the "global village," juxtaposed with contradictory concepts of "developing nations" and the "Third World," society seems still to be speaking to two cities. But these are not the cities of Augustine. They are the contemporary dialectical and hegemonic concepts of materialist thought, ideology, and values. Augustine's ideal of a noble and universal society inspires me, yet ironically, while watching a current affairs television program, I heard former House Speaker Newt Gingrich discussing his fears of illegal immigration, the threat that English might be supplanted as the principal U.S. language, and other ethno-ideocentric views and near-fascist opinionating and campaigning.

To me, that night at the House of Blues evoked not only Augustine's but also Tito Puente's "City of God": a global village, a place where we can all live in peace, which Augustine defined as "the perfectly ordered and *harmonious communion* of those who find their joy in God, and in one another in God" (Bourke 1958, 13; emphasis added). Augustine's philosophy that both cities comprised people of various religions and metaphysical values evokes the idealism and spirit of a growing global village and world culture—a *universal society*.

Etienne Gilson further clarifies Augustine's stance:

> In his notion of a universal religious society is to be sought the origin of that ideal of a world society which is haunting the minds of so many today. . . .
>
> Our contemporaries aspire after a complete unity of all peoples: one world. They are quite right. The universal society which they are endeavoring to organize aims at being a political and temporal society. In this regard they are again right. Perhaps their most serious mistake is in imagining that a universal and purely natural society of men is possible without a universal religious society, which would unite men in the acceptance of the same supernatural truth and in the love of the same supernatural good. (in Bourke 1958, 13)

If one considers the music of Tito Puente to be religious, as I do, then Augustine's ideas become even clearer. What has brought so many diverse philosophies to the floors of places from the Palladium to the Houses of Blues has been a common philosophy based not on rhythm and tones but on the spirit and the spiritual. Puente's music is godlike, as is Augustine's city, and Puente and his society are religious, as is Augustine's universal society. Furthermore, like Augustine, Puente is literally, actively religious: he is Catholic, he practices Afro-Cuban *santería,* and he believes in the religions of the world. As blues is still religious music, so too is there spiritual, magical power in the rumba, cha-cha, and mambo, all descendants of a religious tradition.*

¿Adónde Maestro?

As this book is printed, Tito Puente continues to reign as the king of Latin music. In 1996 he celebrated his fiftieth year in the Latin music industry, still performing at diverse venues throughout the world, ranging from the packed houses at Hollywood's House of Blues to New York's Madison Square Garden to Tokyo's and Greenwich Village's Blue Note jazz clubs. His recordings continue to sell worldwide, both his current projects and rereleases. Puente's record catalog represents a nearly comprehensive historical anthology of the past fifty years of Latin music.

My own professional relationship and personal friendship with the king have been special and rewarding. I have known Tito in a very special way—as a musician, as a fellow artist, and as a young protégé. And I have seen him in some of his greatest moments, as well as in some of his down moments (which are rare). Like all members of the human race, Tito has had to face the challenge of his own inconsistencies, self-contradictions, and vulnerabilities—part of what we call the human condition. But the other side, the strong, positive, and creative side, is the one that Tito has personified through his art, what he leaves as his legacy to society. As his lifelong friend Josie Powell has proclaimed, "He has given the world his music."

For many years I have listened to and played the music of Tito Puente, and I have performed beside him on the bandstand. Not until I started writing this book, however, and began the task of listening to hundreds of his recordings from a historical, analytical, and musical perspective did I begin to really understand the extensive dimensions that this individual has traversed and the accomplishment of his enduring artistry and enterprise. What I am attempting to say is that his body of work is simply overwhelming. Yes, it is clear that Tito Puente ranks with the Ellingtons and the Beethovens—or as those artists might put it, they rank with him.

So where do we go? I know one thing that Tito has told me: "We've got to keep our music alive." I know that we have to go there.

I have also related to Tito on a cultural and spiritual level. I am, like Tito, a multicultural American. We both think in English but sing in Spanish. We are North, Central, and South

---

* I have presented my views on music and faith more fully in Loza 1994.

Americans, and we feel very close to Africans and Native Americans. Beyond this, we believe we also represent the whole world through a music that knows no boundaries, borders, or prejudices. And we feel the beauty and hope of the supernatural—we know that life definitely goes *way* beyond this present phase. It's big, *very big*.

So who will reign after Tito? I don't know that there will ever be another king. But I can say that it has indeed been something special to write down some of the feelings, inspirations, and ideals that have been shared by "the king and I."

¡Adelante Maestro!

Discography

This discography was compiled by Joe Conzo in collaboration with Max Salazar, Steven Loza, and Francisco Crespo. Included are LP (long-play) albums and CDs of ensembles and projects recorded with Tito Puente as leader and thus under his name. Not included are the many recompilations of his recordings or the recordings of other artists on which he has performed or collaborated (as arranger, composer, or producer) or the numerous short-play 78- and 45-rpm disks that he released in his early recording career. A more detailed discography is presently being compiled by Joe Conzo.

Title	Label/No.	Date[a]
1. Tito Puente and Friends	Tropical 5138	1950
2. Mambos	Tico 101-vol-1	1952
3. Mambos	Tico 103	1952
4. Mambos	Tico 107	1952
5. Mambos	Tico 114	1952
6. Mambos	Tico 116	1952
7. Mambos	Tico 120	1952
8. Mambos	Tico 124	1952
9. Cha Cha	Tico 128	1954
10. Cha Cha	Tico 130	1954
11. Mambos	Tico 131	1954
12. Cha Cha	Tico 134	1955
13. Mamborama	Tico 1001	1956
14. Mambo with Me	Tico 1003	1956
15. Cha Cha for Lovers	Tico 1005	1956
16. Dance the Cha Cha	Tico 1010	1956
17. Puente in Percussion	Tico 1011	1956
18. Cha Cha at El Morocco	Tico 1025	1956

19. Cuban Carnival	RCA 1251	1956
20. Puente Goes Jazz	RCA 1312	1956
21. Mambo on Broadway	RCA 1354	1956
22. Let's Cha Cha with Puente	RCA 1392	1956
23. Night Beat	RCA 1447	1957
24. Mucho Puente	RCA 1479	1957
25. Be Mine Tonight, featuring Abbe Lane	RCA 1554	1957
26. Puente Swings, Vicentico Sings	Tico 1049	1957
27. Puente in Love	Tico 1058	1957
28. Woody Herman's Heat Puente's Beat	Everest 5010	1958
29. Top Percussion	RCA 1617	1958
30. Dance Mania	RCA 1692	1958
31. Dancing under Latin Skies	RCA 1874	1959
32. Mucho Cha Cha	RCA 2113	1959
33. Puente at Grossingers	RCA 2187	1959
34. Tambo	RCA 2257	1960
35. Pachanga in NY, with Rolando La Serie	Gemma 1145	1961
36. Pachanga con Puente	Tico 1083	1961
37. The Exciting Tito Puente in Hollywood	GNP 70	1961
38. Vaya Puente	Tico 1085	1962
39. El rey bravo	Tico 1086	1962
40. Y parece bobo	Alegre 842	1962
41. Bossa Nova by Puente	Roulette 25193	1962
42. The Perfect Combination, with Gilberto Monroig	Alegre 853	1963
43. Revolving Bandstand	RCA 2299	1963
44. More Dancemania	RCA 7147	1963
45. Tito Puente in Puerto Rico	Tico 1088	1963
46. Tito Puente bailables	Tico 1093	1963
47. Excitante ritmo de Tito Puente	Tico 1106	1963
48. The World of Tito Puente	Tico 1109	1963
49. Mucho mucho Puente	Tico 1115	1964
50. De mí para tí	Tico 1116	1964
51. The Best of Gilberto Monroig and Tito Puente	Tico 1117	1964
52. My Fair Lady Goes Latin	Roulette 25276	1965
53. Puente Swings La Lupe	Tico 1121	1965
54. Tú y yo: Tito Puente and La Lupe	Tico 1125	1965
55. Carnival in Harlem	Tico 1127	1965
56. Cuba y Puerto Rico son . . . , featuring Celia Cruz	Tico 1130	1966
57. Homenaje a Rafael Hernández, with La Lupe	Tico 1131	1966
58. Stop and Listen, featuring Santos Colón	Tico 1147	1967
59. 20th Anniversary of Tito Puente	Tico 1151	1967
60. El rey y yo, with La Lupe	Tico 1154	1967
61. What Now My Love, featuring Shawn Elliot	Tico 1156	1967
62. Eras, featuring Manny Román	Decca 4879	1967
63. Invitation to Love, featuring Bobby Capó	Musicor 4035	1968
64. El rey Tito Puente	Tico 1172	1968
65. Puente on the Bridge	Tico 1191	1969
66. Quimbo, Quimbumbia, with Celia Cruz	Tico 1193	1969
67. Con orgullo, with Sophy	Tico 1198[b]	1969
68. El fantástico, featuring El Lupo	Cotique 1028	1969
69. Etc., Etc., Etc., with Celia Cruz	Tico 1207	1970

70. Santitos, featuring Santos Colón	Fania 387	1970
71. El sol brilla para todos, featuring La Lloroncita	Tico 1206	1970
72. Imágenes, featuring Santos Colón	Tico 1213	1971
73. Palante	Tico 1214	1971
74. Alma con alma, featuring Celia Cruz	Tico 1221	1971
75. Te reto, featuring Sophy	Tico 1222	1971
76. La bárbara del mundo latino, featuring Noraida	Tico 1223	1971
77. Me voy a desquitar, featuring Noraida	Tico 1226	1971
78. Celia Cruz and Tito Puente in Spain	Tico 1227	1971
79. Pa' los rumberos	Tico 1301	1972
80. Algo especial para recordar, with Celia Cruz	Tico 1304	1972
81. The Many Moods of Tito Puente	RCA 3012	1972
82. Meñique, featuring Meñique	Cotique 1068	1972
83. Tito Puente and His Concert Orchestra	Tico 1308	1973
84. Tito Puente Unlimited	Tico 1322	1974
85. The Legend (La leyenda)	Tico 1413	1978
86. Homenaje a Beny (Moré)	Tico 1425	1978
87. La Pareja: T.P. and La Lupe	Tico 1430	1978
88. Homenaje a Beny (Moré), vol. 2	Tico 1436	1979
89. Dancemania 80's	Tico 1439	1980
90. C'est magnifique, with Azuquita	Tico 1440	1981
91. On Broadway	Concord 207	1983
92. El rey	Concord 250	1984
93. Homenaje a Beny Moré, vol. 3, with Celia Cruz	Tico/Vaya 105	1985
94. Mambo Diablo	Concord 283	1985
95. Sensación	Concord 301	1986
96. Un poco loco	Concord 329	1987
97. Salsa Meets Jazz	Concord 354	1988
98. Goza mi timbal	Concord 399	1989
99. Tito Puente Presents Millie P.	RMM 80375	1990
100. The Mambo King (El número cien)[c]	RMM/Sony 80680	1991
101. Out of This World	Concord 448	1991
102. Mambo of the Times	Concord 4499	1992
103. Live at the Village Gate	Tropijazz/RMM 80879	1992
104. Royal T	Concord 4553	1993
105. Master Timbalero	Concord 4594	1994
106. In Session	Tropijazz/RMM 81208	1994
107. Tito's Idea	Tropijazz/RMM 81571	1995
108. Jazzin': Tito Puente and India plus the Count Basie Orchestra	RMM 82032	1996
109. Special Delivery: Tito Puente and Maynard Ferguson	Concord CCD-4732	1996
110. 50 Years of Swing	RMM 82050	1997
111. En su momento, with Celio González	Teca LLS 555	n.a.
112. Otro descubrimiento de Tito Puente, with Noraida	Millie Latino 1050	n.a.
113. Una tarde de Julio: Fabrizio and Tito Puente	Rhino 501	n.a.
114. Llamado de amor: Tito Puente and Los Hispanos	Musicor 3137	n.a.
115. Brasilia nueve	Decca 74910	n.a.
116. Dancemania '99: Live at Birdland	RMD-82270	1998

a. Date of release or recording.
b. Previously recorded but unreleased.
c. Officially Tito Puente's one-hundredth album.

References Cited

Aparicio, Frances. 1998. *Listening to Salsa: Gender, Latin Popular Music, and Puerto Rican Cultures.* Hanover, N.H.: Published by the University Press of New England for Wesleyan University Press.

Berry, Frank. 1996. "Hollywood Blackout." *People Weekly* 45, no. 11:42–52.

Boggs, Vernon W., ed. 1992. *Salsiology: Afro-Cuban Music and the Evolution of Salsa in New York City.* New York: Excelsior.

Bourke, Vernon J., ed. 1958. *Saint Augustine: The City of God.* New York: Doubleday.

Bradshaw, Paul. 1996. "Nu Yorican Soul: Music Is the Message." *Straight No Chaser: The Magazine of World Jazz Jive* 39 (Winter): 20–27.

Center for Media and Public Affairs (for the National Council of La Raza). 1996. *Don't Blink: Hispanics in Television Entertainment.* Prepared by S. Robert Lichter and Daniel R. Amundson. Washington, D.C.: Center for Media and Public Affairs.

Champagne, Duane. 1989. *American Indian Societies: Strategies and Conditions of Political and Cultural Survival.* Cultural Survival Report no. 32. Cambridge, Mass.: Cultural Survival.

Collier, James Lincoln. 1983. *Louis Armstrong: An American Genius.* New York: Oxford University Press.

Cooper, Carol. 1997. Liner notes to Kenny González and Louis Vega, *Nuyorican Soul.* Cutting Edge CTCR-13084.

Cruz, Alfredo. 1996. Liner notes to Puente, *Jazzin'.* RMM 82032.

Duany, Jorge. 1982. "Latin Jazz Institution: An Interview with Tito Puente." *Esencia,* May–June, pp. 6–7.

———. 1984. "Popular Music in Puerto Rico: Toward an Anthropology of Salsa." *Latin American Music Review* 5, no. 2:187–216.

Ebert, Roger. 1996. *Roger Ebert's Video Companion.* Kansas City, Mo.: Andrews and McMeel.

Echevarría, Domingo G., and Harry Sepúlveda. 1958. Liner notes to Puente, *Dance Mania.* RCA 1692.

Erin, Ronald. 1984. "Cuban Elements in the Music of Aurelio de la Vega." *Latin American Music Review* 5, no. 1:1–32.

Escott, Colin. 1988. Liner notes to *The Drifters 1959–1965: All-Time Greatest Hits and More.* Atlantic 7-81931-2.

Fernández, Enrique. 1986. Liner notes to Puente, *Sensación*. Concord 301.

Flores, Juan. 1988. "Rappin', Writin', and Breakin'." *Centro de Estudios Puertorriqueños Bulletin* 2, no. 3:34–41.

Foucault, Michel. 1993. *The Archaeology of Knowledge and the Discourse on Language*. Trans. A. M. Sheridan Smith. New York: Barnes and Noble.

Glasser, Ruth. 1995. *My Music Is My Flag: Puerto Rican Musicians and Their New York Communities, 1917–1940*. Berkeley: University of California Press.

Glazer, Nathan, and Daniel Moynihan. 1963. *Beyond the Melting Pot: The Negroes, Puerto Ricans, Jews, Italians, and Irish of New York City*. Cambridge, Mass.: MIT Press.

Guzmán, Pablo. 1983. Liner notes to Puente, *On Broadway*. Concord 207.

Kalbacher, Gene. 1993. Liner notes to *Tito Puente Goes Jazz*. RCA 66/48-4 (BMG); reissue of 1956 LP.

Lipsitz, George. 1994. *Dangerous Crossroads: Popular Music, Postmodernism, and the Poetics of Place*. London: Verso.

Lopetegui, Enrique. 1993. "Was the Salsa Too Hot for Bowl Crowd?" *Los Angeles Times,* Sept. 16, pp. F1, F11.

Loza, Steven. 1992. "From Veracruz to Los Angeles: The Reinterpretation of the *Son Jarocho*." *Latin American Music Review* 13, no. 2:179–94.

———. 1993. *Barrio Rhythm: Mexican American Music in Los Angeles*. Urbana: University of Illinois Press.

———. 1994a. "Identity, Nationalism, and Aesthetics among Chicano/Mexicano Musicians in Los Angeles." *Selected Reports in Ethnomusicology: Musical Aesthetics and Multiculturalism in Los Angeles* 10:51–58.

———. 1994b. "Fantasmas enmascarados: pensamientos sobre nuestra investigación y lo académico en etnomusicología." *Heterofonía* 109–10:4–16.

———. 1998. "Latin American Popular Music in Japan and the Issue of International Aesthetics." In Tôru Mitsui, ed., *Popular Music: Intercultural Interpretations*. Proceedings of the Ninth Conference of the International Association for the Study of Popular Music. Kanazawa, Japan: Graduate Program in Music.

Maquet, Jacques. 1979. *Introduction to Aesthetic Anthropology*. Malibu, Calif.: Undena.

Manuel, Peter. 1994. "Puerto Rican Music and Cultural Identity: Creative Appropriation of Cuban Sources from Danza to Salsa." *Ethnomusicology* 38, no. 2:249–80.

Morrow, Buddy, and Tito Puente. 1993. Liner notes to Murrow and Puente, *Revolving Bandstand Sessions*. BMG Music (RCA), Tropical Series, 74321-17448-2.

Murray, Albert. 1973. *The Hero and the Blues*. New York: Vintage.

Puente, Tito. 1981. Recorded interview with Patricia L. Wilson Cryer for the Latin Music Museum of the Boys Harbor School of Performing Arts, New York, Jan. 28.

———. 1984. Recorded lecture, UCLA, May.

———. 1992. Liner notes to *Mambo Macoco: Tito Puente and His Orchestra*. Tumbao Cuban Classics TCD-018 (Camarillo Music).

———. 1994. Videotaped lecture/workshop series, Department of Ethnomusicology, UCLA, Schoenberg Hall, Apr. 4–6.

Roberts, John Storm. 1979. *The Latin Tinge: The Impact of Latin American Music on the United States*. New York: Oxford University Press.

Salazar, Max. 1977a. "Tito Puente: The Living Legend." *Latin Times* 3:15–18.

———. 1977b. "*Latin Times Magazine* Honors Tito Puente at Tower Suite." *Latin Times* 1, no. 4:26–29.

———. 1977c. Program notes. Discovery Day concert honoring Tito Puente, Avery Fisher Hall, Nov. 13.

———. 1993. "Vicentico Valdés: Salsa Hitman." *Latin Beat* 3, no. 5:28–29.

———. 1994. "Tito Puente: The Early Years." *Latin Beat* 4, no. 1:14–20.

————. 1998. "Jimmy Frisaura (1924–1998): The Father of the Tito Puente Orchestra." *Latin Beat* 8, no. 5:24–27.

Sanabria, Bobby, and Ben Socolov. 1990. "Tito Puente: Long Live the King." *Hip: Highlights in Percussion for the Percussion Enthusiast* 5 (Spring/Summer): 1–7, 22–23.

Sandoval, Arturo. 1998. Liner notes to Sandoval, *Hot House.* N2K-10023.

Schillinger, Joseph. 1940. *Kaleidophone.* New York: Chas. Colin.

Smith, Arnold Jay. 1977. "Mongo Santamaría: Cuban King of Congas." *Downbeat* 44, no. 8.

Wilbert, Johannes. 1987. *Tobacco and Shamanism in South America.* New Haven, Conn.: Yale University Press.

Williams, Maria del Pilar. 1996. "Alaska Native Music and Dance: The Spirit of Survival." Ph.D. diss., University of California at Los Angeles.

Wyatt, Hugh. 1984. Liner notes to Puente, *El rey.* Concord 250.

————. 1989. Liner notes to Puente, *Goza mi timbal.* Concord 399.

Ybarra-Frausto, Tomás, and Ana Sol Gutiérrez. 1997. *Towards a Shared Vision: U.S. Latinos and the Smithsonian Institution.* Final report of the Latino Oversight Committee. Washington, D.C.: The Smithsonian Institution.

Index

Music in American Life

Crazeology: The Autobiography of a Chicago Jazzman *Bud Freeman, as Told to Robert Wolf*

Discoursing Sweet Music: Brass Bands and Community Life in Turn-of-the-Century
  Pennsylvania *Kenneth Kreitner*

Mormonism and Music: A History *Michael Hicks*

Voices of the Jazz Age: Profiles of Eight Vintage Jazzmen *Chip Deffaa*

Pickin' on Peachtree: A History of Country Music in Atlanta, Georgia *Wayne W. Daniel*

Bitter Music: Collected Journals, Essays, Introductions, and Librettos *Harry Partch; edited by
  Thomas McGeary*

Ethnic Music on Records: A Discography of Ethnic Recordings Produced in the United States,
  1893 to 1942 *Richard K. Spottswood*

Downhome Blues Lyrics: An Anthology from the Post-World War II Era *Jeff Todd Titon*

Ellington: The Early Years *Mark Tucker*

Chicago Soul *Robert Pruter*

That Half-Barbaric Twang: The Banjo in American Popular Culture *Karen Linn*

Hot Man: The Life of Art Hodes *Art Hodes and Chadwick Hansen*

The Erotic Muse: American Bawdy Songs (2d ed.) *Ed Cray*

Barrio Rhythm: Mexican American Music in Los Angeles *Steven Loza*

The Creation of Jazz: Music, Race, and Culture in Urban America *Burton W. Peretti*

Charles Martin Loeffler: A Life Apart in Music *Ellen Knight*

Club Date Musicians: Playing the New York Party Circuit *Bruce A. MacLeod*

Opera on the Road: Traveling Opera Troupes in the United States, 1825–60 *Katherine K. Preston*

The Stonemans: An Appalachian Family and the Music That Shaped Their Lives *Ivan M. Tribe*

Transforming Tradition: Folk Music Revivals Examined *Edited by Neil V. Rosenberg*

The Crooked Stovepipe: Athapaskan Fiddle Music and Square Dancing in Northeast Alaska and
  Northwest Canada *Craig Mishler*

Traveling the High Way Home: Ralph Stanley and the World of Traditional Bluegrass Music
  John Wright

Carl Ruggles: Composer, Painter, and Storyteller *Marilyn Ziffrin*

Never without a Song: The Years and Songs of Jennie Devlin, 1865–1952 *Katharine D. Newman*

The Hank Snow Story *Hank Snow, with Jack Ownbey and Bob Burris*

Milton Brown and the Founding of Western Swing *Cary Ginell, with special assistance from
  Roy Lee Brown*

Santiago de Murcia's "Códice Saldívar No. 4": A Treasury of Secular Guitar Music from
  Baroque Mexico *Craig H. Russell*

The Sound of the Dove: Singing in Appalachian Primitive Baptist Churches *Beverly Bush Patterson*

Heartland Excursions: Ethnomusicological Reflections on Schools of Music *Bruno Nettl*

Doowop: The Chicago Scene *Robert Pruter*

Blue Rhythms: Six Lives in Rhythm and Blues *Chip Deffaa*

Shoshone Ghost Dance Religion: Poetry Songs and Great Basin Context *Judith Vander*

Go Cat Go! Rockabilly Music and Its Makers *Craig Morrison*

'Twas Only an Irishman's Dream: The Image of Ireland and the Irish in American Popular Song
  Lyrics, 1800–1920 *William H. A. Williams*

Democracy at the Opera: Music, Theater, and Culture in New York City, 1815–60 *Karen Ahlquist*

Fred Waring and the Pennsylvanians *Virginia Waring*

Woody, Cisco, and Me: Seamen Three in the Merchant Marine *Jim Longhi*

Behind the Burnt Cork Mask: Early Blackface Minstrelsy and Antebellum American
  Popular Culture *William J. Mahar*

Going to Cincinnati: A History of the Blues in the Queen City *Steven C. Tracy*

Pistol Packin' Mama: Aunt Molly Jackson and the Politics of Folksong *Shelly Romalis*

Sixties Rock: Garage, Psychedelic, and Other Satisfactions *Michael Hicks*

The Late Great Johnny Ace and the Transition from R&B to Rock 'n' Roll *James M. Salem*

Tito Puente and the Making of Latin Music *Steven Loza*

Typeset in 10.5/13.5 Apollo
with Adobe Mezz display
Designed by Paula Newcomb
Composed by Jim Proefrock
at the University of Illinois Press
Manufactured by Data Reproductions Corp.